Project-Based Learning i Language Acquisition

This book showcases pedagogical tools for learning languages through interdisciplinary project-based learning (PBL). Chapters demonstrate a diverse range of PBL activities that help students build communities of practice within classroom settings and across local and global communities.

Too often, learning a language becomes a static endeavor, confined to a classroom and a singular discipline. But language is dynamic and fluid, no matter the setting in which learning takes place. In acknowledging this, this volume explores how PBL and community-engagement pedagogies serve to combine learning goals and community service in ways that enhance student growth and facilitate second-language development in an interdisciplinary, multilingual, and multicultural higher education learning environment. Chapters touch on activities and approaches, including spoken-word poetry, environmental projects, social activism, study abroad, and in-service learning.

This book will be of interest to researchers, academics, and postgraduate students in the fields of language education, second language acquisition, higher education, and comparative and international education.

Adrián Gras-Velázquez is lecturer in the Spanish and Portuguese Department at Smith College, Massachusetts, USA.

Routledge Research in Language Education

The *Routledge Research in Language Education* series provides a platform for established and emerging scholars to present their latest research and discuss key issues in Language Education. This series welcomes books on all areas of language teaching and learning, including but not limited to language education policy and politics; multilingualism; literacy; L1, L2, or foreign language acquisition; curriculum; classroom practice; pedagogy; teaching materials; and language teacher education and development. Books in the series are *not* limited to the discussion of the teaching and learning of English only.

Books in the series include:

Classroom-Based Research on Chinese as a Second Language
Fangyuan Yuan and Shuai Li

Teaching English for Tourism
Bridging Research and Praxis
Edited by Michael Ennis and Gina Petrie

Post-Colonial Curriculum Practices in South Asia
Building Confidence to Speak English
Asantha U. Attanayake

Teaching Content and Language in the Multilingual Classroom
International Research on Policy, Perspectives, Preparation, and Practice
Edited by Svenja Hammer, Kara Viesca, and Nancy Commins

Project-Based Learning in Second Language Acquisition
Building Communities of Practice in Higher Education
Edited by Adrián Gras-Velázquez

For more information about the series, please visit www.routledge.com/Routledge-Research-in-Language-Education/book-series/RRLE

Project-Based Learning in Second Language Acquisition

Building Communities of Practice in Higher Education

Edited by Adrián Gras-Velázquez

Routledge
Taylor & Francis Group
NEW YORK AND LONDON

First published 2020
by Routledge
605 Third Avenue, New York, NY 10017

and by Routledge
2 Park Square, Milton Park, Abingdon, Oxon, OX14 4RN

First issued in paperback 2021

Routledge is an imprint of the Taylor & Francis Group, an informa business

Library of Congress Cataloging-in-Publication Data
A catalog record for this book has been requested

ISBN 13: 978-0-367-78500-0 (pbk)
ISBN 13: 978-1-138-31378-1 (hbk)

Typeset in Sabon
by Apex CoVantage, LLC

Contents

Contributors

Mariana Achugar, Associate Professor, Department of Media and Languages, School of Information and Communication, Universidad de la República, Uruguay

Inés Arribas, Senior Lecturer, Department of Spanish, Bryn Mawr College, USA

Yasemin Bayyurt, Professor, Department of Foreign Language Education, Boğaziçi University, Turkey

Prajukti (juk) Bhattacharyya, Professor of Geology, Department of Geography, Geology, and Environmental Science, University of Wisconsin-Whitewater, USA

Maria Carreira, Professor of Spanish, Department of Romance, German, Russian Languages and Literatures, California State University, Long Beach, USA

Aurélie Chevant-Aksoy, Assistant Professor of French, Modern Languages and Cultures, Santa Monica College, USA

Julia Chindemi-Vila, Lecturer, Department of Modern Languages and Literatures, Swarthmore College, USA

María José Coperías-Aguilar, Full Professor, Department of English and German Philology, Universitat de València, Spain

Brianna Deering, Associate Lecturer, English Language Academy, University of Wisconsin-Whitewater, USA

Kenya C. Dworkin y Méndez, Associate Professor of Hispanic Studies, Modern Languages Department, Carnegie Mellon University, USA

Felipe Gómez, Associate Teaching Professor, Department of Modern Languages, Dietrich College of Humanities and Social Sciences, Carnegie Mellon University, USA

Adrián Gras-Velázquez, Lecturer, Spanish and Portuguese Department, Smith College, USA

Bruno Grazioli, Resident Director and Faculty, Italian Studies Program in Bologna, Dickinson College, Italy

Claire Hitchins Chik, Associate Director, National Heritage Language Resource Center, University of California Los Angeles, USA

Susan Huss-Lederman, Professor of Applied Linguistics and TESL, Department of Languages and Literatures, University of Wisconsin-Whitewater, USA

Michelle Joffroy, Associate Professor of Spanish and Director, Latin American and Latin@ Studies Program, Smith College, USA

Shushan Karapetian, Associate Director, National Heritage Language Resource Center, and Lecturer, Department of Near Eastern Languages and Cultures, University of California, Los Angeles, USA

Elif Kemaloglu-Er, Assistant Professor, Department of Translation and Interpreting Studies, Adana Alparslan Türkeş Science and Technology University, Turkey

Ericka Knudson, Preceptor of French, Department of Romance Languages and Literatures, Harvard University, USA

Alison Maginn, Associate Professor of Spanish, World Languages and Cultures Department, Monmouth University, USA

CeAnn Chandel Myers, English/ESL Residential Faculty, English Department, Mesa Community College, USA

Susan G. Polansky, Teaching Professor of Hispanic Studies and Head, Department of Modern Languages, Carnegie Mellon University, USA

Emily Skalet, Lead Instructor, Adult Learning Centers, New York Public Library, Bronx, New York, USA

Fredricka L. Stoller, Professor, TESL and Applied Linguistics programs within the English Department, Northern Arizona University, USA

Ah-Young Song, Visiting Assistant Professor, Education, Vassar College, USA

Acknowledgments

I want to thank all the contributors in this volume for their hard work, patience, and enthusiasm. I especially wish to thank Fredricka L. Stoller, who, unbeknownst to her, provided invaluable guidance throughout the writing and editing process. I am also grateful to all my colleagues in the Spanish and Portuguese Department at Smith College for their candor and support. Thanks also to Matthew Friberg and Elsbeth Wright at Routledge for making this a seamless process. On a personal note, I want to thank Josh for, well, everything really. Your support and encouragement mean the world to me. I also thank my parents, Inma and Albert, for instilling in me my love for learning, and Àgueda and Azalea, my sisters – oh what patience you both have! The next helado del Peret is on me. To Peque, thank you for making me laugh every day, and I am sorry if sometimes you do not get as many belly rubs as you would like.

Finally, I want to thank all my students, past, present, and future. You make me want to be a better professor. I truly appreciate your willingness to be my classroom guinea pigs.

Introduction

Adrián Gras-Velázquez

Throughout my career in second and foreign language acquisition, I have consistently been drawn to learning exercises that take students outside of the traditional classroom environment and into a vibrant, experimental one. It is for this reason that I am particularly interested in pedagogies that get students up on their feet and make them physically and mentally a part of the learning process. In my experience, no method has been more effective than project-based learning (PBL). Based on the pedagogical principle of "learning by doing," PBL encourages active student engagement in the learning process as opposed to passive learning. PBL also provides an avenue through which students can transfer their skills to varied and diverse communities outside of the classroom, making it a valuable and powerful pedagogical method.

PBL enhances conventional teaching exercises while simultaneously achieving the learning goals for the course. PBL helps "students engage in many types of learning, including experiential and negotiated learning, problem solving, and research" (Mikulec and Chamness Miller 81). Using PBL, students can explore their own interests, develop higher-level thinking skills, and practice accountability for their own learning experiences. While PBL is not a replacement for other teaching methods, in the words of Haines, it is "an approach to learning which complements mainstream methods and which can be used with almost all levels, ages and abilities of students" (1). More than a "simple incorporation of projects into the curriculum" (Stoller 21), PBL can be summarized as learning through the process of producing and completing a project.

PBL is a set of "complex tasks, based on challenging questions or problems, involving students in design, problem-solving, decision making, or investigative activities; giving students the opportunity to work relatively autonomously over extended periods of time; and culminating in realistic products or presentations" (Thomas in Thuan 329). Although educators approach PBL from multiple perspectives, many acknowledge that the definition contains a number of features including the following:

1) being a process and an end product
2) encouraging student ownership

3) extending over a period of time and not being confined to one class session
4) integrating different skills
5) committing to both language and content learning
6) facilitating both collaborative and individual work
7) requiring students to take responsibility for their own learning (through gathering, processing, and reporting information)
8) giving students and educators new roles and responsibilities in the learning process
9) having an end-product
10) concluding with a reflection of both the process and the product (Stoller 24)

The work in this volume recognizes the benefits of using PBL to engage with communities both inside and outside the classroom. Bringle and Hatcher argue that community engagement is becoming "more salient within higher education" and that community involvement "can change the nature of faculty work, enhance student learning, better fulfill campus mission, and improve the quality of life in communities" (37). Just like PBL, community engagement or service-learning pedagogies reject the model of education where there is a "downward transference of information from knowledgeable teachers to passive students" and encourages an "active pedagogy committed to connecting theory and practice, schools and community, the cognitive and the ethical" (Butin 3). O'Meara (14–23) highlights several benefits and motivations for faculty to implement community engagement in the curriculum, including the following:

1) student learning and growth
2) personal commitments to specific social issues, people, and places
3) the pursuit of rigorous scholarship and learning
4) the desire for collaboration, relationships, and partners

PBL and community engagement have similar principles and goals. As this volume shows, both pedagogical frameworks help students develop their interpersonal and language skills while contributing to the community. PBL and community engagement are ideal for second language acquisition, as they promote and encourage the use of the target language, while building cultural and global competencies, as well as advancing civic involvement. Taking this into consideration, the central research question addressed by this volume is how do project-based and community-engagement pedagogies combine learning goals and community service in ways that enhance student growth and facilitate second language development in an interdisciplinary, multilingual, and multicultural higher education learning environment.

Chapters

This volume is divided into six parts. *Theoretical Intersections* (Part I) establishes frameworks in PBL, community engagement, and second language acquisition in multilingual and multicultural settings. In Chapter 1, María José Coperías-Aguilar discusses how communications in the current global network occur in more than one language, making language teaching a relevant commodity in today's education. Coperías-Aguilar argues that although globalization has promoted cultural and linguistic diversity, it has also brought about homogenization, especially in relation to the use of the English language.

In Chapter 2, Fredricka L. Stoller and CeAnn Chandel Myers present and elaborate upon a five-step process for integrating PBL into language classrooms. Updating Stoller's previous well-known work on PBL, this easily adaptable model guides language teachers in planning, implementing, and evaluating PBL. To bring the model to life, the authors present real-world examples of projects and tasks that have been successfully integrated into a range of L2 and FL classrooms. Chapter 3 continues this exploration on PBL in the classroom as Emily Skalet demonstrates how Vygotsky's sociocultural theory and a multicultural education framework inform PBL and can be utilized to promote active class participation and community engagement. Incorporating an inquiry-based stance and personal classroom examples, the chapter reviews PBL design considerations to engage learners in authentic tasks grounded in their community and interests.

Part II (*Teaching and Learning*) discusses PBL and community engagement in public school tutoring and pre-service teacher education. In Chapter 4, Susan G. Polansky demonstrates how, through a tutoring for community outreach program, university students build a community of practice within the college classroom setting and then move into the local academic community of the public schools. Polansky's project empowers the growth of language learning through reflection and self-critique, overcoming challenges, and appreciating complex roles and perspectives, role modeling, cultural identity, and diversity within communities of learners. Chapter 5 is closely linked to the discussion in Chapter 1 of English as a de-facto language and the need to foster multilingual and multicultural competences in our students. Within the setting of pre-service teacher education in Turkey, Elif Kemaloglu-Er and Yasemin Bayyurt highlight different aspects of non-native speaker realities and multicultural diversity. This chapter reveals how the Standard English-bound attitudes and expectations of some schools and parents put great pressure on pre-service teachers willing to emphasize the multilingual and multicultural diversity in their practicum classes. However, as they assert, this challenge has paved the way for innovative pedagogical practices, and they argue that PBL raises English as Lingua Franca awareness through hands-on practice comprising discovery, creativity, and interaction as well as multilingual and multicultural diversity.

Still within an international background, Part III (*Immersion and the International*) opens with Chapter 6 where Bruno Grazioli discusses how the combination of community-engaged learning and PBL tasks enhances US college students' language learning and supports their intercultural growth while they are participating in a semester of study abroad in Italy. Grazioli posits that spontaneous and practice-based language learning arises from the creation of a community of practice, that is an aggregate of people uniting over a common goal, and through sustained social interaction in the target language (Italian) with native but also non-native individuals. Chapter 7 offers a strong counterpoint to the previous chapter as Susan Huss-Lederman, Prajukti (Juk) Bhattacharyya, and Brianna Deering present a study on international students going to a US college setting and working with domestic students to integrate themselves into the college community. While working in a PBL-driven syllabus focused on environmental sustainability, international students reported increased confidence in their writing skills, improved opportunities to participate in academic discourse, and achieving a sense of belonging within the campus community.

Heritage Learning and Language is the title of Part IV. In Chapter 8, Maria Carreira, Claire Hitchins Chik, and Shushan Karapetian present a model of PBL for teaching heritage language learners (HLLs) developed by the NHLRC at UCLA. Using sample projects from different languages and proficiency levels, the authors illustrate how PBL can facilitate the development of oral and written skills, increase linguistic and cultural awareness, and prepare HLLs to make professional use of the HL. Furthermore, Chapter 8 argues that PBL can help instructors manage a wide range of proficiency levels, interests, and affective needs that HLLs bring to class. Chapter 9 discusses the *Círculo Juvenil de Cultura* program and how it helped create a space where community, bilingualism, and Latino cultures are valued. Mariana Achugar, Felipe Gómez, and Kenya C. Dworkin y Méndez describe how this model of service learning has promoted the university students' interaction (linguistic and cultural) with the immigrant community and members of other partnering organizations of the Latino community.

Part V, *Civic Partnerships*, examines issues of social justice, religious engagement, and action agency. In Chapter 10, Michelle Joffroy discusses how social justice-oriented pedagogies stimulate deeper and more critical engagement with language as a tool to approach dynamic, multifaceted, multisited, and political issues. In the chapter, Joffroy shows how community-based research (CBR) partnerships help harness digital technologies to innovate teaching and develop intellectually sophisticated and publicly-oriented curricula for the second language acquisition classroom. In Chapter 11, Alison Maginn considers how community engagement helps foster an understanding of socio-political and social justice issues, such as educational equity, food insecurity, economic hardship, homelessness, and the discrimination suffered by immigrants. Together, these authors highlight service experience to understand the value of bilingualism, multiculturalism, and the potential for civic agency through intercultural competence.

In the last section, *Case Studies in Creative Communications* (Part VI), Adrián Gras-Velázquez, Julia Chindemi-Vila, and Ah-Young Song discuss the *¿Y tú quién eres?* project in Chapter 12. This project stresses the importance of community and culture within second language acquisition. Most case studies at the intersection of PBL and community engagement have centered on students with high-level proficiency rather than novice learners. In this chapter, the authors demonstrate that many of the benefits of PBL can be successfully implemented and adapted for the beginning-level. In Chapter 13, Inés Arribas explains why oral poetry is vital in both an academic curriculum and language classes. By participating in poetry slams, students learn the language (its lexical wealth, its grammar, its codes, its standards, and its prosody) and also develop an appreciation for language as an instrument of personal expression and communication. By creating and performing their own texts, students embark on a personal journey through the language and become accountable for their language acquisition. Finally, in Chapter 14, Aurélie Chevant-Aksoy and Ericka Knudson explore how language classrooms still draw most of their material from heteronormative narratives despite increasing efforts toward diversity. Through film and PBL, the authors discuss representations of gender and sexuality in the French-speaking world, arguing about the importance of analyzing gendered social constructions and cross-cultural comparisons of the LGBT community while placing special emphasis on French as a gendered language.

Acknowledgments

I would like to thank Jamie Worms in the Latin American and Latino/a Studies Program at Smith College for her comments and sugesstions in this chapter.

References

Bringle, Robert G., and Julie A. Hatcher. "Innovative Practices in Service-Learning and Curricular Engagement." *Institutionalizing Community Engagement in Higher Education: The First Wave of Carnegie Classified Institutions*, edited by Lorilee R. Sandman, et al. Wiley Periodicals, 2009, pp. 37–46.

Butin, Dan W. *Service-Learning in Theory and Practice: The Future of Community Engagement in Higher Education*. Palgrave Macmillan, 2010.

Haines, Simon. *Projects for the EFL Classroom: Resource Material for Teachers*. Thomas Nelson, 1989.

Mikulec, Erin, and Paul Chamness Miller. "Using Project-Based Instruction to Meet Foreign Language Standards." *The Clearing House: A Journal of Educational Strategies, Issues and Ideas*, vol. 84, no. 3, 2011, pp. 81–86.

O'Meara, KerryAnn. "Motivation for Faculty Community Engagement: Learning From Exemplars." *Journal of Higher Education Outreach and Engagement*, vol. 12, no. 1, 2008, pp. 7–29.

Stoller, Fredricka L. "Establishing a Theoretical Foundation for Project-Based Learning in Second and Foreign Language Contexts." *Project-Based Second and Foreign Language Education: Past, Present, and Future*, edited by Gulbahar H. Beckett and Paul Chamness Miller. Information Age Publishing, 2006, pp. 19–40.

Thuan, Pham Duc. "Project-Based Learning: From Theory to EFL Classroom Practice." *Proceeding of the 6th International Open TESOL Conference 2018*, 2018, pp. 327–339.

Part I

Theoretical Intersections

1 Diversity and Second Language Acquisition in the University Classroom

A Multilingual and Multicultural Setting

María José Coperías-Aguilar

Block and Cameron's statement at the beginning of the 21st century saying that there was a "consensus that we are living in an increasingly globalized world" (2) is even more real nowadays. Although the concept of globalization has been approached from many different angles, Giddens's definition, "Increasing interdependence between individuals, nations and regions. Does *not* just mean economic interdependence. Involves accelerated and universal communication, and concerns also political and cultural dimensions" (xii), is comprehensive and tackles most issues concerned with the notion of globalization. Nevertheless, it is a contentious term, and even if for some people globalization would simply refer to a reality in which people, capital, information, and goods move freely across borders, many others are wary of its consequences (Bauman). Very often, globalization is understood as implying the hegemony of the capitalist system and the domination of the wealthy countries and corporations over the poor ones and the consequent loss of their identity features (Green et al. 10). Sometimes, though, the dominance of the powerful over those with fewer means is seen as an opportunity for the resistance of the latter and the homogenization process that globalization may entail as an opportunity for hybridization rather than uniformity (Block and Cameron 6, 3). Some of the factors that have allowed this phenomenon to increase are more advanced communication and transport technologies, which, in turn, have increased people's mobility, or hypermobility (Pauwels 42), and a worldwide connected economic and trade system, thus creating transnational communities.

These global networks are based on the ability to communicate among their members, and, consequently, the development in competences in more than one language as well as in the new literacies required by communication technologies is absolutely necessary. Bordieu introduced the notion of *linguistic capital* to refer to "the capacity to produce expressions *à propos*, *for* a particular market" (18), connecting it with other forms of capital, such as economic or cultural, and considered that differences in terms of accent, grammar, or vocabulary might indicate the social position and linguistic capital of the speakers. Nowadays, this linguistic capital is related to the command of communication skills, oral and written, used in different formats and platforms but also to the competence in several languages (Cameron 72; Pauwels 53). Thus, language teaching as a foreign or a second language,[1] and more specifically the teaching of English, has become a commodity. For some English-speaking countries, like the United Kingdom (Gray "Tesol" 88), Ireland (Sudhershan and Brauen 27), and Australia (Humphreys 94), international education has turned into an important economic asset worth billions of dollars, and higher education has become one of the most important export sectors (Healey 334). Globalization is then changing, on one hand, the ways in which languages are learnt and taught and, on the other, the organization of institutions of higher education (Iglesias de Ussel et al. 14).

Linguistic Diversity, Linguistic Uniformity

Despite the globalizing phenomenon just mentioned, which is often considered to bring along a homogenizing effect, Blommaert contends that "sociolinguistically, the world has not become a village" (1) – echoing McLuhan's global village – and proves this to be so by describing the United States as a *multi-accent* society in reference not only to the existing varieties of English within the country but also to the accents provided by many other languages (49). As for the European Union, it includes almost 30 countries, over 20 official languages, and around 60 regional languages, plus the languages brought by immigrant populations, which makes Europe a highly multilingual and multicultural area (Tudor 21). Similar phenomena can be found in many other countries, as portrayed by Clyne in reference to Australia (53), and across the world (Cadman and Song 5). Other authors have focused, though, on the *super-diversity* that can be found especially in cities as a result of the arrival and settling down of immigrants from many different ethnolinguistic backgrounds (Pauwels 43; Hewings and Sergeant 74). Regarding the sociolinguistic circumstances of Europe, its institutions – the Council of Europe, through its Language Policy Division, and the European Centre for Modern Languages, among others – have fostered multilingualism and multiculturalism by developing a wide range of activities and studies (Coperías-Aguilar "Dealing" 73; Coperías-Aguilar "ICC in the Context" 244), and they have established as an inalienable aim the training of teachers who can teach in more than one language (Kelly et al. ii). Despite the efforts of the European Commission to promote language diversity in language learning, Doiz and her associates ("Internationalisation" 347; "Future Challenges" xvii) highlight the predominance of English as a pan-European language of instruction. However, Alcón argues that if we place English within a framework of hybridity, where it is a language of communication and not of identification, English should not be understood as a threat to multilingualism, but, on the contrary, it might provide conditions for developing multilingual citizens (26–29).

Many other voices in different parts of the world have risen in defense of multilingualism, as well as fostering the learning of several languages and allowing our students to draw on their capacity to use them, and against the idea of building linguistically and culturally monolithic societies (Shohamy 209; Doiz et al. "Internationalisation" 345; Wingate 435; Spiteri 9). However, some of these same voices acknowledge the unavoidable prevalence of English in many contexts since, in a globalized world, a shared linguistic code is necessary in order to get messages across to others, and – as Cameron argues – globalization has given new legitimacy to "the long-lived idea that linguistic diversity is a problem, while linguistic uniformity is a desirable ideal" (67).

Even if languages such as French, Russian, and German have played and still play an important role in international communication, and other languages like Chinese, Spanish, and Arabic are gaining ground, it is English that clearly dominates the international linguistic stage (Pauwels 45). There are several reasons for this pervasiveness of English: it has been adopted as the means of communication by many transnational corporations, and their staff – regardless of the place where they are based – need communication skills in this language; there is an increasing number of world organizations, be they official institutions or charities, that use English as their working language; and English has also become the language of academia, especially regarding the dissemination of knowledge either in conferences or publications, as well as in teaching. Consequently, English has become a transnational language with a majority of users for whom it is a second language, that is, a *lingua franca*. Mauranen defines a lingua franca as "a contact language between speakers or speaker groups when at least one of them uses it as a second language" (8), and Baker emphasizes its intercultural nature and the different linguacultural backgrounds of the speakers (27). At the same time, Wallace argues that this kind of English cannot be standard and will contain regional variations (106), and Janssens and Steyaert prefer the term *multilingual franca*, thus acknowledging the fact that each speaker will bring his/her personal language experience to the linguistic exchange and highlighting the multilingual context (629).

Nonetheless, the rise of English as a lingua franca has brought about some criticism, and issues of linguistic imperialism have been emphasized since the 1990s by several authors, who criticize the way in which English is promoted and taught (Phillipson, Pennycook, Canagarajah *Resisting*; Holborow *The Politics* and *The Language*; Holliday, Gray *The Construction*). The manner in which Western, and more specifically Anglo, communicative norms and scientific ways of knowing has been exported has also been questioned (Cameron 68; Cadman and Song 5), as well as the superior status and prestige that English is granted in relation to other languages (Shohamy 197). Another criticism is associated to the idea that, although generally speaking language is not culturally neutral, a particular language is not necessarily linked to a specific country or culture (Coperías-Aguilar "Dealing" 72; Baker 29). In the case of English, it is difficult to decide which would be the *native* variety that should be taken as the model for the lingua franca, especially considering that for the majority of its users, English is a second language (Walkinshaw et al. 6; Wallace 101). In relation to this, the powerful industry engaged in the production of English textbooks for the international market has also been questioned. These books are mostly produced in English-speaking countries and, as Gray argues, "they are highly wrought cultural constructs and carriers of cultural messages" ("The Global Coursebook" 152), and despite the fact that in recent times guidelines have been issued by publishing companies to their authors to comply with requirements of inclusivity and appropriacy to make them suitable for the global market, and most coursebooks try to deal with a greater variety of materials and sources, ethnocentric values still persist. That is the reason why Corbett contends that rather than producing textbooks for the international market, teaching materials should be addressed to particular communities and become more involved with country-specific publishing (212).

Multilingualism and Multiculturalism in Higher Education Institutions

As Healey argues, universities were born global and, as the term indicates, with a universal disposition (334). In Middle-Age Europe, universities already attracted students and scholars from different parts of the western, and sometimes also the eastern, world, and Latin was used as a shared second language in order to promote scientific exchange. Although not a new phenomenon, internationalization in higher education institutions (HEIs) has acquired a new dimension in this century (Pérez Cañado "Globalization" 397) and, if in the United States and Canada it has become almost an institutional priority, in Europe, its multinational, multicultural and multilingual reality has fostered several institutional initiatives for internationalization (Green et al. 21–22).

Increasing numbers of students decide to engage in higher education in a country other than their own; this may be encouraged by established exchange programs, like the Erasmus/Socrates initiative in Europe, or by the prospect of better social or economic opportunities. Drawing upon an OECD (Organization for Economic Co-operation and Development) survey, Wingate reports that in 2014, around 1.3 million postgraduate students studied outside their country, mostly in universities in English-speaking countries (427). Perrin also reports that Anglophone countries host more than 50% of those students who study abroad (154), proof of which is the fact that, in the academic year 2014–2015, 58% of the students enrolled in full-time postgraduate programs in the UK were international ones or that, in the same year, this kind of student also represented at least 25% of enrolments in Australia, making the United States, the United Kingdom, Australia, and Canada four of the top six study destinations (Heugh et al. 260; Humphreys 94).

Instead of receiving students at home, what some of these Anglophone countries have been doing is export their HEIs overseas, thus creating what is known as Transnational Education (TNE) institutions. Drawing upon a joint Council of Europe/UNESCO document, Healey defines TNE as "all types of higher education programmes and educational services (including distance-learning) in which learners are located in a country different from the one where the awarding body is based" (335). Perrin reports that in 2012, there were more than 220 international campuses around the world established by the same four English-speaking countries just mentioned (154). The third way in which university students can have access to internationalization is by studying either a graduate or postgraduate degree in a foreign language, usually English, in their own countries. English-medium instruction (EMI), that is, the use of English as a lingua franca for content-learning and teaching among students and teachers from different linguistic and cultural backgrounds, is a growing phenomenon in higher education worldwide. In the last decade, there has been an exponential growth in this field, and Walkinshaw and his associates report that in 2016, there were some 8,000 courses taught in English at universities in non-Anglophone countries around the world (2). EMI programs, though, have drawn some criticism and, along with the concerns about ethnocentrism and imperialism associated with the expansion of the English language already mentioned, there is also anxiety regarding some of the challenges involved in the implementation of this way of teaching (Shohamy 208; Sudhershan and Bruen 40).

When we come to think of EMI programs, we usually imagine universities set in non-Anglophone countries offering courses or full degree programs taught in English; however, an increasing participation of immigrants and ethnolinguistic minorities can be observed in HEIs established in English-speaking countries. If we take the US as an example, around 20% of the population speaks English as a second or other language (Russell 152), and although bilingualism – in the shape of speaking English plus one's own language – is encouraged for the international community, immigrants to the US are asked to give up their own language and adhere to English-only monolingualism (García et al. 174, 178). García and her associates also argue that immigrant students in US HEIs are often seen as *strangers in academia* and perceived as unqualified, and they explain how these institutions take different positions on bilingualism and multilingualism depending on who is speaking. So, whereas international students are welcomed and perceived as a financial asset, immigrant students are received with caution; whereas the diverse linguistic background of international students is seen as natural, bilingualism in immigrant students is perceived as a challenge; and whereas international students have full access to content classes, immigrant students are often excluded until they develop English proficiency (192–193). In reference to Canada, Marshall also contends that the bilingual and/or multilingual background of many students who belong to what is often referred to as the 1.5 generation, that is, people living in two worlds and somewhere between first- and second-generation immigrants, is often seen as a deficit rather than a wealth, as a problem rather than an asset (42–43, 47). Cultural clashes may also emerge with international students, as pointed out by Cadman and Song in reference to Australia and the *Asianization* that some of their HEIs are confronting because of the arrival of thousands of students from different Asian countries (7).

According to several authors, the problem lies in the fact that, despite the multilingual and multicultural setting of many of these HEIs, they are monolingual at heart, and the Western style of education no longer reflects or meets the needs of the new students, and, consequently, researchers and practitioners of education often find the situation challenging (Preece and Martin 3–4; Doiz et al. "Internationalisation" 346; Cadman and Song 7; Marshall 42). And although universities welcome cultural difference in general, linguistic diversity in students is often dealt with as a deficit and a problem to be fixed (Preece et al. 288). Shohamy shows a critical standpoint and understands that maybe some problematic issues have been overlooked because of the, sometimes, too hasty implementation of EMI programs. She first wonders how successful achievement of academic content may be if students have a language deficit in English and how successful the improvement of English language is by studying it through content. Next, she poses the inequalities regarding academic achievements that may emerge for some immigrant and language-minority students when they have to study through what can become their third language. Finally, she mistrusts the biases that may result when using a monolingual type of assessment in contrast to the multilingual class discourse (Shohamy 202–205).

The implementation of EMI programs also means a new approach to the learning of English as a foreign or second language, since the main purpose is to increase the exposure of students to the English language. This switch to the use of EMI reflects a big shift in the approach to language teaching (Shohamy 197). As posed by Walkinshaw and his associates, this change means that English becomes a *medium* of instruction rather than an *object* of instruction (2). And this shift in focus from teaching English as a foreign or second language to turning it into both an academic discipline and the mode of delivery makes it necessary to re-think the teaching of English as a foreign or second language (Perrin 153; Heugh et al. 260). This new scenario poses some new challenges too: on one hand, that English language is no longer the possession of those who were born to it and different varieties have to be considered and, on the other, how to combine in the most appropriate way the learning of the English language and the contents taught through this medium.

Second Language Acquisition and the Development of Competences

As stated earlier, linguistic diversity is an extremely valuable asset for Europe and the issue of languages has always been an important concern for the Council of Europe, which – instead of promoting the use of a lingua franca – opted for a model through which multilingualism and multiculturalism are fostered (Coperías-Aguilar "ICC in the Context" 244). After years of joint work by several institutions, in 2001, the final document known as the Common European Framework of Reference for languages (CEFR) was published (Council of Europe). In a previous working paper, Van Ek had argued that foreign language teaching should not only be concerned with training in communication skills but should also involve the personal and social development of the learner as an individual (33). The CEFR, in fact, aimed at developing European citizenship, promoting the learning of several languages as a powerful factor of intellectual development and a tool to enable the acquisition of independence and autonomy as learners, and encouraging open-mindedness. Even if the CEFR was initially designed to be deployed in Europe, it has now been adopted globally (Leung and Lewkowicz 62), and these aims can be applied to language learning in many other parts of the world. In Europe, the CEFR has been developed in parallel to the European Higher Education Area (EHEA), an educational project aimed at making Europe a competitive and dynamic knowledge-based economy that can only become a reality if the different actors involved – students, teachers, researchers, and institutions – are able to communicate with one another in an effective way (Tudor 22). One of the principles underlying the EHEA is engaging both students and teachers in preparing democratic European citizens for the new century through the adoption of multidisciplinary approaches and the acquisition of the skills and attitudes necessary for life in multicultural societies, as well as competences, such as those of listening to, understanding, and interpreting other people's arguments. And this should be achieved through a learner-centered methodology that trains students in critical thinking (Coperías-Aguilar "ICC in the Context" 243–244; Kelly et al. 23).

Even if EHEA is concerned with Europe, the aims and principles just mentioned have been or are being implemented by many other HEIs around the world since, as Jiménez Raya argues, many universities are aware that employers are looking for workers "possessing the capacity to think critically, analyze issues, solve problems, communicate effectively, and take leadership" (120, see also Badger and White 9). In a comparative analysis of foreign language teaching in higher education between the United States and Europe, Pérez Cañado contends that, at present, language studies must have a relevant role on the agendas of HEIs because, if in the past language studies were reserved to specialists, now the acquisition of languages is fundamental for everyone ("Globalization" 394). She also comments on the different circumstances that have fueled language policies on both sides of the Atlantic (diversity, in the case of Europe, and language deficits detected in the US after the events of 9/11) but also on some similarities, among them, the development of competences in order to engage people in lifelong learning (404).

With the arrival of communicative language teaching in the 1970s, the prevalent linguistic competence – the ability to use the forms of a language correctly – to be acquired when learning a second language was superseded by communicative competence (CC), which took into consideration not only linguistic competence but also discourse, sociolinguistic, and strategic competences among others (Coperías-Aguilar "ICC as a Tool" 88; Dooly 78–79). In the 1990s, Byram introduced the concept of intercultural communicative competence (ICC), which recognized the intercultural dimension when communicating in multilingual and multicultural settings. Baker, though acknowledging how useful it has been, especially in relation to education, criticizes ICC for not considering the role of English as a global language of communication when used in settings other than Anglophone ones (32). In turn, he presents two alternatives: Kramsch's symbolic competence ("The Symbolic Dimensions") and Canagarajah's performative competence (*Translingual Practice*). Without rejecting either CC or ICC, symbolic competence takes on a more critical view of culture and addresses ideological, historic, and aesthetic aspects, as well as the complexity yielding from numerous meanings and interpretations when intercultural communication takes place. As for performative competence, it emphasizes the processes of multilingual intercultural communication and the role of communicative strategies. At a different level, an *ad hoc* committee on foreign languages created within the Modern Language Association in the United States and chaired by Mary Louise Pratt, in a position paper on the transformation of college and university foreign language departments in the country, recommended making translingual and transcultural competence (TTC) the goal of language learning. In the paper, the learning of a language in addition to English is encouraged, and TTC is aimed at placing "value on the multilingual ability to *operate between languages*," (289) and the proposed route to achieve this is an integrated curriculum in which language and content go hand in hand.

Changing Models of Speaker and Teacher in Multilingual and Multicultural Second Language Acquisition

As hinted at in previous sections, at present, the number of speakers of English is made up of a minority of native speakers (NS) and a majority of those who speak it as a second or foreign language in a myriad of complex and diverse situations. And despite the fact that, for many, learning English is no longer aimed at communicating with native people but rather with other speakers who are learners of the language themselves, the idealized model of the NS is still prevalent and a target. As several studies have shown (Leung and Lewkowicz 63; Gray "TESOL" 94; Sifakis and Bayyurt 457), this model is supported by some of the best-selling textbooks aimed at the international market, which – incidentally – are produced by publishing companies based on either the United Kingdom or the United States. Consequently, the sources of many of the *authentic* materials used are predominantly from these countries or other countries that are members of the Anglophone world; the topics selected are mostly of interest for people in these nations; and accents are very often British – mainly RP and modified RP – or standard American. The position of textbooks is further reinforced by international examinations, teacher education curricula and policies for teaching English as a second language. Regarding HEIs, the situation is not much different, and the NS is still taken as a yardstick from the very beginning of the students' education process if, for instance, we take into consideration the language tests, which are often an entry requirement (Smit 391). The English language used in academic exchanges is based on that of an NS, and students are required to replicate it (Wingate 427); their linguistic academic competence is also assessed against the model of the educated NS (Pratt et al. 289).

However, the dominance of the native English norms and of the ethnocentric values associated to them (Galloway 470) in the teaching of English as a second language has been long criticized and called into question (Ball and Lindsay 51). The idea that the language used by a learner of English has to be as authentic as possible so as to represent the reality of the NS was one of the tenets of the communicative approach to foreign language teaching and learning, but taking this NS as a model becomes an impossible target, and even if the learner should manage to acquire this degree of perfection, it might not be the correct kind of competence (Coperías-Aguilar "ICC as a Tool" 90). On one hand, this would mean that learners somehow have to abandon their own language; on the other, our knowledge of a language – including our native tongue – is never complete, as there will always be some areas out of our reach

(Coperías-Aguilar "ICC in the Context" 246). Also, as Corbett argues, few native English speakers entirely conform to "standard English in their output and how ironic it is that second language learners are often required institutionally to conform to standards that are more rigorous than those applied to native speakers" (39–40).

In 1993, Kramsch introduced the notion of the learner of a second language as a mediator (*Context and Culture* 233–259), and a year later, Byram and Zarate put forward the idea of the intercultural speaker (IS) as someone who has the ability to manage communication and interaction between people of different cultural identities and languages and is able to handle different interpretations of reality (53). This IS will most probably be less skilled than an NS regarding the mastery of the language but has a privileged vantage position between the home and the target culture, and in no case are the standards of achievement expected of the foreign language learner lowered (Coperías-Aguilar "ICC in the Context" 250). In an attempt to respond to the current complexities of multiculturalism and hybridity, Guilherme took this idea further and developed the notion of the critical IS (124–132). A couple of years later, Phipps and Gonzalez went beyond the idea of the IS and introduced the concept of *being intercultural* – with emphasis on being over knowledge – for which a key tenet is that of *languaging*, that is, emphasis on real communication and dialogue rather than on artificial language tasks, engaging with the other, and reflecting critically (111).

More recently, Llurda has emphasized the distinction between learners and users and established the aim of becoming successful users even if we are incomplete learners of standard native English. In this case, multilingualism is understood as an ordinary accompanying element, and the knowledge of the language by a second language user and an NS will be different but neither better nor worse (520). Then, language mixtures, code-mixing, and translanguaging are considered as legitimate linguistic possibilities to make effective communication possible, rather than being constantly discouraged or even banned from the language classroom. In light of this, code-switching can be seen as an expression of the bilingual or multilingual competence of the speakers and not as a deficiency (Cogo 359), and translanguaging – which has been defined as "the adoption of bilingual supportive scaffolding practices" (Doiz et al. "Future Challenges" 218) and focuses on the languaging process rather than the code of the language – is even more readily accepted (Heugh et al. 264).

The figure of the second- or foreign-language teacher has also revolved around an idealized NS (Llurda 523) who thus represented a prescriber of linguistic rules, an ambassador of the cultural mores, or a custodian of correct English, whatever *correct* might mean. Instead, the teacher of a second language should become a mediator or a facilitator who has to give priority not to the amount of knowledge to be acquired but to the development of new attitudes, skills, and critical awareness in the student. This educator will have to be concerned with empowering students and helping them to develop strategies to become autonomous users in diverse settings (Jaleniauskienė 274; Jiménez Raya 524). In this context, Blair argues that "the ideal teachers of English are well-trained, multilingual, ELF-aware, pragmatically and interculturally competent – *regardless of their first language*," that is, a "'post-native', multilingual model for teacher education" (99). Corbett also finds that non-native teachers become particularly valued for their ability to move between the home and target culture, although the best teacher will be the person who can awaken curiosity in students (12).

Toward Collaboration and Learner-Centered Approaches

Jaleniauskienė presents a series of important tendencies in education at the moment that could be summarized in two approaches: those related to moving from individual to collaborative learning and those moving from teacher-centered to learner-centered environments, which actually overlap (266). The idea that teachers and students have to work collaboratively in the language classroom, even sharing the power and transforming each other has been highlighted by several authors (Coffey 28; Cadman and Song 12; Jiménez Raya 127). And Ehrenreich defines a community of practice as "a group of people who regularly interact with each other by means of a shared communicative repertoire in order to accomplish a common task" (37); in this process, she argues, a lot of informal learning also takes place, and, in our present globalized world, it brings together people from many diverse linguistic backgrounds. Relationships in these kinds of communities inevitably involve the acquisition of sociolinguistic competences. For Dooly (78), "project-based learning is founded on contextualized, learner-centered outcomes and social practices that emerge as the participants collaboratively move toward shared goals and output," and more specifically, project-based language learning should be based on contextualized cooperative learning. And the final output, Dooly adds, should also have an impact on people outside the classroom and be incorporated into the surrounding community (81).

At the same time, as contended by several authors (Coperías-Aguilar "ICC as a Tool" 92; Jiménez Raya 124), making autonomous people should be a primary and highly desirable goal of education. In this sense, in the context of higher education in Europe, learning autonomy received a considerable boost with the emergence of both the CEFR and the European Language Portfolio (Sudhershan and Bruen 29), since the emphasis in the CEFR is on language being action-based not knowledge-based, the learner's empowerment, and the achievement of competences. Although competence-based language teaching and the notion of observable and measurable learning outcomes emerged in the US in the 1970s, Pérez Cañado argues that in higher education, it only came to the forefront with the beginning of the EHEA in the late 1990s ("Introduction and Overview" 4). However, it is now here to stay, as it is a way to adapt teaching methods to the demands of our time.

Note

1. Although aware of the literature dealing with the differences between them, in this paper, the terms second and foreign language are used indistinctly

References

Alcón-Soler, Eva. "Linguistic Unity and Cultural Diversity in Europe: Implications for Research on English Language and Learning." *Intercultural Language Use and Language Learning*, edited by Eva Alcón and Pilar Safont. Springer, 2007, pp. 23–29.

Badger, Richard, and Goodith White. "The Use of Technology to Promote Critical Thinking and Creativity in Language Learning." *Higher Education and Second Language Learning: Promoting Self-Directed Learning in New Technological and Educational Contexts*, edited by Rosario Hernández and Paul Rankin. Peter Lang, 2014, pp. 7–24.

Baker, Will. "English as a Lingua Franca and Intercultural Communication." *The Routledge Handbook of English as a Lingua Franca*, edited by Jennifer Jenkins, et al. Routledge, 2018, pp. 25–36.

Ball, Phil, and Diana Lindsay. "Language Demands and Support for English-Medium Instruction in Tertiary Education. Learning From a Specific Context." *English-Medium Instruction at Universities: Global Challenges*, edited by Aintzane Doiz, et al. Multilingual Matters, 2012, pp. 44–61.

Bauman, Zygmunt. *Globalization: The Human Consequences*. Polity, 1998.

Blair, Andrew. "Evolving a Post-Native, Multilingual Model for ELF-Aware Teacher Education." *Current Perspectives on Pedagogy for ELF*, edited by Y. Bayyurt and S. Akcan. De Gruyter Mouton, 2015, pp. 89–101.

Block, David, and Deborah Cameron. "Introduction." In *Globalization and Language Teaching*, edited by David Block and Deborah Cameron. Routledge, 2002, pp. 1–10.

Blommaert, Jan. *The Sociolinguistics of Globalization*. Cambridge University Press, 2010.

Bourdieu, Pierre. *Language and Symbolic Power*, edited by J. B. Thompson and translated by G. Raymond, and M. Adamson. Harvard University Press, 1991.

Byram, Michael. *Teaching and Assessing Intercultural Communicative Competence*. Multilingual Matters, 1997.

———., and Geneviève Zarate. *Definitions, Objectives and Assessment of Socio-Cultural Competence*. Council of Europe, 1994.

Cadman, Kate, and Xianlin Song. "Embracing Transcultural Pedagogy: An Epistemological Perspective." *Asian Languages and Cultures in Global Higher Education*, edited by Xianlin Song and Kate Cadman. University of Adelaide Press, 2012, pp. 3–26.

Cameron, Deborah. "Globalization and the Teaching of 'Communication Skills'." *Globalization and Language Teaching*, edited by David Block and Deborah Cameron. Routledge, 2002, pp. 67–82.

Canagarajah, Suresh. *Resisting Linguistic Imperialism*. Oxford University Press, 1999.

———. *Translingual Practice: Global Englishes and Cosmopolitan Relations*. Routledge, 2013.

Clyne, Michael. "Multilingualism, Multiculturalism and Integration." *Multiculturalism and Integration: A Harmonious Relationship*, edited by Michael Clyne and James Jupp. ANU Press, 2011, pp. 53–71.

Coffey, Margaret. "Building Cultural Community in English Language Programs." *TESOL Journal*, vol. 8, no. 2, 1999, pp. 26–30.

Cogo, Alessia. "ELF and Multilingualism." *The Routledge Handbook of English as a Lingua Franca*, edited by Jennifer Jenkins, et al. Routledge, 2018, pp. 357–368.

Coperías-Aguilar, María José. "Dealing With Intercultural Communicative Competence in the Foreign Language Classroom." *Intercultural Language Use and Language Learning*, edited by Eva Alcón and Pilar Safont. Springer, 2007, pp. 59–78.

———. "Intercultural Communicative Competence in the Context of the European Higher Education Area." *Language and Intercultural Communication*, vol. 9, no. 4, 2009, pp. 242–255.

———. "Intercultural Communicative Competence as a Tool for Autonomous Learning." *Revista Canaria de Estudios Ingleses*, vol. 61, 2010, pp. 87–98.

Corbett, John. *An Intercultural Approach to English Language Teaching*. Multilingual Matters, 2003.

Council of Europe. *Common European Framework of Reference for Languages*. Cambridge University Press, 2001.

Doiz, Aintzane, et al. "Internationalisation, Multilingualism, and English-medium Instruction." *World Englishes*, vol. 30, no. 3, 2011, pp. 345–359.

———., et al. "Future Challenges for English-Medium Instruction at the Tertiary Level." *English-Medium Instruction at Universities: Global Challenges*, edited by Aintzane Doiz, et al. Multilingual Matters, 2012, pp. 213–221.

Dooly, Melinda. "Promoting Competency-Based Language Teaching Through Project-Based Language Learning." *Competency-Based Language Teaching in Higher Education*, edited by María Luisa Pérez Cañado. Springer, 2013, pp. 77–91.

Ehrenreich, Susanne. "Communities of Practice and English as a Lingua Franca." *The Routledge Handbook of English as a Lingua Franca*, edited by Jennifer Jenkins, et al. Routledge, 2018, pp. 37–50.

Galloway, Nicola. "ELF and ELT Teaching Materials." *The Routledge Handbook of English as a Lingua Franca*, edited by Jennifer Jenkins, et al. Routledge, 2018, pp. 468–480.

García, Ofelia, et al. "Educating International and Immigrant Students in US Higher Education: Opportunities and Challenges." *English-Medium Instruction at Universities: Global Challenges*, edited by Aintzane Doiz, et al. Multilingual Matters, 2012, pp. 174–195.

Giddens, Anthony. *Europe in the Global Age*. Polity, 2007.

Gray, John. "The Global Coursebook in English Language Teaching." *Globalization and Language Teaching*, edited by David Block and Deborah Cameron. Routledge, 2002, pp. 151–167.

———. *The Construction of English: Culture, Consumerism and Promotion in the ELT Global Coursebook*. Palgrave Macmillan, 2010.

———. "TESOL and the Discipline of English." *Futures for English Studies: Teaching Language, Literature and Creative Writing in Higher Education*, edited by Ann Hewings, et al. Palgrave Macmillan, 2016, pp. 81–98.

Green, Madeleine, et al. *The Brave New (and Smaller) World of Higher Education: A Transatlantic View*. www.acenet.edu/news-room/Documents/2002-brave-new-world.pdf. Accessed 10 October 2018.

Guilherme, Manuela. *Critical Citizens for an Intercultural World*. Multilingual Matters, 2002.

Healey, Nigel M. "Is Higher Education *Really* 'Internationalising'?" *Higher Education*, vol. 55, 2008, pp. 333–355.

Heugh, Kathleen, et al. "Multilingualism and Translanguaging in the Teaching of and Through English: Rethinking Linguistic Boundaries in an Australian University." *English-Medium Instruction in Higher Education in Asia-Pacific*, edited by Ben Fenton-Smith, et al. Springer, 2017, pp. 259–280.

Hewings, Ann, and Philip Seargeant. "English Language Studies: A Critical Appraisal." *Futures for English Studies: Teaching Language, Literature and Creative Writing in Higher Education*, edited by Ann Hewings, et al. Palgrave Macmillan, 2016, pp. 61–77.

Holborow, Marnie. *The Politics of English*. Sage Publications, 1999.

———. *The Language of Neoliberalism*. Routledge, 2015.

Humphreys, Pamela. "EMI in Anglophone Nations: Contradiction in Terms or Cause for Consideration." *English-Medium Instruction in Higher Education in Asia-Pacific*, edited by Ben Fenton-Smith, et al. Springer, 2017, pp. 93–114.

Iglesias de Ussel, Julio, et al. *Sistemas y Políticas de Educación Superior*. Consejo Económico y Social, 2009.

Jaleniauskienė, Evelina. "Revitalizing Foreign Language Learning in Higher Education Using a PBL Curriculum." *Procedia – Social and Behavioral Sciences*, no. 232, 2016, pp. 265–275.

Janssens, Maddy, and Chris Steyaert. "Re-Considering Language Within a Cosmopolitan Understanding: Toward a *Multilingual Franca* Approach in International Business Studies." *Journal of International Business Studies*, vol. 45, no. 5, 2014, pp. 623–639.

Jiménez Raya, Manuel. "Exploring Pedagogy for Autonomy in Language Education at University: Possibilities and Impossibilities." *Competency-Based Language Teaching in Higher Education*, edited by María Luisa Pérez Cañado. Springer, 2013, pp. 119–138.

Kelly, Michael, et al. *The Training of Teachers of a Foreign Language: Developments in Europe*. European Commission, 2002.

Kramsch, Claire. *Context and Culture in Language Teaching*. Oxford University Press, 1993.

———. "The Symbolic Dimensions of the Intercultural." *Language Teaching*, vol. 44, no. 3, 2011, pp. 354–367.

Leung, Constant, and Jo Lewkowicz. "English Language Teaching. Pedagogic Reconnection With the Social Dimension." *The Routledge Handbook of English as a Lingua Franca*, edited by Jennifer Jenkins, et al. Routledge, 2018, pp. 61–73.

Llurda, Enric. "English Language Teachers and ELF." *The Routledge Handbook of English as a Lingua Franca*, edited by Jennifer Jenkins, et al. Routledge, 2018, pp. 518–528.

Marshall, Steve. "Re-Becoming ESL: Multilingual University Students and a Deficit Identity." *Language and Education*, vol. 24, no. 1, 2009, pp. 41–56.

Mauranen, Anna. "Conceptualising ELF." *The Routledge Handbook of English as a Lingua Franca*, edited by Jennifer Jenkins, et al. Routledge, 2018, pp. 7–24.

McLuhan, Marshall. *The Gutenberg Galaxy: The Making of Typographic Man*. Toronto University Press, 1962.

Pauwels, Anne. "Rethinking the Learning of Languages in the Context of Globalisation and Hyperlingualism." *Plurilingualism and Multiliteracies: International Research on Identity Construction in Language Education*, edited by Dagmar Abendroth-Timmer and Eva-Maria Henning. Peter Lang, 2014, pp. 41–56.

Pennycook, Alastair. *English and the Discourses of Colonialism*. Routledge, 1998.

Pérez Cañado, María Luisa. "Globalization in Foreign Language Teaching: Establishing Transatlantic Links in Higher Education." *Higher Education Quarterly*, vol. 64, no. 4, 2010, pp. 392–412.

———. "Introduction and Overview." *Competency-Based Language Teaching in Higher Education*, edited by María Luisa Pérez Cañado. Springer, 2013, pp. 1–18.

Perrin, Stuart. "Language Policy and Transnational Education (TNE) Institutions: What Role for What English?" *English-Medium Instruction in Higher Education in Asia-Pacific*, edited by Ben Fenton-Smith, et al. Springer, 2017, pp. 153–172.

Phillipson, Robert. *Linguistic Imperialism*. Oxford University Press, 1992.

Phipps, Alison, and Mike Gonzalez. *Modern Languages: Learning and Teaching in an Intercultural Field*. Sage, 2004.

Pratt, Mary Louise, et al. "Transforming College and University Foreign Language Departments." *The Modern Language Journal*, vol. 92, no. 2, 2008, pp. 287–292.

Preece, Siân, and Peter Martin. "Imagining Higher Education as a Multilingual Space." *Language and Education*, vol. 24, no. 1, 2009, pp. 3–8.

———., et al. "Examining Linguistic Diversity as a Resource for Higher Education in the Anglophone World." *Shaping Higher Education With Students: Ways to Connect Research and Teaching*, edited by Vincent C. H. Tong, et al. UCL Press, 2018, pp. 288–293.

Russell, David. "The Literacy and the Literate: The Study and Teaching of Writing in US English Departments." *Futures for English Studies: Teaching Language, Literature and Creative Writing in Higher Education*, edited by Ann Hewings, et al. Palgrave Macmillan, 2016, pp. 139–157.

Shohamy, Elana. "A Critical Perspective on the Use of English as a Medium of Instruction at Universities." *English-Medium Instruction at Universities: Global Challenges*, edited by Aintzane Doiz, et al. Multilingual Matters, 2012, pp. 196–210.

Sifakis, Nicos, and Yasemin Bayyurt. "ELF-aware Teaching, Learning and Teacher Development." *The Routledge Handbook of English as a Lingua Franca*, edited by Jennifer Jenkins, et al. Routledge, 2018, pp. 456–467.

Smit, Ute. "Beyond Monolingualism in Higher Education. A Language Policy Account." *The Routledge Handbook of English as a Lingua Franca*, edited by Jennifer Jenkins, et al. Routledge, 2018, pp. 387–399.

Spiteri, Damian. *Multiculturalism, Higher Education and Intercultural Communication: Developing Strengths-Based Narratives for Teaching and Learning*. Palgrave Macmillan, 2017.

Sudhershan, Aleksandra, and Jennifer Bruen. "Dealing With 'Educational Baggage' in the Language Classroom: Developing Autonomy Among International Students." *Higher Education and Second Language Learning: Promoting*

Self-Directed Learning in New Technological and Educational Contexts, edited by Rosario Hernández and Paul Rankin. Peter Lang, 2014, pp. 25–43.
Tudor, Ian. "From Content to Competency: Challenges Facing Higher Education Language Teaching in Europe." *Competency-Based Language Teaching in Higher Education*, edited by María Luisa Pérez Cañado. Springer, 2013, pp. 21–32.
Van Ek, Jan. *Objectives for Foreign Language Learning*. Council of Europe, 1986.
Walkinshaw, Ian, et al. "EMI Issues and Challenges in Asia-Pacific Higher Education: An Introduction." *English-Medium Instruction in Higher Education in Asia-Pacific*, edited by Ben Fenton-Smith, et al. Springer, 2017, pp. 1–20.
Wallace, Catherine. "Local Literacies and Global Literacy." *Globalization and Language Teaching*, edited by David Block and Deborah Cameron. Routledge, 2002, pp. 101–114.
Wingate, Ursula. "Transforming Higher Education Language and Literacy Policies. The Contribution of ELF." *The Routledge Handbook of English as a Lingua Franca*, edited by Jennifer Jenkins, et al. Routledge, 2018, pp. 427–438.

2 Project-Based Learning

A Five-Stage Framework to Guide Language Teachers

Fredricka L. Stoller and CeAnn Chandel Myers

Project-based learning (PBL) has been advocated as an effective means for promoting purposeful language learning, content learning, and community engagement for more than three decades: in the 1980s and 1990s (e.g., Carter and Thomas; Fried-Booth; Haines; Legutke, "Project Airport: Parts 1 and 2"; Legutke and Thomas) and since 2000 (e.g., Beckett and Miller; Beckett and Slater; Brown and Brown; Galante; Hsu; Mikulec and Miller). Reports of service-learning projects that engage language students in their communities demonstrate the value of such engagement for academic success and student empowerment (e.g., Askildson et al.; Perren et al.; Russell; Yankura Swacha). The literature is consistent in highlighting that PBL entails much more than the simple incorporation of projects into instruction and that it is adaptable to bilingual, multilingual, and multicultural classrooms. The literature also emphasizes the many benefits that accrue from student engagement in PBL, itemized here (and reviewed by Stoller, "Establishing a Theoretical Foundation"):

- authenticity of experience and language
- improved language, academic, and real-life skills
- improved abilities to make decisions, be analytical, think critically, solve problems, and work collaboratively
- enhanced confidence, self-esteem, and attitudes toward learning and using the target language
- increased content knowledge
- increased autonomy, independence, initiative, and willingness to take responsibility for learning
- repeated opportunities for interaction (output), modified input, and negotiated meaning
- opportunities for purposeful attention to form and other aspects of language
- intensity of motivation, engagement, enjoyment, and creativity

In this chapter, we introduce an iterative five-stage framework that can guide language teachers' planning, implementation, and evaluation of PBL. The framework can be adapted for (a) second, foreign, and additional language contexts; (b) young, adolescent, and adult learners; (c) learners with general, academic, vocational, and social language aims; (d) various student configurations (i.e., individual, pair, group, or class); (e) diverse language-skill emphases; and (f) different time frames. Following the five-stage framework description are authentic case studies written to highlight each stage of the framework.

PBL Five-Stage Framework

The PBL five-stage framework introduced here builds upon insights gained over three decades, during which the first author of this chapter regularly integrated project-based learning into her own teaching and trained second and foreign language teachers to do the same. The framework is the result of an evolution in thinking that began with an eight-step process (Sheppard and Stoller), transitioned to a ten-step model (Alan and Stoller; Stoller, "Project Work"), and is now depicted as a five-stage framework. As seen in Figure 2.1, the framework comprises five distinct cycles of student engagement and scaffolded instruction.

It is our belief that the framework addresses the limitations of earlier thinking. It does so by recognizing (a) the iterative nature of PBL, (b) the different types of student engagement and scaffolded instruction that are needed, (c) the skill and strategy demands of each stage, (d) teachers' evolving roles, and (e) the value of two types of reflective/evaluative tasks that bring projects to their conclusion. The framework explicitly recognizes the importance of students' language-development needs, an element that is sometimes unintentionally neglected because teachers and students become so focused on project content. Overall, the five-stage framework prepares teachers – new to and experienced with PBL – to plan, implement, and assess projects that

- give students a clear sense of the progression of their projects (from beginning to end)
- enhance student motivation and engagement
- help students improve their language skills and strategies
- introduce students to additional skills and strategies required for information gathering, processing, and display cycles
- give students the confidence to work independently or collaboratively to succeed
- provide students and teachers with opportunities for reflection

Stage 1: Preparation Cycle

The preparation cycle entails the determination of project theme and topics, final outcomes, and a plan for progressing from start to finish. When determining theme and topics, the goal is to identify those that further course goals. Themes oftentimes spring from textbook materials or

Stage	Cycle	Iterative process for teachers and students
1	Preparation Cycle	Determine project theme/topic(s)[1,2] ↔ Agree on project outcome(s)[1,2] → Plan project[1,2]
2	Information Gathering Cycle	Scaffold instruction[1] ⇄ Gather information[2]
3	Information Processing Cycle	Scaffold instruction[1] → Organize information[2] → Scaffold instruction[1] → Analyze information[2] → Scaffold instruction[1]
4	Information Display Cycle	Scaffold instruction[1] → Display outcome(s)[2]
5	Reflections Cycle	Reflect on learning[1,2] ↔ Reflect on project[1,2] Reflect on learning → Content, Language skills, Academic skills, Life skills, Strategies, Technology skills Reflect on project → Process, Product

[1] = teacher;
[2] = student
Note: Scaffolded instruction, planned by the teacher, addresses skills and strategies needed for successful student engagement in each project stage. Scaffolding can emphasize language skills and strategies; technology skills; data collection, organization, and analysis skills; life skills, etc.

Figure 2.1 PBL Five-Stage Framework

student interests. The most effective projects (a) center on themes viewed by students as relevant to their communities, studies, and lives; (b) are supported by plentiful resources, (c) arouse student curiosity, (d) motivate students, and (e) have the potential to stimulate pride among students.

Also during this cycle, tangible final outcomes, a characteristic that distinguishes PBL from numerous forms of task-based language teaching, are decided upon. Final outcomes should align themselves with curricular aims, course goals, and student needs. As indicated in Table 2.1, final outcomes can result in written work, oral activities, and other tangible products.

Intertwined with these planning decisions are determinations about project type (Table 2.2) and methods for information collection (e.g., correspondence, face-to-face encounters, library or Web searches, student creativity, surveys). Throughout the preparation cycle, the teacher makes preliminary decisions about what types of scaffolded instruction to provide and at what points in the project to do so.

Teacher and student roles can vary during this stage. In some instructional settings, projects are defined by the teacher, specified in the curriculum, or included in the course textbook. In other settings, teachers decide

Table 2.1 A Sampling of Tangible Project Outcomes

Possible Final Outcomes[a]		
Written	*Oral*	*Other*
Brochure Bulletin board display Email or letter Literary magazine Newsletter, wall newspaper Paper (e.g., argumentative, descriptive, narrative, opinion, proposal, research, report) Poem Poster Scrapbook Summary Synthesis	Debate Oral presentation (with or without a handout) Panel discussion Poetry reading Role play Simulation (e.g., board meeting, model United Nations meeting, trade fair) Theatrical production	Community event (e.g., booth at Earth Day fair, charity/fundraising event, food drive, Peace Pole proposal through to ceremony, presentation at a local school, recycled-art show, tutoring of underserved children) Creation of materials for a local school Digital story Multimedia presentation PowerPoint presentation Video or website creation

[a]Some outcomes may require teaching technology skills for project completion.

Table 2.2 Sampling of Project Types

Performance (e.g., play written by students) Production (e.g., trash-to-fashion show, video)
Real-world (e.g., website to promote tourism in community) Simulated (e.g., proposed solution to a global problem) Social-welfare (e.g., community wheelchair-accessibility proposal)
Temporary (e.g., poster fair, newsletter) Semi-permanent (e.g., wall newspaper) Permanent (e.g., school recycling program)

on select aspects of a project and students provide input on other project elements; in this way, project preparation becomes more of a teacher-student collaborative effort. For instance, the teacher may select a textbook theme (e.g., pollution) and students identify topics of interest (e.g., community air, water, and noise pollution). As another example, students (individually, in groups, or as a class) may be given the opportunity to decide on the project's final outcome. In settings with advanced students or students in language-for-specific-purposes courses – especially if they have had previous experience with projects or have well-defined goals – students may be granted considerable freedom to define the nature of their projects during the preparation cycle. Despite this variation in teacher and student roles, students in *all* contexts benefit from having some voice in project preparation so that early on, they develop a commitment to the project.

Stage 2: Information Gathering Cycle

After preliminary decisions are made, students engage in information gathering (Stage 2). The types of information gathered and methods for information collection vary, as does the scaffolded instruction provided by the teacher to set students up for success at this stage. In Table 2.3, five methods of information gathering and examples of scaffolded instruction, appropriate for the stage, are itemized. What and how teachers scaffold is inextricably linked to course goals and students' language-, strategy-, and content-learning needs. A review of or introduction to theme- and topic-related vocabulary is typically central to this project stage, as is a review of key grammatical structures.

Stage 3: Information Processing Cycle

The third stage of the framework engages students in the processing of information (i.e., organization and analyses of data) collected in Stage 2. Whatever types of information have been collected, students benefit from being guided in the processing of that information. With the goal of setting students up for success at this stage, scaffolded instruction can guide students in (a) reconsidering the purpose of their projects to inform organization and analysis tasks; (b) reviewing information collected; (c) distinguishing between pertinent and less pertinent information (in light of project goals); (d) keeping relevant information and setting aside the rest; (e) coding or reconfiguring data (with grids, note cards, outlines) to discover categories, characteristics, patterns, relationships, and trends; (f) summarizing or synthesizing data; and finally (g) deciding if additional information is needed.

Some types of information require other forms of scaffolded instruction. For instance, if students have recorded interviews, they may need

Table 2.3 Information-Gathering Methods and Examples of Scaffolded Instruction

Information-Gathering Methods	*Possible Emphases of Scaffolded Instruction*	
Correspondence	Contrast language in formal letters and emails Contrast formats of formal letters and emails Review conventional openings and closings	Review language for polite requests Engage students in process writing: brainstorm, draft, revise, edit, peer review, revise
Interviews	Review question formation Address pronunciation, intonation, and stress Teach language of openings and closings	Introduce gambits for requesting repetition, clarification, elaboration, and so on Guide practice in listening and note taking
Reading	Guide students in establishing a purpose, making and later checking predictions, inferencing Guide students in skimming for main ideas and scanning for details	Guide students in using discourse structure for main-idea comprehension Review ways to take notes while reading Discuss reasons for rereading Guide students in filling in outlines or graphic organizers
Surveys & questionnaires	Cover question formation Contrast formal and informal language Teach question types (e.g., fact, opinion, clarification; multiple choice, open ended, true/false)	Introduce technology skills for creating instrument(s) Make time for piloting of instrument(s) Teach language for inviting participation
Web searches	Guide students in establishing a purpose, posing guiding questions, and selecting key words Teach students how to navigate the Web and preview sites to determine suitability, reliability, authorship, and bias Teach strategies for minimizing distractions (inherent in Web searches)	Guide students in (a) skimming for main ideas and scanning for details, (b) listening for the gist and details, (c) rereading or listening again for well-defined purposes Discuss ways to take notes Guide students in exploring hyperlinks to extend information gathering

to learn how to transcribe them and interpret the transcripts. If students have collected written texts, as another example, some attention to paraphrasing might be appropriate to assist them in transferring information from text to notes.

Table 2.4 Examples of Scaffolded Instruction Provided in Stage 4

Final Outcomes	*Possible Emphases of Scaffolded Instruction*
Oral or written	Review pertinent transition words, vocabulary, and grammar Emphasize the importance of attribution and paraphrasing Discuss issues related to plagiarism
Oral	Review (and practice) pronunciation, intonation, and stress Discuss manner of presentation (openings, closings, eye contact, voice projection) Provide opportunities for rehearsal and feedback
Written	Review quoting, paraphrasing, and methods of attribution (in-text and in references) Provide opportunities for rounds of revision, editing, and feedback Review formatting conventions and final-product expectations

Stage 4: Information Display Cycle

It is during Stage 4 when students finalize and share (i.e., display) project outcomes with the teacher and possibly other audiences. Like in the other stages of the process, the teacher incorporates scaffolded instruction into classroom activities to assist students with finalizing project outcomes and then "displaying" them (when, e.g., submitting a written paper, participating in a poster fair, giving a PowerPoint presentation, engaging in a debate). Table 2.4 itemizes possible forms of teacher scaffolding for this penultimate project stage.

Stage 5: Reflections Cycle

It is commonplace for teachers and students to view Stage 4 as a project's logical conclusion. It is at the end of Stage 4 when teachers typically assign grades to students' final outcomes. We, however, advocate for two rounds of student (and teacher) reflection to serve as the real culmination (even though reflection can occur during other project stages as well). During this culminating stage, with teacher encouragement and modeling, students reflect (through, e.g., discussion, journal entries, meditation) on what they have learned from project engagement in terms of (a) content, language, skills, and strategies and (b) process and product (i.e., final outcome). Teachers learn a tremendous amount from students' reflections, yet teachers too should engage in the same types of reflective processes to identify project strengths and weaknesses in addition to implications for future projects.

Case Studies

Our five case studies are sequenced to highlight each cycle in the PBL five-stage framework. The case studies depict projects that the second author of the chapter has implemented in English language classes in second- and foreign-language settings. We chose these particular projects because they highlight the versatility of PBL. Each project can be adapted, in small or large ways, for other target languages and instructional settings; different lengths of time; students at different educational and proficiency levels; linguistically homogeneous classes; linguistically and culturally heterogeneous classes; and students with distinct language-learning aims. In almost all cases, some involvement with communities beyond the confines of their own classrooms (e.g., the classroom next door, another school, the local community, or communities in other countries or on other continents) could be incorporated, if it is not already. (See Boss and Krauss, for discussions of extending learning experiences beyond the classroom.)

In our case studies, we do not directly address the assessment of students' performance. Dependent upon course and project goals, teachers might (a) engage in assessments *of* learning (summative) or assessments *for* learning (formative) and (b) grade holistically or analytically. Nor do we address the inevitable challenges that teachers might face in planning and implementation (e.g., scarcity of target-language resources; limited bandwidth for in-class Internet searches; student, and possibly teacher, discomfort with PBL because it diverges so much from traditional teaching methods). Because each instructional setting is distinct, we assume that teachers adopting a project-based approach will (a) aim for context-appropriate assessment and (b) be vigilant about challenges that arise and work to resolve them so that students gain the most from PBL.

Case Study 1: Sustainability Grant Proposal Project

Box 2.1

Theme	Environmental sustainability
Final outcome(s)	Sustainability event planning and written grant proposal
Student proficiency	Advanced
Time allotment	6 hours/week for 4 weeks (~24 hours total)
PBL highlight	Preparation cycle (Stage 1)

Goals

By the end of the project, students will

- think critically about real-world problems centered on sustainability and propose an educational "intervention" as a step toward a solution

- conduct research on a sustainability topic and successfully integrate it into a grant proposal
- write persuasive and informative paragraphs justifying an education-oriented event
- understand the value of and write using agreed-upon style-guide conventions
- experience improved confidence in abilities to complete an authentic target-language written genre

Overview

For this project, students (individually, in pairs or groups) plan an environmental sustainability event and apply for event funding through a grant offered by their educational institution, the local community, or a local business. The project requires students to complete a grant proposal, following award specifications. While students are not required to submit their proposals for consideration, they are encouraged to do so. The project comprises two major parts:

1. Students envision and plan an educational sustainability event to take place at their educational institution, nearby school, or other community venue. To help students structure the project, they are given three general event options to choose from: (a) educating the campus community about energy waste at an Earth Day booth, (b) establishing a school composting program, or (c) conducting research about local recycling habits and educating the campus community about them.
2. Students complete a five-part grant proposal (Table 2.5).

Highlights: Preparation Cycle (Stage 1)

With this project, we highlight the preparation cycle, which entails determining project theme/topics, agreeing on project outcome(s), and planning the project. The sustainability theme, commonly addressed in language textbooks, is selected by the instructor. The instructor also narrows down the theme to three topics that are relevant to students' lives

Table 2.5 Grant Proposal Guidelines (adapted for language students)

1. Cover Page 2. Project Description • Project Overview (1 paragraph) • Methods (1 paragraph) • Benefits (1 paragraph) • Time Line (1 list with 5 events)	3. Statement of Community Interest (1 paragraph) 4. Budget and Budget Justification (1 paragraph and 2 tables) 5. References (4 sources minimum)

and communities. Students choose one of the topics for their projects, resulting in increased motivation and a greater sense of project ownership.

The two project outcomes (i.e., sustainability event planning and a written grant proposal, the latter an authentic written genre with a well-defined audience) are also decided upon by the instructor. If necessary, the teacher modifies grant-proposal expectations to complement students' abilities and account for time constraints, while still preserving the benefits accompanying an authentic project. The project is structured around steps (Figure 2.2) aligned with the PBL five-stage framework cycles. The steps guide not only the students but also the teacher who facilitates the project. The project builds upon a textbook unit and provides opportunities for students to learn and practice new skills (e.g., persuasive writing, research), language (e.g., environmental lexicon), and fixed phrases, such as those used when making reference to sources (e.g., "*According to,*" "*Based on*"). The project configuration leads students through incremental steps that result in project completion.

What is not readily apparent in Figure 2.2 are the scaffolded activities incorporated throughout. For example, in the third step, students research their topics. Because conducting research in the target language is a skill that students are learning, teacher scaffolding is needed. To assist students with their research, students and instructor co-create research

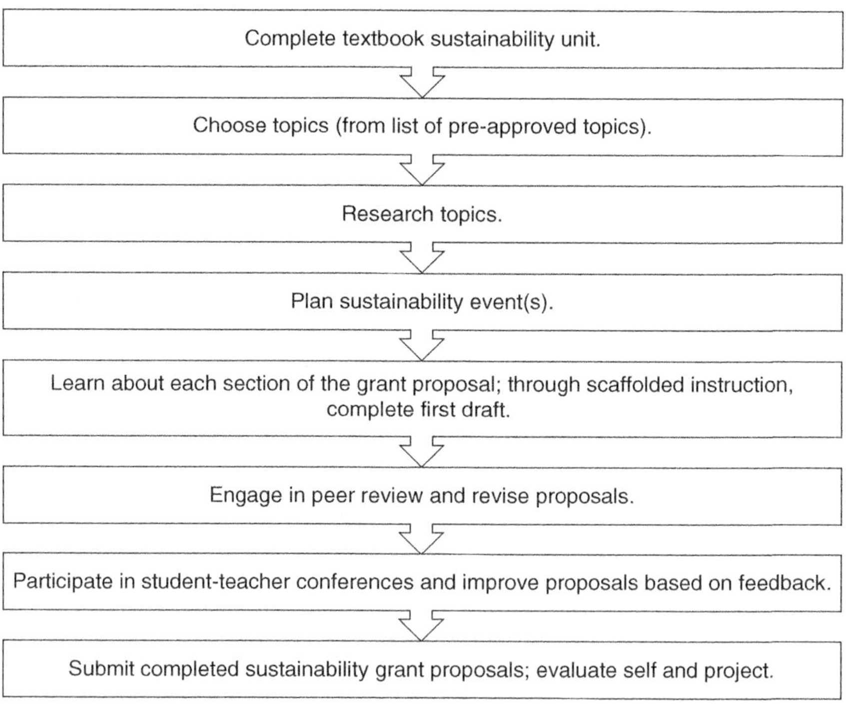

Figure 2.2 Sustainability grant proposal project in eight steps.

questions, students consult the textbook and reliable (and comprehensible) websites (the latter provided by the teacher), the instructor provides assistance during class time allotted for student research, and students are introduced to issues related to plagiarism and citation conventions. Finally, when students are ready to incorporate research results into their proposals, the instructor provides feedback on students' written work, citations, and compliance with proposal expectations.

Reflections

The sustainability grant proposal project has many strengths. Its structure sets students up for success and makes it possible for them to see how their linguistic, academic, and research skills build upon and support each other. Furthermore, the structure permits students to witness improvements, celebrate small accomplishments, and complete the project confidently. Students are motivated by the fact that the project (a) is inextricably linked to an authentic genre, (b) connects learning goals to community service, and (c) encourages creative thought. By means of this project, students gain not only real-world communication skills but also opportunities for critical thinking. The authentic nature of the project resonates with students and motivates them to work through the steps required to apply for the grant. At its conclusion, students feel secure that they can participate in and contribute to their communities.

This project is easily adapted for students with different needs or in other contexts. For example, the project could be modified to prepare students to (a) give oral presentations to inform classmates about their events or (b) participate in simulated interviews during which students answer questions about their events. To match the project to a different theme or authentic genre, instructors can search the Internet and community resources to find alternative grant proposals or project options. The project can then be modified to best suit the students and teaching context. Whatever the adaptation, linking class projects to authentic final outcomes can be motivational and confidence-inspiring for language students.

Case Study 2: Survey-Interview-Video Project

Box 2.2

Theme	What do people really think?
Final outcome(s)	Video and support materials
Student proficiency	Intermediate
Time allotment	1 hour/week for 12 weeks (~12 hours total)
PBL highlight	Information gathering cycle (Stage 2)

Goals

By the end of the project, students will

- use a variety of question forms accurately in writing and speaking
- gather information from various sources
- orally refer to sources using "citation language"
- list sources accurately on a reference page
- draw connections between research and previously learned information
- utilize technological tools to convey information learned during the project
- present information utilizing effective presentation skills

Overview

For the survey-interview-video project, students work in small groups to gain a better understanding of a topic covered earlier in class (e.g., the pros and cons of television). Using textbook knowledge as a base, groups investigate their own topics further, compile a list of relevant references, and use their expanded knowledge to create two research instruments: a ten-item survey and a five-item open-ended interview protocol. Then, they gather additional information from a minimum of ten target-language-speaking informants for the survey and five for the interviews. These target-language informants can be students in other classes at their school, other teachers, neighbors, friends, or individuals in their communities. (See Table 2.6 for a sample topic, survey item, and interview question.) Next, groups analyze survey and interview data, synthesize results, and report them in an informative 5–7 minute video presentation. At the conclusion of the project, each group submits its survey, interview questions, video presentation, reference page, and completed group evaluation form. When project videos are then shown in class, students experience a sense of pride in their accomplishments.

Highlights: Information Gathering Cycle (Stage 2)

With this project, we highlight the information gathering cycle, which involves an iterative process of student information gathering and

Table 2.6 Sample Topic, Survey Item, and Interview Question

Topic	*Survey Item*	*Interview Question*
Television	Do you think children should be allowed to watch television?	Do you think television has more positive or negative influences on people's lives? Explain.

instructor scaffolded support. This project has a large data-gathering component. Students spend a considerable amount of time (a) revisiting previously learned topic-related content, (b) exploring the Internet, (c) compiling information from various sources, and (d) collecting survey and interview data.

The project hinges upon students asking stimulating questions and gathering pertinent information from informants (i.e., survey and interview respondents). To accomplish this, students need a good understanding of their topics. During initial information gathering, each group member finds and shares one relevant information source (e.g., magazine article, Internet site) with group members. From among the compiled resources, groups select at least two to inform their survey and interview questions, refer to in their videos, and include in their reference lists. At different points, students participate in teacher-led tutorials to review question forms and learn basic techniques for creating research instruments. They also learn techniques for conducting surveys and interviews, with the goal of gathering large quantities of data from survey items and more refined data from open-ended interview questions.

Building upon what students learn from teacher-led sessions on (a) question formation; (b) question types to elicit facts, opinions, clarification, and so on; and (c) instrument development, students create a ten-item survey and share it with peers and the instructor for feedback. Then, students learn and practice language to introduce themselves, explain their projects, and invite participation in their research (e.g., "Excuse me, do you have two minutes to answer a survey for a project in my English class?"). Groups are then ready to go beyond their classrooms, into their communities, to gather survey data.

In addition to collecting survey data, group members collaborate to write interview questions. After revising their interview questions, students learn language for conducting interviews (e.g., how to request clarification, elicit additional information). They then practice in mock interviews. The final step in the information gathering cycle is to conduct and record interviews with five people.

Reflections

The major strengths of the survey-interview-video project are that it leads to improvements in many skill areas (Table 2.7), increased confidence as a result of communicating in the target language for authentic purposes, and an expanded network resulting from real interactions with informants. Furthermore, the project can be easily adapted by teachers in different contexts. For example, the project can be modified in relation to content area, information sources (e.g., academic journals), task complexity (e.g., the number of required surveys and interviews), and final outcome (e.g., a written report). Such changes lead to different forms of teacher scaffolding and

Table 2.7 Skills Improved Through the Survey-Interview-Video Project

Skills Improved	*Examples*
Linguistic Skills	• Form questions accurately • Refer to sources using "citation language"
Academic Skills	• Think critically about a topic • Synthesize ideas from various data sources
Information Gathering Skills	• Search the Internet for appropriate websites • Decide relevance of different information sources
Technology skills	• Create a well-formatted survey (using Microsoft Word) • Create and edit a video (using iMovie)

skill emphases. Whatever changes are made, guiding students in information gathering tasks represents an excellent forum for the development of varied skills and an ideal avenue for linking course content with students' communities. Students who complete the project improve a wide range of skills and become better prepared to succeed in the future.

Case Study 3: Model UN Problem Resolution Project

Box 2.3

Theme	Current world problems
Final outcome(s)	PowerPoint presentation
Student proficiency	Intermediate to advanced
Time allotment	3 hours/week for 4 weeks (~12 hours total)
PBL highlight	Information processing cycle (Stage 3)

Goals

By the end of the project, students will

- gather information from varied sources
- think critically about the causes and effects of real-world problems
- state ideas and respond to others' ideas
- debate and negotiate respectfully with classmates who represent different cultures
- ask clarification questions to gain a better understanding of others' ideas
- compromise pragmatically, using context-appropriate language and politeness strategies
- collaborate with peers to generate possible solutions to real-world problems
- give a persuasive presentation

Overview

This project simulates the exploration of issues faced by the United Nations (UN) and leads to students' generation of possible solutions to real-world problems. The project progresses through a sequence of individual, group, and whole-class tasks, culminating with a Model UN meeting. Students begin by selecting one real and distinct country (to research and represent). Then, they conduct research about their country to learn more about it and the problems that it faces. Next, they use their new knowledge to nominate one country-specific problem, which they think has global implications, for the Model UN to consider. From among all the problems proposed, the class narrows down the pool, by vote, to the four most serious problems, which become the focus of the remainder of the project. Next, in small groups, students brainstorm and list possible solutions to all four problems.

At this juncture, each student selects one of the four problems to work on. Four new groups are formed by clustering students who have chosen the same focal problem. Groups conduct research on their problem, consider the possible solutions listed during previous group deliberations, and negotiate to craft a resolution that proposes steps for a comprehensive solution. Upon completion of a jointly written group resolution, groups create a three-minute PowerPoint presentation to (a) introduce the problem and resolution to the Model UN and (b) persuade other member-states to vote for their resolution. On the last day of the project, Model UN members listen to group presentations, one at a time, ask questions, state opinions, and vote to pass or reject each resolution. (Students from other classes could be invited to attend and participate in the Model UN meeting.) In the final stage of the project, students take part in reflection activities and evaluate themselves, group members, and the project.

Highlights: Information Processing (Stage 3)

Here, we highlight the information processing cycle of the Model UN project, focusing on (a) students' organization and analysis of information and (b) teacher scaffolding. Throughout this cycle, students (a) organize ideas from multiple sources, (b) analyze the strengths and weaknesses of ideas through discussion and negotiation, and (c) make individual, group, and whole-class decisions. During the various rounds of the project, students have different types of data to compile (e.g., country-specific and global problems to sort through, solutions to consider). To organize these data, the teacher introduces students to organizational strategies (e.g., categorization, clustering, and pattern-identification techniques) and linguistic frames for communicating about them (e.g., "These two ideas are similar" or "We can combine these two solutions"). Utilizing these strategies and linguistic frames, students sort and assemble data in preparation for subsequent analysis cycles.

During each cycle of analysis, students collaborate with group members and/or the whole class. The teacher prepares students for the language demands of collaborative tasks by introducing them to speech acts that will likely be needed (Table 2.8). After students have practiced the language for each speech act, they are better prepared to participate in each cycle of analysis, during which they communicate, negotiate, compromise, and finally make decisions.

Reflections

In this project, students choose a country to represent, problems to focus on, and the content of a resolution to present to the Model UN. Throughout the project, students think critically about multifaceted world problems and possible solutions. Because students control these aspects of the project, they develop a sense of ownership in the project and participate fully, thereby contributing to the project's success. The multiple opportunities for scaffolded instruction permit the teacher to address students' language, research, and collaborative skills.

To adapt this project to different teaching contexts, teachers can (a) alter the number of students representing each country; (b) increase or decrease the number of problems selected; (c) make initial decisions about focal problems, with the possibility of, for example, designating one overarching problem that students explore from various perspectives (e.g., drugs, explored at individual, community, and societal levels); and (d) modify the final outcome to match course goals (e.g., a written report instead of or in addition to an oral presentation).

Overall, this project brings real-world issues and evidence-based solutions into the classroom; it prepares students to communicate about

Table 2.8 Speech Acts and Corresponding Language to Support Students' Engagement

Speech Act	*Examples*
To share data with the goal of organizing information	"These two solutions are similar because . . ."
To express opinions	"Generally speaking, I think this solution is strong because . . ."
To express agreement	"I think that [name] brings up a good point because . . ."
To express disagreement	"I see what you're saying, but . . ."
To express cultural attitudes/traditions	"That is a problem for _____ culture because . . ."
To facilitate compromise	"Why don't we try to use both of these ideas and . . .?"
To encourage group member participation	"How does __(country)__ feel about _____?"
To seek clarification	"Could you explain how that might work?"

diverse topics, a skill that can be transferred to future academic endeavors and everyday interactions.

Case Study 4: Imitation-Speech Video Project

Box 2.4

Theme	Super suprasegmentals
Final outcome(s)	Imitation-speech video, with annotated transcript
Student proficiency	High beginner to advanced
Time allotment	1 hour/week for 8 weeks (~ 8 total hours)
PBL highlight	Information display cycle (Stage 4)

Goals

By the end of the project, students will

- learn and use meta-language to identify suprasegmental features of spoken English
- listen for and interpret pragmatic functions of English suprasegmentals appropriately
- use suprasegmental features of spoken English to be pragmatically appropriate
- gain confidence in controlling pronunciation
- utilize technological tools to convey information learned during the project.

Overview

As part of the imitation-speech video project (adapted from Stacy and Grode), students learn about English suprasegmentals (i.e., word stress, sentence stress, intonation, and connected speech) and their importance for comprehensible pronunciation. The project requires students to choose a video of someone whose pronunciation they imitate in their own videos. By the project's conclusion, students can (a) recognize and name different pronunciation features and (b) modify their own pronunciation.

While viewing one- to three-minute segments of popular movies, students analyze different speakers' pronunciation and annotate suprasegmental features on a video transcript. After students become familiar with pronunciation-related terminology and have adequate practice listening for different pronunciation features, they then choose a one- to three-minute video segment of a speech or monologue (which has an available written transcript) to imitate. Students can find their videos from a variety of sources including TED Talks, Oscar speeches, movies, and YouTube. After they select their videos, students listen to and analyze them for the same four pronunciation features that were practiced in class. Next, students video record themselves imitating the original speaker as meticulously as possible. Finally, upon completion of their videos, students enjoy a "video day" when they compare the original videos with their peers' imitation videos.

Highlights: Information Display Cycle (Stage 4)

With this project, we highlight the information display cycle. This project culminates with two tangible outcomes: (a) a transcript of students' selected videos with accurate annotations of pronunciation features and (b) an imitation-speech video. These two outcomes permit students to showcase their abilities to identify pronunciation features and produce them in their own speaking. Leading up to the two final outcomes, the teacher guides students through numerous cycles of focused listening practice (analyzing the pronunciation features of different speech samples) and guided repetition (imitating different people's pronunciation, accompanied by feedback from the instructor and peers). To prepare students for their imitation speeches, the teacher encourages students to listen to and analyze their selected video segments as many times as they deem necessary (in and out of class) to accurately annotate the pronunciation. The second phase of speech preparation entails students doing their best to imitate their chosen speaker using the same suprasegmental features as the original. After spending several hours modifying their pronunciation and recording their videos, students can confidently share their completed imitation speeches with classmates.

Reflections

The effective interpretation and use of English suprasegmental features are important for successful spoken communication (Celce-Murcia et al.). Thus, the imitation-speech video project prepares students to achieve personal and professional goals that involve speaking the target language. While this project allows more theatrical students to shine, even shy students enjoy creating and watching their imitation videos; all students feel confident about final project outcomes because they can record their videos as many times as they feel is needed. An additional benefit of this project is that students become proficient in the meta-language of suprasegmental pronunciation features, which can help them communicate with teachers about pronunciation in future classes.

Case Study 5: My Blog Project

Box 2.5

Theme	Self-discovery
Final outcome(s)	Blog with seven entries
Student proficiency	Intermediate
Time allotment	1 hour/week for 8 weeks (~8 hours total)
PBL highlight	Reflections cycle (Stage 5)

Goals

By the end of the project, students will

- think critically about personal choices, beliefs, and culture
- use previously learned vocabulary, grammar, and content knowledge in meaningful ways
- gain increased motivation for reading and writing in the target language
- effectively convey ideas, thoughts, and beliefs about familiar topics in writing
- use technological tools to enhance reading and writing in the target language

Overview

For the My Blog project, students learn to create a simple blog using free blogging sites (e.g., wordpress.com). Over eight weeks, students create seven blog posts that take them on a journey of self-discovery. They write their thoughts and opinions, share current and past photographs, and post a video. Additionally, students search for and introduce classmates to other interesting blogs. They also read and comment on peers' blog posts.

The students' seven blog topics are as follows:

1. **Who am I?:** Students write a ten-sentence blog post introducing themselves by providing information about their origins, families, favorite foods, and so on.
2. **Relationships:** Students select one of ten questions about relationships to answer (e.g., Who makes the best bosses: males or females? Why? What are the qualities of a good leader?). In their short paragraph responses, they explain their personal opinions and/or experiences.

3. **Awesome blogs:** Students are introduced to five different blogs in class, and using a worksheet, they analyze each blog for different features (e.g., design, language, creativity, content). The instructor prepares students to search for other blogs of interest because, in their third post, students introduce three new blogs to their readers, accompanied by a three- to five-sentence explanation of why they like each blog.
4. **My culture through photographs:** Students post ten pictures (five of which must be taken themselves) along with a short description that explains how each photo relates to their personal culture. Students select the types of pictures to post (e.g., photos of themselves engaged in hobbies; more personal photos of family and friends; less personal and more artistic photos of landscapes or sunsets).
5. **Predicting my future:** Students imagine what their lives will be like at 40 years of age and write a letter to their future selves. In their letters, they first explain their current lives. Then, they predict what their lives will be like in the future (e.g., job, family, hobbies). Finally, they give themselves a piece of advice (e.g., if you stopped playing the guitar, start again!).
6. **My dream job:** Each student prepares for and takes part in a five-question mock interview for a dream job. Students ask someone they know to interview them using a set of general questions distributed in class (e.g., "What are your strengths?"). The interview is videotaped on their cell phones and saved for later uploading. Additionally, students write their ideal answers to a subset of the interview questions; they do not transcribe what had been videotaped. At week's end, students post the video of their mock interview and written answers to interview questions.
7. **My childhood:** Students locate an old picture of themselves and post it with a three- to five-sentence description of how the picture depicts their childhood.

Highlights: Reflections Cycle (Stage 5)

With this project, we highlight the reflections cycle, which entails reflections on what has been learned and what the project experience was like. In actuality, reflective tasks occur throughout the project, for teacher and students alike. As the teacher assesses and provides feedback (on language, content, and organization) on weekly blogs, she reflects on students' progress and needs. Students reflect on feedback and consider ways to improve future posts.

Students engage in other types of conscious self-reflection as well. At the beginning, middle, and end of the project, students engage in reflective tasks that spotlight the content, language, strategies, academic skills, and life skills that they hope to learn, are learning, and have learned. Such reflections help students reach a fuller understanding of skills that have improved and those that need improvement.

The culminating reflective task (completed anonymously by students) leads to an evaluation of the process and product of the project and the instructor. Students are encouraged to be honest in their feedback; the teacher assures students that the feedback will have no impact on their grades. This last component of the reflections cycle provides teachers with valuable insights into students' project experiences and ways to improve future projects.

Reflections

Using blogs as project outcomes provides a platform on which students can communicate about a variety of topics. Blogs, on the topics noted earlier, provide an optimal way to encourage students to work autonomously to personalize posts. Such autonomy invites students to (a) reflect on their lives, families, choices, and world views and (b) use the target language to communicate personally meaningful ideas. Writing and posting blogs also creates opportunities for recycling vocabulary, grammar, and content that students learned previously. For students with more academic goals, the blog project could be restructured to focus on academic topics and more scholarly information gathering and processing tasks. It is worth noting that while the technological demands of blogging might make some students uncomfortable, teacher scaffolding and a focus on content, as opposed to blog design, can put students at ease.

Conclusion

The incorporation of project-based learning (PBL) into our teaching repertoires has the potential to promote meaningful language and content learning, strategy training, and community engagement. The many benefits that accrue from PBL – in terms of language improvement; increased content knowledge; student motivation, confidence, and empowerment; real-life skills; and critical thinking – are relevant to students with a range of language abilities, in bilingual, multilingual, and multicultural classrooms. PBL permits teachers to extend learning opportunities beyond the classroom, thereby putting students into contact with new audiences, in, for example, the classroom next door, the local community, and beyond. As suggested by Fitzgerald and colleagues in their broader discussion of the centrality of engagement in higher education, PBL can shift the educational experience of language learners from an internally classroom-based focused one to an experience that is broader and more enriching in scope.

In this chapter, we introduced a five-stage framework that can guide teachers in the planning, implementation, and evaluation of PBL. Our case studies of projects that have been successfully implemented in language classrooms in second and foreign language contexts demonstrate how versatile the PBL approach is and how the framework can be translated into practice. It is our hope that readers gain insights that can be used to enhance the teaching and learning in their classes.

References

Alan, Bülent, and Fredricka L. Stoller. "Maximizing the Benefits of Project Work in Foreign Language Classrooms." *English Teaching Forum*, vol. 43, no. 4, 2005, pp. 10–21.

Askildson, Lance R., et al. "Developing Multiple Literacies in Academic English Through Service-Learning and Community Engagement." *TESOL Journal*, vol. 4, no. 3, 2013, pp. 402–438.

Beckett, Gulbahar H., and Paul Chamness Miller, editors. *Project-Based Second and Foreign Language Education: Past, Present, and Future*. Information Age Publishing, 2006.

———., and Tammy Slater. "The Project Framework: A Tool for Language and Content Integrations." *English Language Teaching Journal*, vol. 59, 2005, pp. 108–116.

Boss, Suzie, and Jane Krauss. *Reinventing Project-Based Learning: Your Field Guide to Real-World Projects in the Digital Age*. 3rd ed. International Society for Technology in Education, 2018.

Brown, Cherie J., and Erina M. Brown. *Partners in the Classroom: Collaborative English Language Teaching and Learning Projects*. Akita International University Press, 2014.

Carter, Graham, and Howard Thomas. "'Dear Brown Eyes': Experiential Learning in a Project Orientated Approach." *English Language Teaching Journal*, vol. 40, 1986, pp. 196–204.

Celce-Murcia, Marianne, et al. *Teaching Pronunciation: A Course Book and Reference Guide*. 2nd ed. Cambridge University Press, 2010.

Fitzgerald, Hiram E., et al. "The Centrality of Engagement in Higher Education." *Journal of Higher Education Outreach and Engagement*, vol. 16, no. 3, 2016, pp. 7–28.

Fried-Booth, Diane L. *Project Work*. Oxford University Press, 1986.

Galante, Angelica. "Developing EAL Learner's Intercultural Sensitivity Through a Digital Literacy Project." *TESL Canada Journal*, vol. 32, no. 1, 2014, pp. 53–63.

Haines, Simon. *Projects for the EFL Classroom: Resource Material for Teachers*. Nelson, 1989.

Hsu, Li-Yuan. "Integrating Culture With Project-Based Instruction in an EFL Classroom." *English Teaching & Learning*, vol. 38, no. 1, 2014, pp. 61–90.

Legutke, Michael. "Project Airport: Part 1." *Modern English Teacher*, vol. 11, no. 4, 1984, pp. 10–14.

———. "Project Airport: Part 2." *Modern English Teacher*, vol. 12, no. 1, 1985, pp. 28–31.

———, and Howard Thomas. *Process and Experience in the Language Classroom*. Longman, 1991.

McPherron, Paul, and Patrick T. Randolph. "Thinking Like Researchers: An ESL Project That Investigates Local Communities." *TESOL Journal*, vol. 4, no. 2, 2013, pp. 312–331.

Mikulec, Erin, and Paul Chamness Miller. "Using Project-Based Instruction to Meet Foreign Language Standards." *The Clearing House a Journal of Educational Strategies, Issues and Ideas*, vol. 84, 2011, pp. 81–86.

Perren, James, Nuray Grove, and Julie Thornton. "Three Empowering Curricular Innovations for Service-Learning in ESL Programs." *TESOL Journal*, vol. 4, no. 3, 2013, pp. 463–486.

Russell, Natalie M. "Teaching More Than English: Connecting ESL Students to Their Community Through Service Learning." *Phi Delta Kappan*, vol. 88, no. 1, 2007, pp. 770–771.

Sheppard, Ken, and Fredricka L. Stoller. "Guidelines for the Integration of Student Projects in ESP Classrooms." *English Teaching Forum*, vol. 33, no. 2, 1995, pp. 10–15.

Stacy, Adrienne, and Jennifer Grode. "Targeting and Assessing Spoken Accuracy in English." *TESOL Convention*, March 2013, Dallas, TX. Presentation.

Stoller, Fredricka L. "Project Work: A Means to Promote Language and Content." *English Teaching Forum*, vol. 35, no. 4, 1997, pp. 2–9, 37.

———. "Establishing a Theoretical Foundation for Project-Based Learning in Second and Foreign Language Contexts." *Project-Based Second and Foreign Language Education: Past, Present, and Future*, edited by Gulbahar H. Beckett and Paul Chamness Miller. Information Age Publishing, 2006, pp. 19–40.

Yankura Swacha, Kathryn. "Service-Learning in the Second Language Writing Classroom: Future Directions for Research." *TESOL Journal*, vol. 9, no. 2, 2018, pp. 278–298.

3 A Theoretical Approach to Project-Based Learning in Community-Based Settings

Emily Skalet

Project-based learning (PBL) is a collaborative and communicative instructional strategy in which educators work alongside learners to create meaningful opportunities in academic contexts that extend to real-world application. Authentic opportunities to practice language in the classroom enhance students' self-efficacy when encountering similar literacy and language tasks within their community. Educators working with adult English language learners can use PBL to support students as they explore, analyze, and respond to texts and concerns they may experience in their everyday lives (Jacobson et al. 34).

Adult English language learners are active participants in the communities in which they live, work, and attend school (Cone and Harris 44). They are regularly required to balance their everyday responsibilities in a new culture and therefore are constantly negotiating language and literacy demands in varying contexts. Developing a student-centered approach and communicative standards with PBL supports students' language learning because it reflects the day-to-day needs of their lives and also encourages civic engagement. Carefully considering the scope of responsibilities and everyday tasks and challenges students may encounter, and most likely already do (Lakin et al. 21), educators are in an exceptional position to integrate community and civic engagement into our daily lesson plans in order to best support our students.

The theoretical frameworks useful for planning PBL integrate consideration for an equitable and participatory classroom culture and the social components of learning. Sociocultural theory (1978) and multicultural education can help prepare practitioners to design and incorporate projects relevant to language learners' needs. The theoretical frameworks further inform the sequential nature to planning small-group and whole-class projects to be completed over a course of time. Maintaining an inquiry-stance positions all of us in the classroom to ask questions about the project purposes and address why it may reflect personal and community needs.

PBL, as informed by students' real-life needs, is strategic and often begins with expansive language goals that cannot be achieved in a single lesson but rather are intentionally built toward with daily learning objectives, assignments, and classroom routines that support the project goal throughout a specified time line. Educators may use planning strategies to consider how the language and literacy work assigned in lesson one supports the students' expected outcomes in lesson ten. Authentic PBL considers student and community needs so that students may feel more confident approaching community service contexts (DuBord and Kimball 320). Explicit in authentic PBL is the understanding that this something students can take with them when they leave the classroom and in community and service learning contexts (320). In PBL with specific goals and clear expectations, instructors scaffold assignments and prepare students for more complex tasks, group work, and application ahead.

This chapter explores how PBL with adult English language learners in academic settings can support students' self-efficacy in approaching language and literacy tasks in varied community contexts. Reviewing three primary frameworks: sociocultural theory (Vygotsky 1978), multicultural education, and inquiry-based learning, I explore methods and strategies to incorporate and design PBL that encourages community involvement. Utilizing class time to expand on students' experiences and needs navigating a new culture, I will review how PBL with an inquiry-based stance can create and maintain a supportive classroom culture where students' ideas and needs intersect with real-world application and reflective learning.

Sociocultural Theory (1978)

Through developing meaningful PBL, we consider the needs of our students within the social context of our communities and classrooms (Kutz and Roskelly 58). Vygotsky's sociocultural theory (1978) informs this collaborative learning style because of the focus on learning as it pertains to social and cultural practices and our potential for accessing new knowledge over time through a variety of interactions (Lantolf et al. 207). One of the primary tenets of sociocultural theory is that learning is dependent on our participation in cultural situations. Second is the zone of proximal development (ZPD), which posits information and knowledge circulating between learners and learners and learners and instructors encourages and expands the depth of comprehension (213). The ZPD invites us to think carefully about how students' learning is enhanced when they are provided with consistent opportunities to collaborate with others who may have more experience on a particular unit of study. Viewing PBL in the classroom through the theory's two central components permits us to consistently include varied learning styles and real-world contexts for learners.

Social Learning

Meaningful PBL will consider the language required to adequately approach different environments and provide the requisite instructional support as students are asked to take more responsibility for their learning and language processes (Ajayi 643). In practice and as I will discuss later, this may mean preparing beginner-level students to request medical assistance, or it could be supporting higher-level students in completing case studies for a service learning project. Assigning adequate space for learners to explore a particular topic of interest or need provides generative opportunities for language learning. Additionally, small-group or whole-class projects where students are engaged in obtaining knowledge and skills for a specific goal provide multiple opportunities for students to interact with peers and instructors so that we incorporate varied perspectives into prior established knowledge (Nyikos and Hashimoto 508).

We are oriented to connect "tools and signs" to help us make choices that reflect our evolving understanding of the context (John-Steiner and Mahn 192). Working toward a project in a language classroom provides space to hone skills needed to complete the academic project and can then be applied to participating in the community. Identifying and analyzing the aforementioned "tools and signs" is paramount to discussing effective strategies to take part in and access community-based services.

Operating with the assumption that most people regularly and successfully travel through and negotiate both familiar and unfamiliar contexts, it is helpful to remember that we are always linked with our environments. The actions we perform and the language we use in those spaces (Lantolf et al. 221) can subsequently inform classroom needs and interests. Elevating language learners' day-to-day needs and participation in the community helps to ensure active and confident participation in their community. PBL can then be utilized to incorporate and teach the language specific to certain contexts (Ajayi 641) as we will see in the following classroom examples. Pertaining to community engagement, sociocultural theory positions us to also think about the theory and methods to access and participate in service learning (Crabtree, 26).

ZPD: Zone of Proximal Development

The nature of PBL is to begin with a larger assignment that students complete over a specified time. ZPD is not scaffolding, but when planning, it is helpful for instructors to consider strategies to scaffold assignments in order for students to approach the final project successfully and with confidence. Collaborative learning strategies, such as completing group case studies or problem-solving assignments support students' engagement in the classroom and creates experiential learning opportunities so that learners can eventually complete a similar task independently and support others in the same context as needed (Lantolf et al. 217). In this way, ZPD and scaffolding intersect as we work with students to help them to effectively and efficiently strategize their classwork (Verenika 4). Adult students working with other students or the instructor are linking the new information with what they know, thereby adding to their experience and self-efficacy approaching the material and community need (John-Steiner and Mahn 192).

The Cognitive Apprenticeship model within social learning promotes a collaborative classroom culture with an emphasis on students' self-reflection. Students review their progress with the designated learning objectives and consider it alongside more experienced learners and instructors (Nyikos and Hashimoto 511). Instead of it being comparative, which often contains negative associations, we are instead asking learners to reflect on their personal progress and look to more experienced people for support, strategies, and advice. Cognitive Apprenticeship can encourage students to learn from more experienced practitioners, allowing for a more mutually productive experiential learning especially in international service-learning opportunities (Crabtree 25).

PBL, in its variety of forms, relies on a classroom culture that acknowledges students' immense background knowledge and interpersonal experiences. Expanded in academic contexts, it is a commitment to strategically developing communicative opportunities for students to further develop their language skills (Lee 30). When we consider the social aspect of learning and how we gain access and incorporate new knowledge into existing personal frameworks, collaborative projects provide the space for new ideas and personal growth.

Classroom Example: Language Experience Approach

In a multilingual and multicultural beginner level ESOL/literacy class for people without formal literacy education in their native language, we completed a five-week unit on the topic of health. The coursework focused extensively on language needed in emergency situations. We incorporated print awareness as it relates to identifying health-related signs (e.g., poison, danger, emergency) and discussed what community services are available when a person needs medical assistance. Interpreting and analyzing "tools and signs" (John-Steiner and Mahn 192) and an overview of available resources were requisite components of our project and supported our learning as we strategized methods to access and potentially later collaborate with community-based services.

Our project focus was a written document completed through the Language Experience Approach method (LEA). LEAs are collaboratively generated texts in which learners contribute ideas to the story. In traditional literacy-based LEAs, students dictate sentences to the facilitator, who transcribes them as they are said, thus co-creating class materials. We used a picture-based narrative detailing a caregiver's understandably frantic response after a baby accidentally ingests poison (Lignon and Tannenbaum 7).

In small, mixed-level groups, students discussed what the pictures represented to them and described the narrative in English. While some of the language detailed in the scenes of the story may have been above the students' independent level, through collaborative group work, students were able to formulate possibilities as they compared ideas and contributions as a group (Anton 304). Students shared opinions and asked questions that demonstrated life experience that extended beyond the formal class environment (Nyikos and Hashimoto 513). Our culminating project, which took place over the course of several days, was very much a creative pursuit demanding higher-level thinking combined with real-life practicality.

Multicultural Education Framework

A multicultural education framework fosters an emphasis on teaching and learning to include perspectives and values reflective of our cultural backgrounds. In addition to a comprehensive and inclusive philosophy, one of the primary components of multicultural education is to support equitable education opportunities that will build and promote social responsibility and justice (Nieto and Bode 5). Using this framework to structure community and civic-engagement-based PBL allows us to think of ways for all learners to become participatory members of society (Aydin 33) through an inclusive understanding of background knowledge and perspectives as well as the potential for relevant application.

Students' access to and knowledge of their cultures, communities, and community needs is an unequivocal strength in a language classroom and should be part of classwork in teaching and learning to support civic-engagement and service (Bringle et al. 1). Increasing student involvement through multicultural education creates a participatory classroom where projects can reflect student needs and choice in addition to what they want to see and become part of in their communities.

The purpose of authentic PBL is centered on real-world application. Multicultural education complements and strengthens a commitment to community service and engagement through incorporating students' cultural and language strengths. Through promoting student needs and values in the classroom, a multicultural education framework helps to support self-efficacy as students engage in the multifaceted components of community and academic settings (Campano 5). Projects that are focused in the community where students live or work and are service-based utilize students' existing cultural and language knowledge (DuBord and Kimball 300) and position students to analyze concerns and connect it to larger frameworks (Crabtree 25).

Sonia Nieto writes of a multicultural education framework, "It is no longer simply a question of transmitting important knowledge to students, but rather of working with them so that they can reflect, theorize, and create knowledge" (Nieto 36). In addition to a collaborative view of strengths, this idea of critical inclusivity (Aydin 35) focuses on student engagement in co-constructing learning opportunities and application. Examining this further, PBL encourages students to explore and to take leadership roles that recognize and embrace different learning styles to apply to real-world application (Jenks et al. 90). Planning spaces for students in PBL invites us to look closer at how our classroom is situated and our access to appropriate, inclusive, and validating teaching materials that can support multilingual and multicultural learners and perspectives. In addition to creating a participatory classroom where projects reflect student needs and choice, PBL can position and prepare our classrooms to become change agents (Aydin 36).

When determining purposeful and level-appropriate projects to support community engagement, it is paramount to consider what students continually engage with outside of traditional academic structures and how needs and experiences can be subsequently supported with classroom learning objectives (Nieto 33). Multicultural education is a way for educators to think about the people in their classrooms and how their values, communities, and languages are subsequently incorporated into the curriculum and community engagement.

PBL as Inquiry-Based

As mentioned, authentic PBL in an adult language classroom gives students genuine opportunities to take ownership of their learning and language goals. An inquiry-based stance supports the reflective planning and practice component of PBL because it provides instructors an opportunity to thoughtfully review what we regularly use as curriculum resources, classroom strategies, and learning objectives. Cochran-Smith and Lytle write,

> the notion of inquiry as stance is the idea that educational practice is not simply instrumental in the sense of figuring out how to get things done, but also and more importantly, it is social and political in the sense of deliberating about what to get done, why to get it done, who decides, and whose interests are served
>
> (Cochran-Smith and Lytle 121)

To determine authenticity and value in class projects with an inquiry-based stance, it is imperative to consider conversations with learners and colleagues to evaluate objectives, assignments, and success (Cochran-Smith and Lytle 28). Approaching PBL with this framework means that learning will be collaborative and self-reflective because it is mutually informed by what the students are bringing to the classroom and what they want to study. Exploring and subsequently validating this meaning-making process allows us to assess language and literacy progress and extend it beyond traditional classroom contexts.

Connected to language acquisition, sociocultural theory, and multicultural education, an inquiry-based stance includes students' questions and experiences in curriculum choices and PBL development to formulate and co-construct meaningful projects. Encouraging collaboration with colleagues, students, and community partnerships to review understandings and classroom needs expands what community and classroom engagement can be because we are all positioned as learners (Cochran-Smith and Lytle 28). Consistently striving to ask questions about student perspectives, values, and interests with subsequent reflection supports an inquiry stance.

When we work with students to integrate community-based elements into our curriculum through PBL, we also establish and further legitimize the everyday lived experiences of English language learners (Campano 4). It can be validating to incorporate the experiences adult learners face in their communities in academic space to grapple with everyday issues thus integrating "more immediate life-world experiences with school-based knowledge and instruction" (Campano 31). Collaborating with community organizations and members enables us to expand our knowledge of available resources, services, and events, which can then inform what is brought into the classroom (19). Discerning what students know and is valuable to them will enhance their participation in the community and further support participation in and application of language skills (Dubord and Kimball 303).

An inquiry-based approach promotes strategic consideration of the language and literacy skills people require to access the resources they want. Reflecting on the scope of needs and interests, this could mean students become active participants in community organizations through open dialogues about needs and services offered with eventual partnerships (298), or it could mean that classes may return to concepts close to survival English or functional literacy. Regardless of class level, the skills and strategies demonstrate a nuanced understanding of social context and language that supports a more inclusive and investigative approach.

Classroom Example

While teaching a summer semester of beginner-level ESOL/literacy in New York City, our primary theme was "transportation," and I had a whole unit planned based on what I assumed was important. Very early in the unit, I overheard students talking about their difficulties purchasing public transportation tickets using the standard MetroCard machine. The students' range of time in New York varied, but the conversations' general consensus was that using technology in this capacity, combined with being unable to read and respond to the instructions and prompts on the interactive touch screen, could be prohibitively challenging. The literacy, language, and technology obstacles caused some students to wait for a willing passerby to help purchase a ticket when they needed to travel within the city. For some students, if no one was available to help, they would return home unable to complete their errands and appointments for the day. The conversation was deeply informative for me, and the concern motivated a complete change in curricular plans. Instead of my original ideas, we constructed a project-based unit around using MetroCard machines in New York City.

We spent five weeks preparing to purchase public transportation tickets. We actively reviewed general machine and payment information with ample pictures taken from the actual machines. We studied the requisite travel vocabulary – asking for and giving directions and reading transportation-related signs. Students worked in small groups to practice modified touch screens and share personal experiences and effective strategies for independent travel (Anton 304). Our small group work prepared us for our culminating project – a field trip to our nearby subway station to purchase tickets.

The final project was entirely informed by students' personal experiences and concerns when traveling independently in our community. Through incorporating our background knowledge and what we practiced in class, we were able to plan our field trip together. Once at the subway station, the class applied the language and literacy we studied to its most authentic context. Completing a complex task such as this with the support of more experienced peers can be extraordinarily beneficial when learners are asked to recall and integrate concepts and vocabulary (Cone and Harris 49). For assessment, I informally observed the students purchase or scroll through the screens and practice the vocabulary and supported them as needed. Students more experienced and confident with MetroCard machine use were also invited to assist less-experienced users.

After our field trip, we reflected on the experience together. We spoke and then wrote about what students could do now that they could not do before. Through a combination of open dialogue and teacher-generated prompts to discuss and consider what independent access to transportation brings, the students dictated their sentences to me, and I transcribed. Through our whole class reflection, students compared and contrasted their initial goals and subsequent achievements, often expanding thinking based on contributions from other students (Nyikos and Hashimoto 506). Our story began with "I can speak English. I can write my name." As we thought more about our field trip, the sentences became more specific to the potential for independent travel opportunities, i.e., "I can go to school. I can go to work. I can go somewhere. I can leave." Our classroom and local subway station became what Campano refers to as "collaborative sites of inquiry" (Campano 5), where learners interpreted an authentic task, collaborated with peers to successfully complete it, and then reflected on the experience.

Developing Meaningful Projects to Encourage Community Engagement

Beginning with a particular theme or general purpose advises what direction PBL takes in the classroom. Strategic community-based PBL provides the space for students to ask questions while navigating a new language in their communities and classrooms. Through thinking about what is important to them (Anton 311), PBL builds on what students want to know or are already familiar with and want to expand. Once a theme or purpose is determined, the following step is designing the project with the preceding objectives and assignments. The backward design approach (Tomlinson and McTighe 27) helps to adequately support students so that they are prepared to successfully complete the tasks leading to the larger learning objectives.

Project Ideas for Varying Levels

A strong initial step is to brainstorm ideas for projects given the course theme or unit purpose. My preference is to begin with broad project ideas operating with the assumption that this is not something to be completed in a single lesson or even a week, but rather a goal that all of our language and literacy learning is building toward. Some instructors and learners prefer PBL where the culminating project is tangible, such as completing a group case study or creating a class text. Other PBL units have projects that emphasize oral and listening skills as the product, perhaps incorporating a presentation as the culminating project. The most innovative projects in my classroom have originated with learner ideas because they are the true experts on what they need to successfully engage with to become active participants in their community.

Surveying students through informal and formal platforms is an effective strategy to ensure classwork connects to the students' communities. Once an authentic question or concern for the project is determined, class time can be utilized to articulate strategies to then analyze and respond to community-based texts (Cone and Harris 47). With the three aforementioned frameworks in mind, I sought to gather this information from beginner-level ESOL/literacy learners through introducing a picture-based needs assessment. I posted pictures representing different themes (e.g., health, housing, shopping) around our classroom and asked students to place a sticky note with their name on the paper that represented what they most wanted to study in English class. Once we counted all the votes for our general theme, we did a similar activity to determine the unit project.

Using a picture-based needs assessment is a participatory approach that allows students at all levels a clear method to self-assess and communicate their interests with their peers. The needs assessment, whether it is picture- or text-based, is completed in an interactive and collaborative style reflecting the ZPD (Nyikos and Hashimoto 507). It asks learners to engage in self-reflection and discuss personal experiences with those particular topics. In my class, this meant that students shared times they asked for directions at the hospital or requested a particular product at the supermarket. When introducing a new project at any level, students can compare their interactions in the community and collaborate to determine which areas they seek to grow. Encouraging the class to reflect on experiences and to express and respond to opinions is inherently generative and the essence of creating meaningful PBL.

Another strategy to identify potential project ideas is conversations with colleagues about issues learners have discussed in their classrooms. Concerns that higher level students encounter will likely be identical to those that lower level students do, simply the approach to teaching to support it in the classroom will differ. Through an informal discussion with a colleague, I learned about a student genuinely struggling with the written forms and language needed to actively participate in teacher conferences for her child. I brought the issue of navigating K–12 schools to my classroom to gauge student interest and was met with enthusiasm. Our central project for the unit based on that conversation was focused on completing a form and communicating with school personnel. We steadily worked to practice reading school lists and completing important forms. With a community-service perspective, the same project idea could evolve to include volunteering at the school or completing assignments to support family involvement.

How Do Classwork and Community Partnerships Support the Project?

In order to successfully complete the project, students will need access to the appropriate resources, collaborative classroom work, and a working concept of the expected language they will both encounter and be asked to use. Established community partnerships for students to access service learning opportunities are conducive to bringing the project outside of traditional academic space and into communities. From a pragmatic and inclusive perspective, this planning process also asks that we return to community experts for guidance (Crabtree 19). As discussed earlier in relation to ZPD, consider the nature of the project and what spaces are available for students to work together and independently to achieve language and academic results.

Considerations for Implementing PBL

Organized PBL that integrates classroom and community engagement reflects strategic co-construction and planning on behalf of the instructor and students. In practice, the theoretical frameworks guide how we integrate the four language skills, structure expectations for learners, and provide scaffolding so that students can successfully complete projects with meaningful and authentic application. Language and literacy are context specific. The specific social components, vocabulary, and grammatical structures needed to access specific spaces (Vygotsky 28–29 as cited in Nyikos and Hashimoto 509) are introduced and practiced as part of the project. While PBL is structured to be student-centered, there is the need for explicit instruction to guide students to access new skills for real world application. Instructors can introduce literature, grammatical structures, and vocabulary as it intersects with everyday concerns (Campano 114).

PBL in an inquiry-based and learner-centered classroom is well situated for small group work and student inquiry but requires careful structure reflecting academic rigor. The instructor can explain the expectations for the project (Cone and Harris 45) or expectations can be co-constructed as a class. Articulating the purpose of the project and the reasoning behind instructional choices contributes to a clear structure where students are part of the planning process and understand the reasoning behind expectations. As we dedicate class time to particular projects, instructors may identify and subsequently seek to reduce the scaffolding needed so that learners can participate in this cultural engagement independently (Lantolf et al. 215). Thinking beyond traditional formal assessments, PBL that is completed over the course of time will give educators a chance to think about learner development (211).

PBL allows us to think about how to include varied learning objectives and real world applicable outcomes to see how language learning can enable students to feel more confident engaging with their communities (Campano 10). We can define success here in two ways: (a) is the student more confident approaching similar situations and (b) what is the student's reflection of the project and is this something the student can do independently now? As mentioned earlier, the most successful project ideas come from students who become engaged in their learning and will support learning both in and out of the classroom.

References

Ajayi, Lasisi. "ESL Theory-Practice Dynamics: The Difficulty of Integrating Sociocultural Perspectives Into Pedagogical Practices." *Foreign Language Annals*, vol. 41, no. 4, 2008, pp. 639–659.

Aydin, Hasan. "A Literature-based Approaches on Multicultural Education." *Anthropologist*, vol. 16, no. 1–2, 2013, pp. 31–44.

Bringle, Robert G., et al. "Partnerships in Service Learning and Civic Engagement." *Partnerships: A Journal of Service Learning & Civic Engagement*, vol. 1, no. 1, 2009, pp. 1–20.

Campano, Gerald. *Immigrant Students and Literacy: Reading, Writing, and Remembering*. Teachers College Press, 2007.

Cochran-Smith, Marilyn, and Susan L. Lytle. *Inquiry as Stance*. Teachers College Press, 2009.

Cone, Dick, and Susan Harris. "Service-Learning Practice: Developing a Theoretical Framework." *Michigan Journal of Community Service Learning*, vol. 3, no. 1, 1996, pp. 31–43.

Crabtree, Robbin D. "Theoretical Foundations for International Service Learning." *Michigan Journal of Community Service Learning*, vol. 15, no. 1, 2008, pp. 18–36.

DuBord, Elise, and Elizabeth Kimball. "Cross-Language Community Engagement: Assessing the Strengths of Heritage Learners." *Heritage Language Journal*, vol. 13, no. 3, 2016, pp. 298–330.

Jacobson, Erik, et al. "Creating Authentic Materials and Activities for the Adult Literacy Classroom." *A Handbook for Practitioners, NCSALL*, 2003. www.ncsall.net/fileadmin/resources/teach/jacobson.pdf. Accessed 5 February 2019.

Jenks, Charles, et al. "Approaches to Multicultural Education in Preservice Teacher Education: Philosophical Frameworks and Models for Teaching." *The Urban Review*, vol. 33, no. 2, 2001, pp. 87–105.

John-Steiner, Vera, and Holbrook Mahn. "Sociocultural Approaches to Learning and Development: A Vygotskian Framework." *Educational Psychologist*, vol. 31, no. 3–4, 1996, pp. 191–206.

Kutz, Eleanor, and Hephzibah Roskelly. *An Unquiet Pedagogy Transforming Practice in the English Classroom*. Boynton/Cook Publisher Heinemann, 1991.

Lantolf, James P., et al. "Sociocultural Theory and Second Language Development." *Theories in Second Language Acquisition*. 2nd ed., edited by Bill VanPatten and Jessica Williams. Routledge, 2015, pp. 207–226.

Lee, Michele S. "Implementing the Sociocultural Theory While Teaching ESL." *Student Perspectives About Civic Engagement*, vol. 1, no. 1, 2015, pp. 28–35.

Lignon, Fred, and Elizabeth Tannenbaum. "911." *Picture Stories: Language and Literacy Activities for Beginners: 1st (first) Edition*. Longman, 1990, p. 7

Nieto, Sonia. *The Light in Their Eyes: Creating Multicultural Learning Communities*. 10th ed. Teachers College Press, 2010.

———, and Patty Bode. *Affirming Diversity: The Sociopolitical Context of Multicultural Education*. Pearson Education, Inc., 2012.

Nyikos, Martha, and Reiko Hashimoto. "Constructivist Theory Applied to Collaborative Learning in Teacher Education: In Search of ZPD." *The Modern Language Journal*, vol. 81, no. 4, 1997, pp. 506–517.

Tomlinson, Carol Ann, and Jay McTighe. *Integrating Differentiated Instruction and Understanding by Design*. ASCD, 2006.

Vygotsky, Lev S. *Mind in Society: The Development of Higher Psychological Processes*. Harvard University Press, 1978.

Part II

Teaching and Learning

4 Community Bridges and Interdisciplinary Language Learning Projects

Stepping Out of Comfort Zones and Building Ways to Grow

Susan G. Polansky

Scholarship on communities of practice has expanded over the years from initial focus on the business world to apply to a broad range of spheres of work, study, and service. In communities of all sorts, individuals form dynamic groups around shared interests and values. Whatever the domain, although what members of a community hold in common is fundamental to the development of its goals, group interactions that incorporate a diversity of perspectives in the process of sharing expertise can foster the community's vitality, success, and sustainability. Productive communities of practice invite openness. They cultivate a familiar rhythm that welcomes change, and they allow for different voices and levels of individual and group participation.

This chapter shares how university students who pursue a variety of academic disciplines and engage in community- and project-based learning in partnership with the local public school system enhance second language development and promote student growth in multiple dimensions. Their "community of practice" develops through *Tutoring for Community Outreach*, a longstanding collaboration established in 1996 between the Department of Modern Languages at Carnegie Mellon University and the Pittsburgh Public Schools. This is a community-based, semester-long course for undergraduate and MA students who work four to six hours per week with K–12 students and teachers of Chinese, English as a Second Language, French, German, Japanese, and Spanish. Most of the university students who enroll pursue double majors with a modern language and another academic field or pursue minors in a modern language, and a number have been students in the department's MA program in Applied Second Language Acquisition. As the university tutors deepen appreciation of their own and others' language learning, they bring together their capabilities from diverse fields (sciences, technology, fine arts, social sciences, history, creative writing, linguistics, business, and more) and carry their expertise into a wide variety of tutoring and teaching assistant activities and into the final projects they create in collaboration with cooperating teachers and their students in the public schools. It bears mention that in institutions where students may not carry additional majors, they likely have interests and talents they can link with their language proficiency in the ways to be described in this course model. In the on-campus class sessions and through weekly journal writing, the tutors reflect on experiences, discuss strategies, and design learning activities they implement at their school sites. This is an iterative process that promotes growth through reflection and self-critique, role modeling, learning to deal with challenges, and coming to appreciate complex roles and perspectives, cultural identity, and diversity within the wider context of the communities of learners in the urban public school setting.

Wenger and colleagues have set forth a widely recognized structural model for communities with three key elements: domain, community, and practice (27). A look at these three components in the tutoring course will provide, first, a profile of the *community*, the participants who create "the social fabric of learning" (28). Second, a description of the *domain* or main foci will outline the fundamental goals and key features of this curricular model. Third, examples of *practice*, the university students' community engagement activities, projects, final synthesis reflections, and post-semester work will demonstrate how with their diverse backgrounds and interdisciplinary interests, they come together in a community of practice. Their interactions in the multicultural context of the local academic community of the public schools with younger students with a variety of needs and learning styles contribute to their tutees' growth as well as their own. This practice is "the knowledge the community develops, shares, and maintains" (Wenger et al. 28). Concluding considerations focus on factors contributing to the positive outcomes of this community- and project-based learning experience.

The Community: A Diverse Group of Participants

For more than two decades, the communities of students taking the *Tutoring for Community Outreach* course have studied languages and cultures in creative combinations with other fields across the university, such as Chinese studies and business or biological sciences, French and Francophone studies and psychology or linguistics, German studies and professional writing, Hispanic studies and computer science or chemical engineering, and Japanese studies and information systems or design. To date, 175 students, roughly five to ten each semester, have enrolled, and they have been placed at 13 different school sites: two high schools, three middle schools, and eight elementary schools with language magnet programs. Most schools are walking distance or a short bus ride from the university. Students with intermediate-level target language proficiency have worked at elementary or middle schools, and those with at least intermediate-level proficiency have worked in the high schools.

Their schooling prior to college often differs a great deal from the urban school settings they enter. Some are international students from Asia, Latin America, or Europe; some come from small, rural US districts, more homogeneous private schools, or city schools with less diverse environments. Their motivations for taking the course vary. Some are attracted to community service or seek to explore the field of education in an institution where there is no school of education or education major or are fulfilling a requirement for the modern languages major that directs students to courses about acquisition of language and culture or topics related to language policy and contexts for language learning.

The screening process during pre-registration aims to maximize the potential for positive outcomes for all concerned. This first step initiates the tutors' engagement with other stakeholders – the course professor and university faculty liaison and the individuals who facilitate the clearance process – and prepares for making connections with the school site liaisons, the cooperating teachers in the schools, and their elementary, middle, and high school students. Prospective enrollees consult with the course professor, submit information forms, and give the name of a faculty contact who can provide input about their language proficiency and suitability. The course professor stresses the importance of meeting commitments and students' roles as ambassadors of the university as well as learners in this community partnership. The intention is that the community they are joining evolves as "a group of people who interact, build relationships, and in the process develop a sense of belonging and mutual commitment" (Wenger et al. 10). They should develop and become part of a network "held together by shared understandings and a sense of obligation" (Bender 7).

After receiving permission to enroll, students complete the process of obtaining state and federal clearances in order to work with minors. The university faculty liaison makes contact with the public school site liaison to assess interest in having tutors at the school and supplies information about the tutors: names, contact information, majors and minors, year of graduation, languages, and available hours. The school site liaison communicates with cooperating teachers, facilitates matching and scheduling arrangements, and conducts an orientation at the school site at the beginning of each semester. Decisions about placements and adjustments take into account both the matching of convenient schedules and the preferences of cooperating teachers and tutors.

Every semester, just as the tutors represent a diverse group, so does the population of teachers and students with whom they interact. Spanning stages and ages, some of the world languages teachers have worked many years and are well established in their schools, while others are recent graduates or very new to their classrooms. Tutors learn to engage with different levels of experience, styles, and personalities, and some work with more than one cooperating teacher per semester. The public school students also display great variation in learning styles, proficiency levels, motivation, and need. The goal is for the community engagement arrangements and activities to address these differences. Tutors may offer remedial help to those who are behind or who have been absent, or they may provide enrichment to academically talented students. They may work one-on-one or in small groups in and out of the classroom, guide conversation practice, help with quiz and test review, process writing, or observe and work alongside teachers and assist as needed. They may create and teach mini-lessons or entire class periods or help integrate the use of technology. Cooperating teachers offer suggestions and guidance through the semester. In the search for optimal ways to support the students, participants learn and grow within a stable, flexible framework. Fundamental to the strength of the partnership is the ability of key stakeholders to function in an established structure while addressing positively a broad range of needs.

The Domain: Key Goals and Stable, Flexible Features

In broad terms, the domain of the community in *Tutoring for Community Outreach* has focused on cultivating students' civic engagement, their appreciation of diverse contexts and approaches for language learning, and their reflective, applied learning. The university students increase familiarity with cultural contexts in which language learning occurs, with education in an urban setting and teaching as a profession, and with different education systems and programs for learning and teaching world languages. They gain insight into how to work with K–12 students with diverse needs and learning styles. They make connections between the field of education and other professional fields and disciplines. They develop their interpersonal and communicative skills in their target languages and English as they reflect, explore, prepare, implement, and refine strategies for promoting successful language learning. In addition to activities at the school sites, course readings, weekly journal writing, and exchanges in class provide opportunities for dedicated and continuing reflection and discussion, which foster growth and tutors' recognition of subtleties, and thus support the success of the experience.

The domain is grounded in the learning objectives for the course. As listed on the course syllabus, students will

- engage in a community outreach service-learning experience to gain deeper understanding of the cultural contexts in which language learning occurs
- partner with the local schools in the learning of world languages by either elementary, middle, or high school students and gain insight into how to work with students with diverse needs and learning styles
- gain appreciation of different education systems and approaches to world language learning and teaching

- reflect on strategies for promoting successful language learning
- reflect on topics related to education in an urban setting and teaching as a profession
- draw connections between the field of education and other professional fields and disciplines

These goals interconnect with the perspectives and needs of the community partners in the public schools. Cooperating teachers and their students appreciate that tutors increase possibilities for differentiated learning, improve their students' proclivity to learn, and build their skills and knowledge in concrete ways. Tutors can devote attention to individual students that teachers may not be able to offer. Students who have been absent or are having difficulty in understanding a concept have been able to work individually or in small groups with tutors outside of the classroom, and tutors often have a different approach to delivering information that correlates more closely with a particular student. Tutees may return to their classrooms readier and abler to participate. Transmitting their enthusiasm for second language learning, tutors can build positive connections as near peer tutors to increase tutees' interest and motivation. Tutees may see the college students as novel and new compared to their regular teacher. Given the youth, dress, and often colloquial and age-related methods of the tutors, students often do not perceive the tutors as authority figures, and this can facilitate positive rapport building and dynamic interactions. Tutors may offer unique as well as task-based contributions to building cultural and linguistic knowledge and application. From different backgrounds, nationalities, and experiences abroad, with their special personal touches, tutors may engage students with new perspectives and thought patterns and serve as sources of cultural customs and nuances that may not be otherwise available.

Within the domain's anchoring framework, each semester brings new happenings and each tutor encounters some of the same as well as very different experiences from fellow participants. In a given semester, a tutor may assume a fairly predictable pattern of responsibilities with the same tutees or groups over many weeks and also, on given days, encounter the unexpected. Inevitably, tutors face challenges as well as situations to celebrate. Some tutors have difficulty delineating the boundaries between being a young adult and an adolescent and need to find the appropriate balance for giving directions and guiding tutees effectively. Some tutees feel so comfortable with a tutor that they begin to share personal information, some of which might place the tutor in an awkward situation. Some students initially perceive working with a tutor, or the mere act of leaving the classroom to work with one, as a sign of stupidity or an embarrassment, and tutors try to increase their sensitivity to these individual circumstances as they seek productive connections with tutees.

The course professor, university tutors, school site liaisons, cooperating teachers, and their students address challenges of balancing stability with flexibility so that the community can learn and grow.

> Knowledge boundaries and the leading edge of a domain enables members to decide exactly what is worth sharing, how to present their ideas, and which activities to pursue. It also allows them to recognize the potential in tentative or half-baked ideas.
>
> (Wenger et al. 28)

In the community of practice within the university classroom and at the school sites, much sharing and testing of ideas takes place. To promote the goals of the domain, tutors are encouraged to innovate, adapt, and make adjustments based on suggestions and discussions about weekly activities. Some activities they design serve for particular lessons unconnected to their final projects for the course or may inform the creation of their final projects. Near mid-semester, consultation about final projects begins with the university faculty member, cooperating teachers, and fellow tutors. Examples of practice and bodies of knowledge developed and shared by the community, these culminating projects connect closely with the topics of the domain.

The Practice: Learning Activities and Project Development

For the final major assignment in the community engagement experience, tutors have the choice of writing an essay on a topic related to second language learning or contexts of learning in connection with their work with the students and teachers at their school site, or they may undertake a hands-on project to implement in their final days at the school site. The guidelines for both options emphasize the need for members of the community to develop their plans by consulting, investigating, discovering, testing, and refining. The vast majority of students opt to create a project to put into action at their schools. "Successful practice development depends on a balance between joint activities, in which members explore ideas together, and the production of 'things'" (Wenger et al. 39). A look at the development process for tutors' projects, including examples, will demonstrate this dynamic interaction of sharing and producing and how in practice students embrace challenge and grow.

> The term *practice* . . . denotes a set of socially defined ways of doing things in a specific domain: a set of common approaches and shared standards that create a basis for action, communication, problem solving, performance, and accountability.
>
> (Wenger et al. 38)

While there is great variation in what tutors' practice entails, their projects are rooted in the individual and collective experiences of the semester and the cultural contexts and needs of the school community members. The course guidelines for the projects also set forth standards for process and product to help meet criteria for successful practice. During the eighth or ninth week of the 15-week semester, tutors should have begun to brainstorm and consult with cooperating teachers and the university professor. By the beginning of week 10, students submit a paragraph-length abstract with their preliminary plan. Between weeks 11 and 14, tutors continue to share ideas with cooperating teachers and meet individually at least two more times with the course professor to provide progress updates and to confirm the dates for presentation at the school site so that the course professor is able to attend. During the on-campus class sessions of these weeks, tutors share ideas with each other and continue to make changes. During week 14 or 15, tutors execute their projects, and where schedules permit, fellow tutors also attend these presentations.

To complete their projects, tutors prepare a reflective self-assessment to submit during the final exam period. It should include 1) a clear description of the project with the goals; 2) a version or elements of the content of the project, for example: the lesson plans, visuals, or a show-and-tell collection of handouts, teaching materials, or a copy of the finished "product" (slide presentation, game, story, and so on); 3) a thoughtful narrative of the process and results, often with input from tutees (How did things go?); and 4) the tutor's evaluation of the results: Were you satisfied with the outcome? What might you change if you could implement again? In an additional end-of-semester session, the community of practice – tutors and course professor – meets for lunch, dinner, or dessert to recap experiences in a final exchange. Given the multiple language areas of the tutors in all but a few semesters over the years, class discussions are conducted in English. Given the course instructor's knowledge of Spanish and French, tutors with proficiency in these languages are encouraged to write weekly journals in their target languages all semester, and many do so as well for their final submissions.

Tutors have typically implemented their projects during single or multiple full-period classes and delivered engaging, culturally and linguistically rich lessons that have reflected their interdisciplinary talents and interests. With adaptations and then interesting comparative assessments, some tutors have repeated a single lesson project with more than one group of students. This list gives a brief sampling of final project titles through the years, with examples from each language area and notation of tutors' academic concentrations and interests. Details will follow for the projects with asterisks.

- The Chinese Dragon Boat Festival* (Chinese and linguistics)
- Chinese Calligraphy: History and Practice (Chinese and fine arts)

- Shopping and Bargaining in Chinese* (Chinese and English)
- A Collection of Poems about Peace by ESL Students (French, psychology, and creative writing)
- French Bingo and Interaction with French-Speaking University Exchange Students* (French and psychology)
- Ionesco's *Rhinocéros*, Theater of the Absurd, and French Opera (French, cognitive science, human-computer interaction, and voice)
- A German Autobahn Game to Learn Geography and Vocabulary (German and civil engineering)
- Japanese New Year Traditions and Zodiac Symbols (Japanese, science and humanities, and history)
- Monuments and Festivals in Japan: Adventures During Study Abroad (Japanese and computer science)
- News Interviews with Famous Spanish Speakers (Hispanic studies and professional writing)
- Learning and Drawing Animals in Spanish (Hispanic studies and design)
- Creating Instagram Slogans in Spanish* (Hispanic studies and global studies)
- Games in Spanish and the "Head Fake" Method* (Hispanic studies and chemistry)
- A Virtual Trip to Bolivia and a Letter Exchange with a Study Abroad Family (Hispanic studies and global studies)

The following five excerpts from tutors' self-assessments of their projects – two from Chinese, one from French, and two from Spanish – give a sense of their interactions with tutees, their own growth, and that of their tutees. To maintain the anonymity of the participants, names have been redacted in the quoted passages. These five selections exemplify how students have developed projects that combine their language and culture area with another key area of academic interest. They show a variety of styles and attitudes along with evidence of the methodologies, content, or perspectives of the academic area that complements the target language and culture focus. These accounts of events and second language learning outcomes point to diverse aspects of development related, for instance, to identity, investment in a community of learning, motivation, nervousness, confidence, empathy, dealing with the unexpected, need for improvement, and feeling personal satisfaction.

Example 1: The Dragon Boat Festival Project

A tutor collaborated with two classmates to create her part for a three-day lesson on the Dragon Boat Festival. For the first day, a tutor with concentrations in Chinese and history developed a lesson on the history of the festival. For the second day, a tutor with concentrations in Chinese and English designed a lesson on a ballad associated with the festival. For the third day, this tutor drew on her background in Chinese and linguistics to create a lesson integrating language, culture, and step-by-step application to make sticky rice dumplings. In this excerpt from her reflection, she justifies with confidence the design of her lesson, is generally pleased with the learning outcomes, and envisions improvement with additional focus on linguistic elements and some competition to encourage even more interest. The tutor writes,

> This lesson is organized well to help students learn both making sticky rice dumplings and the phrases related to it. It has three merits. First of all, the lesson provides students good quality input in learning the phrases and making sticky rice dumplings. For example, in order to teach them how to make sticky rice dumpling, I played the video and demonstrated it step by step. Before they make the real sticky rice dumpling the students did the activity "I say you act" to familiarize themselves with the steps of making sticky rice dumplings. To my surprise, the students are able to remember the steps well. Some of them made a more beautiful sticky rice dumpling than I did. As for the phrases about making sticky rice dumpling, the students first learnt the new phrases by having the "passing and reading word" activity, and then they practiced saying the phrases by putting them in order and watching the video. They practiced speaking the phrases for at least five times during the class. These activities serve as scaffolding and comprehensible inputs for the students to grasp the usage of these phrases. I was very happy to see the students say out the steps fluently. Secondly, students practiced their listening, speaking and reading skills in Chinese. Thirdly, the passing the bag and reading the word activity involve all the students in an interesting way to learn new words. The music also livened up the class atmosphere.
>
> To sum up, I think the class has reached my goal and the students enjoyed the learning process very much. But I am not sure whether the students can recognize the characters or not since all the phrases I gave them was marked with pinyin. If I can have the class again, I will not have pinyin on the handouts and encourage students to read the characters. I will also invite the teacher to choose the best sticky rice dumpling so as to motivate the students to make a beautiful one.

Example 2: Shopping and Bargaining in Chinese

A tutor majoring in Chinese and English helps her students develop skits. Like the previous tutor, she is satisfied with the students' performance. She is also content with the goals she has set for herself to maintain use of the target language and generate a positive climate for learning. She also recognizes ways she could have increased students' exposure to the target culture and language. The tutor writes,

> Generally speaking, I am very satisfied with my presentation. The students achieved the intended goals and they even exceeded beyond what I taught them. In the end, I assigned them a free skit, where there was a bossy girlfriend requesting her boyfriend an iPhone. He ended up buying her one after bargaining with the shop assistant. Students were able to create funny dialogues by reactivating what they had learned before. Besides the learning outcome, the classroom also had a warm, pleasant and friendly atmosphere. There was laughter in the classroom from time to time. Besides, they were working actively with each other when preparing for group work as well the competition. (three people one group, they needed to find the right money for several objects and said the number in a timely fashion). Furthermore, there are two things I think lived up to my expectation. One is the near 100% use of target language, and two is the good rapport building with the students.
>
> There were some parts I think I can make improvements. For one part, I should have used more "market-like" objects for the skit performance. Since the skits are about bargaining, the commodity should have been something like fruit, meat, rather than an iPhone. The shift of realia could have enhanced the authenticity of the lesson and also built a more real market landscape for the students. For the other part, I think I could have done a better job in incorporating some readings in class. Since the whole lesson was about listening and speaking practice, I could have spent 5–10 minutes practicing either character recognition or writing practice. It would have given students a short break from talking and moving around to sit and think.

Example 3: French Bingo and Interaction With French-Speaking University Exchange Students

With this project, a tutor of French and Francophone Studies and psychology opens the community of practice to include French-speaking university exchange students. She feels elated after her lesson day and reflects on the relative success of the lesson she implemented with variations in periods 1, 2, and 4. She compares students' levels of participation and creativity. She hypothesizes about student behaviors, assesses the way she has prepared the classes for the visit of exchange students, and defends her decision to encourage students by allowing the use of English. Although she sees that her orchestration of the visit has brought French culture alive to the high school students, since the reception is not consistent across classes, she is not completely pleased. Still, evidence of her progress is apparent in her understanding of the need for flexibility and her transmission of this message to the visitors who are brand new to this context. The tutor writes,

> I'm happy to say the day went amazingly well! X, a French student, joined me for Madame's first period class. The students seemed a bit more reserved at first but eagerly began asking questions. Surprisingly, the three students who asked the most questions were the ones who typically didn't participate at all (i.e., head down, refused to speak French, always unprepared). They were actually excited and asked really insightful questions! I think allowing the students and X to speak in English was a key decision. I had given the students BINGO sheets with words that they would expect to hear, and some students were getting creative in asking X questions that would elicit him using those words in a response. I think the tool itself was somewhat helpful in guiding their introductory questions. X (the French-speaking foreign exchange student) was enjoying himself so much that he volunteered to stay for Madame's second period class. The students were much more reserved, but part of that might have been because they didn't know me or him. Their French was more advanced, so he began testing their comprehension skills. In both classes, there were a number of students who spoke more than one language (myself, X, a number of Hispanic and Middle Eastern students, and the Brazilian exchange student). We actually began a conversation about why we learn all these languages and the benefits. I really hope it gave the students some insight into the value of bilingualism! . . . J and R (both Swiss) joined for Madame's fourth period class. The class as a whole was much more reserved, and I'm not exactly sure why. There were a couple of star students missing, but one star student was asking and answering all of the questions. With encouragement from Madame, the foreign exchange students asked more directed questions to elicit more detailed responses. It was a bit like pulling teeth, but both parties seemed to be enjoying themselves. I did feel a bit let down, however. After the success of first period, fourth period's involvement and interest wasn't as obvious. Before starting, I had talked with J and R (the exchange students) about flexibility and expecting the unexpected. Having that mentality did help me appreciate the success of the project, despite it not being what I originally had in mind.

Example 4: Creating Instagram Slogans in Spanish

This tutor, a major in Hispanic studies and global studies, infuses elements of her senior honors thesis project into her school site project. Her research focuses on the history of tourism in Cuba and the impact of social media's contribution to forming collective images and forging identities. With her project, she helps students appreciate the power of images and technology. Her lesson links students' familiarity with social media to bring them closer to Spanish language and culture. Like the previous tutor, she compares student response in her repeated lesson presentations in different classes. She also comments on her increased appreciation of the teacher's role and its challenges dealing with multiple requests and the unexpected and on her adjustment to challenge in assuming the position of teacher. She also considers particular refinements to promote Spanish language acquisition. The tutor writes,

> In order to demonstrate the life of Spanish in today's world, I used Instagram, a popular social media tool, to show how technology that is used daily brings students much closer to the language than they may have realized. The main goal of the project was to show cultural themes familiar to the students from class in the context of Instagram posts in order to bring what they had learned in to a practical and fun context. . . . Having such few students in the first presentation made for a little less lively of a class, especially considering that class period is a bit quieter to begin with. However, the group contributed and that makes the job of presenting easier. In the second presentation, the class had over twenty students who are mostly in ninth-grade, which brought a much different energy. . . . Due to the fact that there was a full class in the second presentation, I had the smallest taste of what a teacher has to handle in balancing time. During the small group sessions to create the new hashtags for the picture, I felt like I had explained the task 15 times and that my name was called 20 times. It was a small example of how teachers have twenty people who all need their attention and they are only one person. Nonetheless, I dealt with it by just making rounds to the different groups.
>
> Speaking in front of others never goes as planned, especially when that is dependent on audience interaction. I was feeling even more nervous considering the audience is high school students and they are not exactly predictable. However, I felt that it generally went well. Overall, I was satisfied with the results. . . . If I were to present again, I would have picked specific new vocabulary to learn from the presentation. I had Spanish sprinkled in, but I think I could have targeted specific words to focus on by showing these words highlighted through hashtags. It seems obvious to me now, but I did not think of the idea until after the fact.

Example 5: Games in Spanish and the "Head Fake"

In this final example, a tutor with majors in Hispanic studies and chemistry designs a project in the form of an experiment with data collection.

With the purpose of cultivating students' focus on achievement and enjoyment through play and competition and diverting their attention from explicit learning of Spanish, she creates a series of games. In her reflection, she evaluates her data, suggests changes that could have improved her experiment, and analyzes with a critical eye an unexpected result that demonstrates her understanding of the limitations of her study as well as her concern for the growth and development of the students. The tutor writes,

> This project report will analyze the implementation of the "head-fake" method of teaching with high school Spanish students. This method involves having the students perform some sort of task or play a game, with the explicit intention of completing an end goal related to that game itself. However, the achievement of the actual learning objective should happen subconsciously, and was therefore not explicitly indicated to the students. . . . In conclusion, a definite correlation between learning associations was found in the reflections of the students. It was evident that when the students felt like they learned a lot from the game, they were more clear as to what that was specifically, thereby indicating it as the purpose of the game. As to whether the head fake method of teaching was effectively applied, some of the data suggests that certain students kept game objectives and learning separate, but there is not enough data to provide a definitive result.
>
> The most difficult day, in terms of the in-class work, was the second day with Ms. D's Spanish 3's. This was the first day that the "Dice" game was being played, and the group ended up being much larger than usual. However, the games still worked out, and some of the students were able to provide helpful evaluations. In the other classes, the games went very well and the students gave lots of feedback. If I could repeat this project, I might have instead broken up Ms. D's class into two groups in order to have more focused gameplay. This could have allowed for more participation from the quieter students and therefore helped them learn more. Additionally, I would create even more games and try to get a larger group of students for feedback.
>
> The last conclusion drawn from the results is possibly the most important, and is not even directly related to the initial project goals. I found in gathering the data that most of the students rated the lowest (eleven 4s and nine 3s) in terms of feeling more confident in their Spanish after playing the games. This perhaps reflects that they are lacking confidence in their language study. This finding is consistent with most of my experiences at the school over the semester. One student even added in the comments that confidence really has nothing to do with Spanish class, when it is actually one of the

most important goals in my opinion. Confidence in learning is a difficult issue because it requires the right reinforcement at the right time. However, it is something that should be implemented more into language study in order to help students reach farther, and therefore achieve farther. From my results, I determined that confidence cannot really be taught subconsciously, as it is a conscious decision to approach learning a certain way. Therefore, in the future it would be helpful for teachers to explicitly address to the students the importance of building up a healthy level of confidence in their language abilities. Part of the confidence deficiency comes from the feeling of knowing so little about such a vast language, but it should be emphasized that using whatever amount they do know with conviction provides great benefits and more effective communication.

Additional Practice: Reflective Synthesis Beyond the Projects

In addition to the project presentations with accompanying written submissions, tutors compose and share with each other a final narrative journal entry as part of their concluding gathering of practice. They respond to a prompt about the totality of the service-learning experience, its high points and challenges, and ways of meeting them. These excerpts from five final narratives offer further insight into their perspectives on growth and their sense of place and fit in the community of practice. In the first example, a tutor reviews her earliest narrative of the semester to assess her learning, growth, and adaptation within the broader community. She has recognized her tendency to be "too attached," calibrated her interactions with others, and worked to adjust them. She has negotiated aspects of the domain to balance flexibility with stability and validated the significance of her engagement in this community of practice:

> This tutoring experience at the school site has been nothing short of transformative and a truly pleasurable experience. I recently looked back and read my very first journal entry before writing my final entry and realized a few things. I noticed that the anticipated fear/concerns were not actual concerns throughout the semester, and those that were (like being afraid of being wrong) I was able to quickly overcome. . . . My biggest challenge as a tutor this semester was being flexible and not getting attached. I tutored the students of Ms. N's class, Ms. O, and Ms. P. The structure and my role was different in each class. For Ms. N's class I was responsible for working outside of the classroom and tutoring one "at risk" student the entire semester. This structure was very different compared to Ms. O's class and Ms. P's. In the former I tutored 4–6 students at a time and for the latter I served the role as an assistant teacher or classroom management monitor. Despite the differences in expected role I grew accustomed to these structures and when something changed

> abruptly I was caught off guard. . . . This challenge of flexibility and developing an attachment for my tutees was resolved, as I started to see the bigger picture, I was committed to helping all students with Spanish not just those I had developed relationships with. Once I became aware of my tendency to get attached to students I started to realize that another way my challenge can be "resolved" is by continuing to engage in similar experiences this new found perspective impacted my personal goals and development because I am considering tutoring or teaching post graduation. Additionally, I have learned that aside from tutoring I personally struggle with being flexible having this insight is enabling me to work on accepting the unknown. In short, tutoring Spanish at this high school helped me to successfully push myself outside of my comfort zone, to be incredibly patient, and to solidify my passion for education and commitment to improving student's language skills as well as my own.

While the first example shows a tutor's evolution involving some appropriate detachment from tutees, this second narrative reveals a tutor's attention to building closer connections with them:

> What was most difficult about my school site experience was my ability to connect with the students and to truly feel as if I was contributing to the classroom. At first, my time in the classroom was spent observing the teachers' different teaching styles and answering individual questions, so I didn't feel a strong bond with any of the students. Moreover, I wasn't in class every day, so there was much that I missed on my days off. Eventually, I began taking the lead more and more in the classroom. This began with offering a song to help memorize conjugation endings. . . . This was my first move towards having a stronger role in the class as a whole. On more individual levels, I began learning students' names more quickly and having more conversations about their likes and dislikes. Incorporating it into our informal conversations helped them to understand the material and let me build a stronger, more personal connection with many of the students.

This third narrative, like the first two, shows the tutor's growing appreciation of connection with the diverse participants and complex dimensions of the community of practice and the accompanying adjustment toward feeling more comfortable:

> As I wrap up my semester and my time at the school site, I started reflecting back on my tutoring experience. This class really helped me grow and pushed me to step outside of my comfort zone. I came into the class not knowing exactly what to expect and what I would gain from the experience. Although I was excited to pick up tutoring from

> where I had left off in high school, I was very nervous to go back into education and interact with all the students. Back when even standing up in front of the classroom and being introduced as "Ms. E" was absolutely nerve wrecking, I thought I would never become comfortable enough to build relationships with the class. Fast-forward four months now, I think I received more help and improvement on myself than what I gave to all my students at the school site. Interacting with all these students of very different background and race has led me to be more aware and open-minded.

This excerpt underscores a fourth tutor's recognition that while working together within this community of practice, in the face of circumstances that are unpredictable, the agency of one's students is as important as one's own:

> Although it was uncomfortable at first, becoming comfortable with the unexpected was easy enough to learn. Everyone always says how important of a trait that is to have, and I feel that teaching in a foreign and intimidating situation for a semester has helped me accept this lack of control. I won't be able to control the situation, but part of being a teacher is learning from the students as well. It's a relationship between myself and those I'm trying to help. Realizing that they can be in control of their own education is sometimes more important than following an agenda.

This fifth example echoes the previous tutor's attention to the importance of students' agency, and it also highlights the value of reflective assessment to promote a kind of closure that at the same time opens to forward thinking and further learning:

> When it came down to any challenge as tutor, the first step was to reflect. These journals have helped me immensely throughout the semester. I think this can apply to the students as well. If I could redo the tutoring sessions where I worked with the small groups in the library or in the hallways, I would've made more of an effort to bring closure to the sessions, so the students didn't leave with the things that they had learned left floating in the air. Reflection, as a tutor, has given me the chance to consider, and reconsider my purpose and goals, emphasizing the relevance of teaching of foreign language in school.

Enduring Communities of Practice: Growth Beyond the Semester

Over the many offerings of this course, during two particular semesters, the community of practice of the university students extended several semesters beyond the fifteen weeks through their collaboration with the course professor on writing projects that resulted in published articles (Polansky et al. 2010, 2015). Toward the end of spring semester 2008, and again toward the end of fall semester 2012, given fruitful exchanges of the students enrolled, the course professor invited each group to develop their stories. The 2008 community of seven students spanned language areas and disciplines with majors in English and French and Francophone studies, computer science and Japanese studies, business and Japanese studies, information systems and Japanese studies, Japanese and Chinese studies, decision science and Hispanic studies, and electrical and computer engineering and Hispanic studies. The 2012 group of four students also represented a diverse group with majors in French and Francophone studies, cognitive science and human computer interaction, Chinese studies and information systems, and Hispanic studies and chemical engineering, as well as an MA student in applied second language acquisition with a concentration in Chinese.

Each group was able to weave together individual as well as collective experiences to assess growth in various ways. The first group produced "Tales of Tutors: The Role of Narrative in Language Learning and Service-Learning" to highlight the value of storytelling as a reflective practice. The second group's article, "Tutoring Modern Languages and Cultures Through Service Learning: Flexibility with Growth in Multiple Ways," revealed how the tutors developed appreciation of the complexities of their roles and place as they built connections, dealt with obstacles, gained a deeper view of their local practice, and broadened their perspectives on the social contexts of an urban public school system. Via collaborative composition, community members shared expertise, perspectives, and procedures that led to work exemplifying this assertion by Wenger and colleagues:

> Stories are the best way to traverse the knowledge system in a way that explains the linkages between community activities, knowledge resources, and performance outcomes. Only a story can describe these complex causal relations while incorporating implicit contextual factors that may be crucial to appreciate but hard to codify or generalize. (168)

The communities of practice of university tutors that have evolved each semester have also contributed to the decades-long overarching community of practice between the university's department of modern languages and the public school system. University faculty members and a number of cooperating teachers and school site liaisons have participated for several or many semesters over the years, and a few tutors have enrolled for a second semester or continued their engagement with the public schools. Wenger and colleagues enumerate seven principles for cultivating communities of practice: design for evolution, open dialogue between inside and outside perspective, invite different levels of participation, develop both public and private community spaces, focus on value, combine familiarity and excitement, and create a rhythm for the community (51–62). In contrast, Probst, Gilbert, and Borzillo offer the main reasons for failure: lack of a core group, low level of one-to-one interaction between members, rigidity of competences, lack of identification with the community of practice, and practice intangibility (343). The factors related to failure have for the most part been absent from the enduring university–public school partnership that integrates a significant project-based learning component. Its key features coincide with the positive principles for cultivation: orienting participants at the beginning of each new semester to clarify goals and facilitate entry into new contexts; reinforcing a structure for the domain that is stable yet flexible; maintaining clear, punctual, and frequent communications among participants; and interacting with gestures of respect, sensitivity and appreciation whether through low points or high points.

After graduation, students' community- and project-based learning has led to a variety of paths of study and careers, including education-related areas: Fulbright TA programs and other international teaching experiences for ESL, education policy work, development of educational games, elementary and secondary teaching, medical school and pediatrics, doctoral programs in second language acquisition, informatics and learning, and legal work with immigrants and refugees. From their community of practice experiences, they have realized noteworthy transformation observable through the semesters and also in subsequent years.

The examples in this chapter, while specific to a particular institution of higher learning and its partnership with the local public schools, underscore the value of project-based learning and community engagement for participants' growth in multiple dimensions. It takes considerable effort and commitment to develop community partnerships that are sustainable. Some communities of practice last longer than others, and evolve, reshape, or dissolve naturally with longer or shorter term goals. To start modestly, an instructor might include a component in a course that provides a group of students with an opportunity to collaborate with diverse others around shared goals – in a local school, hospital, community center, library, or other civic setting – and to develop a project that responds to the needs of others while bringing together their academic interests, second language skills, and other talents. Through such experiences, university students can develop self-awareness and empathy, improve their communication skills, learn to appreciate and deal with complexity, and carry these lessons on their paths forward.

References

Bender, Thomas. *Community and Social Change in America*. Johns Hopkins Press, 1982.

Polansky, Susan G., Timothy Andrianoff, Jaclyn Bernard, Ana Flores, Isabel Gardocki, Ryan Handerhan, Jihea Park, and Lisa Young. "Tales of Tutors: The

Role of Narrative in Language Learning and Service-Learning." *Foreign Language Annals*, vol. 2, no. 43, 2010, pp. 304–23.
———, Amritha Mallikarjun, Jonghyun Thom, Laura Valcarce, and Lin Zhu. "Tutoring Modern Languages and Cultures Through Service Learning: Flexibility With Growth in Multiple Ways." *ADFL Bulletin*, vol. 43, no. 2, 2015, pp. 72–87.
Probst, Gilbert, and Stefano Borzillo. "Why Communities of Practice Succeed and Why They Fail." *European Management Journal*, vol. 26, 2008, pp. 335–347.
Wenger, Etienne, Richard McDermott, and William M. Snyder. *A Guide to Managing Knowledge: Cultivating Communities of Practice*. Harvard Business School Press, 2002.

5 Project-Based and ELF-Aware Pre-Service Teacher Education in Turkey

Sample Cases of Discovery, Creativity, Interaction, and Multilingual and Multicultural Diversity

Elif Kemaloglu-Er and Yasemin Bayyurt

An attempt to define English as a Lingua Franca (ELF) should first start by appreciating the complexity and variability of this construct. Today, English is the global language of our planet, and every second, millions and millions of people from diverse sociocultural and linguistic backgrounds interact using English as one of their means of communication in their professional, academic, and personal lives. The constant dynamism, fluidity, and variability of these interactions underlain by multilingualism and their integrated roles in human communication as well as the unique experiences of the interlocutors with their own ways of speaking to achieve mutual intelligibility in varying contexts increase the complexity of the ELF phenomenon (Baird et al. 173–178). According to Jenkins, in this "online" age, ELF presents tremendous variability and ultra-dynamic fluidity so it cannot be considered with boundaries (Jenkins 55). It is an entity transcending boundaries beyond description. On the basis of this reality of variability and functionality in ELF use deviating from native norms, ELF can also be taken as an accepting and flexible way to understand the English language and English language teaching. Accordingly, ELF is a perspective that acknowledges the non-native varieties of English in their own right and the non-native users of language with their own unique characteristics (i.e., with their own use of English, L1s, and sociolingual and sociocultural backgrounds) (Kemaloglu-Er 18–19). Given that ELF is a ubiquitous aspect of the global use of English, it is necessary to integrate it into English language teaching as well as English language teacher education and raise the awareness of the stakeholders of the meaning and significance of ELF and its pedagogy. However, it is challenging to achieve this goal since the deeply-seated convictions of most English users in the world seem to have a native-speakerist orientation. In order that this can change, it is crucial to not only make the pre- and in-service teachers aware of the ELF concept but also give them opportunities to experience ELF as a living and pedagogical phenomenon. Herein, project-based learning as a "quintessence of experiential learning" can be an effective way to gain this consciousness (Eyring 336). This study presents a theory- and practice-based model for pre-service teacher education where the participants not only received intense theoretical training but also discovered their own meanings given to ELF and their own ways of practicing its pedagogy through the ELF-aware teaching projects they personally developed and applied in the form of peer teaching and practicum. In this chapter, having highlighted the meaning of ELF-awareness and its integration into teacher education, the project-based learning model used in this study will be introduced. Then the project outputs (i.e., how the pre-service teachers integrated ELF into their English lessons) will be explored. The opinions of the participants about their ELF-aware projects and the project-based program will also be presented along with pedagogical implications and suggestions.

Defining "ELF-Awareness" in ELF-Aware Teacher Education

In ELF-aware teacher education, the term *ELF-aware* was intentionally used to refer to ELF-aware teaching and by extension teacher learning and development (Bayyurt and Sifakis, *Developing an ELF-Aware Pedagogy* 55–76; Bayyurt and Sifakis, *ELF-Aware In-Service Teacher Education* 117–135; Bayyurt and Sifakis, *Foundations of an EIL-Aware Teacher Education* 3–18; Sifakis, *ELF-Awareness as an Opportunity* 317–335; Sifakis, *ELF-Awareness in English Language Teaching* 288–306; Sifakis and Bayyurt, *Insights from ELF* 471–484; Sifakis and Bayyurt, *ELF-Aware Teacher Education* 147–153; Sifakis and Bayyurt, *ELF-Aware Teacher Learning* 456–467). Both ELF-aware teacher education and ELF-aware teaching are underlain by the concept of ELF-awareness, which is

> the process of engaging with ELF research and developing one's own understanding of the ways in which it can be integrated in one's classroom context, through a continuous process of critical reflection, design, implementation and evaluation of instructional activities that reflect and localize one's interpretation of the ELF construct.
> (Sifakis and Bayyurt, *ELF-Aware Teacher Learning* 465)

Thus ELF-awareness paves the way for teachers to appreciate ELF research and its implications on the ELT practice as well as to understand how theoretical aspects of ELF can be incorporated into their own teaching context through continuous and collaborative critical reflection. In becoming ELF-aware, one must go through an extensive intermediary process through which one can link the implications of ELF in theory and research to their own teaching practices.

The process consists of three phases: a theoretical phase, an application phase, and an evaluation phase (Bayyurt and Sifakis, *ELF-Aware*

In-Service Teacher Education 124–125). The theoretical phase familiarizes the pre- / in-service teachers with ELF- and WE-related literature so that they can gain insights into the global use of English and the status and role of non-native speakers, the meanings of the ELF construct, and the changes experienced about ELF in theory and practice from its earlier phases until now. The teachers are expected to read about these issues and reflect on them by responding to the given reflection questions. They are also encouraged to discuss the readings and their reflections with their colleagues.

The application phase involves integration of ELF into their teaching contexts in their own authentic ways with their accumulated ELF-related knowledge via lesson plans and instructional activities. Critical awareness is a *sine qua non* of this stage; thus, it is significant that teachers be sensitive to the needs and idiosyncrasies of their learners and take into consideration as much information as possible about the school setting and the attitudes and expectations of other stakeholders (e.g., learners, directors of studies, learners' parents, school advisors, and so on). In experimenting with ELF in the English classroom, teachers should avoid judging EFL teaching as irrelevant or even downright wrong. Instead, they are supposed to enrich the EFL practices with insights gained from ELF (Sifakis, *ELF-Awareness in English Language Teaching* 294). The evaluation phase involves online- and face-to-face meetings to assess the implementations as well as raise questions, discuss issues, and reflect on new ideas in the path of potential perspective transformation.

Sifakis and Bayyurt define the term *ELF-aware* in contrast to *ELF-informed* and describe the essential characteristics of "ELF-aware teaching" (Sifakis and Bayyurt, *ELF-Aware Teacher Learning* 463). First of all, it is stated that "ELF-aware" was intentionally chosen by the researchers instead of "ELF-informed." According to them, "ELF-aware" describes a process of becoming, but "ELF-informed" a process of being. The latter also implies a passive form of receiving knowledge. In the process of the former, the teachers should be actively and critically involved with ELF in theory and practice, thus there is design, experimentation, evaluation, and co-construction of ELF lessons.

As defined by Sifakis and Bayyurt, ELF-aware teaching has two important qualities: it is ecological in nature and potentially transformative (463). The ecological nature of ELF-aware teaching comprises teachers' awareness of the micro- and macro-ecosystem around themselves and the idiosyncratic local features, as well as the constraints and problems. Thus "ELF-aware" teachers must be conscious of both ELF theory and research and the ecological contexts around them, including their own classroom as well as the wider institutional and social settings. Being ecological refers to being aware of the context; yet being in a transformative process refers to one being fully aware of one's deepest beliefs about language use, teaching, and learning. In this way, it would be possible for the teachers to question and possibly change their established beliefs about ELF-related issues, such as the nature and role of Standard English (SE) in interactions among non-native speakers (NNSs), the role and the status of native and non-native speakers, and the function of feedback and correction methods in the classroom. Teachers engaged in transformative learning possibly take a more proactive, more autonomous position (Bayyurt and Sifakis, *ELF-Awareness in English Language Teaching* 294–297). Questioning, discovering, and efforts in changing the external conditions and one's convictions about these issues are in the very nature of this type of learning.

Project Work in ELF-Aware Pre-Service Teacher Education

Aiming to raise the language teachers' awareness of the concept of ELF and make them tangibly and critically aware of key ELF-related concerns, the model in this study, namely ELF-aware pre-service teacher education, focuses on raising the pre-service English teachers' awareness of ELF and ELF-aware pedagogy and ultimately changing them into ELF-aware practitioners through intense theoretical training, active teaching practice, and continuous critical reflection, as well as reflective interactions with colleagues. The model has been applied with successive groups of pre-service teachers in their senior year. The data analyzed in this study comes from the second application of the model. *Project work*, both as a term and an educational stance, has been integrated into the education program because of our interests as the researchers in project-based language learning and our beliefs in its pedagogical benefits, such as real-life-based self-discovery, self-initiated experimentation, and multivariate interaction opportunities, and also because we are in agreement with Sifakis's view that the ELF approach is indeed an "ESP approach" in terms of curriculum design and instruction and Sheppard and Stoller's opinion that project work is very effective in ESP settings since it embraces meaningful and purposeful language use, focus on meaning rather than form, authentic tasks, and learner centeredness, all features of ESP (Sheppard and Stoller 10–12; Sifakis *ELF-awareness in English Language Teaching*). We also thought project work would be a good tool for their content learning, as it requires active involvement in real life outside the classroom and cooperating with the community (Bandy, *Service Learning*; McLeod 20; Power 57). Our pre-service teachers are often not engaged with their community. As student teachers, their education is mostly theory-based, and they are in need of real-life classroom teaching experience. We thought if teachers could actively engage with real-life-based ELF-aware teaching projects out of the confines of their university classrooms and interact with students as well as the in-service teachers in their local environments, they would be more effective in solving the ELF-related problems that are important to them and their communities. This would broaden the horizons of not only the teachers but also their communities, where native norms are dominant according to our observations and lead to reduced stereotypes and greater intercultural understanding. Also, we believed community engagement could be meaningful for our student-teachers, as they would have opportunities to witness the real-world impacts of what they have learned and planned with regard to ELF pedagogy with real community partners by devising and testing their lesson plans. As such lesson plans would aim to integrate a novel component in pedagogy (i.e., ELF), the process would also be new and potentially transformative for both the recipient and provider of the service. By implementing ELF-aware pedagogy in real classrooms, it would also be possible for these prospective teachers to set their career goals regarding linguistic and cultural diversity to be applied within their in-service teaching period. Lastly, through community engagement, the pre-service teachers would be able to experience civic responsibility for raising ELF awareness in their local community mostly governed by native norms.

The pre-service teachers accordingly investigated how to integrate ELF into ELT outside the classroom by doing a literature survey and interviewing the teachers within their local community, and then they tried to develop their own ELF-aware lesson plans and test them with their peers as well as with real classes outside the classroom at their practicum schools followed by collective lesson evaluations. Thus, there was a focus on content learning and real world subject matter, an emphasis on cooperation as well as autonomy, and an authentic integration of skills and processing from various sources, all of which are stated to be characteristics of project work by Stoller (117–114). Lastly, we have also seen that practices of integration of project work into English language pre-service teacher education are rare (Holst, *Implementing Project-Based Learning*; Orlova, *Incorporating Project Work*) and even non-existent in terms of ELF-aware pre-service teacher education; thus, this can be a novel contribution to the field.

The training lasted two academic semesters. In the theoretical phase, with an intense exposure to readings, discussions, and reflection papers, the teachers gained insights into the general concepts of the global use of English and the status and role of NNSs, the issues raised by the ELF construct, and the changes ELF has undergone from its earlier phases until now. Then, in the application phase, the teachers were prompted to devise their own teaching projects aiming to raise ELF-awareness. Inspired by the project-based learning model proposed by Kemaloglu, the project-based phase was designed in a way to comprise three essential components in project-based learning: i) research, ii) creativity, and iii) interaction (218–219). Accordingly, the basic phases in the project process were researching ELF-aware pedagogy, creating ELF-aware lesson plans and implementing them by peer teaching and practicum teaching, and assessing these lessons with the relevant stakeholders. There was also one essential component we added to the projects to specify the global and diverse use of English and to refer to the multifaceted cultural characteristics of ELF users in constant interaction in today's world, and this component was multilingual and multicultural diversity. Project work was thought to be an excellent tool to promote this global aspect since it has particular relevance for ELT with the potential to act as a bridge between "classroom" and "real life" (Booth 5). By being involved with projects, the pre-service teachers would therefore reflect on the multilingual and multicultural aspects of their community in an active manner and become more competent in devising solutions for pedagogical issues in their local settings that concern the imposition of Standard English and native norms.

As for the research component, the pre-service teachers were asked to do their own research involving literature surveys and interviews with English teachers about how to integrate ELF into ELT and write a research report. Our expectation was that the research would be a challenging one since we were already aware that the field of ELF pedagogy is a new field with few available publications focusing on exactly the how aspect of ELF pedagogy. From our previous studies, we were also informed that in-service teachers, aware of ELF and its pedagogy, were very few (Kemaloglu-Er 271, 289; Kemaloglu-Er and Bayyurt, *ELF-Aware Teacher Education* 265). So the teachers were told that they might have such difficulties, but they were also encouraged to find as many ELF-related aspects as possible regarding the multilingual and multicultural diversity in the pedagogical applications around them. Following their research process, the pre-service teachers also stated that there were almost no teachers around themselves aware of ELF, but they reported examples of multilingual and multicultural diversity included in the English classroom without an explicit awareness of ELF pedagogy, such as inclusion of not only native but also non-native cultures in the classroom, allowing L1s when need be, or presenting spoken or written discourse samples from non-native speakers. The research reports pre-service teachers wrote were evaluated by their instructor in online and face-to-face meetings and set the grounds for pre-teachers' forthcoming lesson plans and their implementations.

As for creativity, the prospective teachers were asked to create their ELF-aware lesson projects to be implemented. For this step, they not only devised ELF-aware lesson plans but also implemented them. The pre-service teachers in this study had very little teaching experience or none at all. The only opportunities of these teacher candidates to practice teaching in their teacher education program were peer teaching with their colleagues and practicum in the assigned K–12 schools where they were supposed to practice teaching. Thus, they were asked to practice ELF-aware pedagogy by means of both ways, namely, peer teaching and practicum. They were not confined to the walls of their university classrooms. They did peer teaching in those places to get ready for teaching in real life. Yet they also got engaged with their local community by practicing ELF with real students and being guided and monitored by in-service teachers from real life. How they incorporated ELF into their lessons is mentioned in detail in the following section. The interaction component of ELF-aware project work was actualized by interactions of the pre-service teachers with both their peers as their sample students in peer teaching and their students in their practicum classes and the collective evaluations of these practices via discussions with their colleagues. The pre-service teachers' opinions about their projects are also presented here. Lastly, the component of multilinguistic and multicultural diversity in the projects was specified as a requisite to be included in each ELF-aware teaching project, and the teachers were told to use their own initiative to decide on how to do this.

It should be underlined that the project-based pre-service teacher education model applied in this study espoused full teacher autonomy (i.e., throughout the entire training process, there was no prescription or persuasion of any kind by the educators; participant-teachers were perpetually told they should negotiate their own ways of defining ELF and implementing ELF-aware pedagogy). Essentially, the model offered participants the tools, facilitated the process, and responded to queries and problems posed but was in no way involved in influencing their perspectives about ELF-related concerns.

Project Outputs: How ELF Can Be Integrated Into English Lessons

In this study, ELF-aware pedagogy was put into action by pre-service teachers through various forms of explicit and implicit ways in their one-shot experimentations through peer teaching with their colleagues and practicum in real school settings. The explicit ways were implemented by i) introducing ELF and the related concepts to the students openly and directly via videos, readings, and discussions and ii) helping them discover their non-native identity through critical reflection and reflective interactions as well as real life experience. However, implicit ways did not include a direct and open reference to the ELF concept but aimed to include ELF-related elements in the English lessons covertly. To illustrate, i) video displays of NNSs from different backgrounds, ii) NNSs' and learners' own local cultures, and iii) learners' intelligible variations as well as iv) their own L1s were seen to be a part of these lessons, yet they were integrated without any accompanying direct reference to the ELF concept or any explicit explanations about it.

Explicit ELF integration was put into implementation in several ways. For instance, one teacher, after highlighting the fact that English is a global language of today's world, had the students listen to different accents and discussed how intelligible they were with the students referring to their deviations from the standard norms, variations, and communication strategies. Then the teacher had the students act out the accents they had chosen and talk about how they felt in this experience. Another teacher first had the students talk about their English learning backgrounds and then talked about the status of English in the globalized world, introducing Kachru's circles. Then she had the students discuss the status of English in Turkey and how it affects the use of English in Turkey and whether they see any differences between themselves and their native friends in the use of English in terms of fluency, accuracy, and pronunciation, and if so, what these differences are like. Some other teachers brought English texts, namely stories and news items written by writers from different linguacultural backgrounds and had the students discuss the variations.

In implicit ways, the teachers preferred to refer to ELF-related multilingual and multicultural topics in an indirect way. For example, one teacher introduced Japan first and had the students listen to a Japanese woman telling a Japanese story about origami dolls. The students then read a passage about Japan and compared the Japanese culture and the Turkish culture. Another teacher introduced different festivals from the world through the videos of speakers from the countries where the festivals are held, speaking with their own accents. A teacher had a lesson with the class about how to conduct interviews successfully and had the students watch parts of interviews in English not only between native English speakers but also between native speakers and some non-native celebrities. The only reference he made to ELF in those displays was his saying that non-native speakers were relaxed and confident, and he suggested students should be confident like them in their interview practices. Other forms of implicit practices included intentional pedagogical implementations like not correcting intelligible variations in students' spoken communication, allowing L1 in the class for functional purposes, such as praising, warning, and giving complex instructions and even deliberately showing a confident attitude as a non-native English-speaking teacher speaking English with his or her own accent and variations in front of the class.

This explicit-implicit distinction in the ways to apply ELF-aware pedagogy was first defined by Kemaloglu-Er and Bayyurt (*ELF Awareness* 163–173). In this study, we again see the same category actualized in varied ways. Especially implicit ways reflect the creativity of ELF-aware practitioners willing to apply ELF-aware pedagogy in settings dominated by EFL norms. In this study, we saw that the implicit ways, namely, implementing ELF-related pedagogical practices without direct reference to the ELF concept, originated from the pressure of the Standard English-bound attitudes of the stakeholders, including the learners, the parents, and the school director/s on ELF-related practices. That is, in most EFL settings in their local communities that were strictly abiding by the native speaker norms, it would be challenging to introduce the ELF construct openly and straightforwardly in the classes, as it is likely to be disturbing or even annoying for the stakeholders, and this drove the participants to find novel and safe ways to apply ELF-aware pedagogy. Thus, the implicit ways were chosen, as they were thought to provide a safe space for ELF-aware teachers willing to integrate ELF into their lessons and help them enrich their lessons in the EFL-based curricula. Also implicit ways involved minor additions to the curriculum, thus they did not hamper the normal curricular pace. However, the reflections also revealed that it is not possible to apply only implicit ways in a real ELF syllabus. To ensure the ELF-awareness of the learners, we should also use explicit ways, through which they are expected to get "conscious" of ELF at least to a certain level. Thus, the explicit and the implicit approaches are complementary and should be thought in a continuum where both should be applied in varying levels depending on the contextual factors. The ELF-aware pedagogical applications were one-shot experimentations in our study, but it was thought by the teachers that in an ELF syllabus, one can start with the explicit or the implicit but the flow should be toward a point where these two should meet. The teacher can also opt for a syllabus where the explicit and the implicit can form different combinations and complement each other (e.g., more explicit here and somewhat implicit there or vice versa) or a syllabus that is predominantly implicit or predominantly explicit. For instance, in exam-focused ESP classes, the tendency may be toward a predominantly implicit syllabus, while in communication-focused general English classes, the syllabus may display a combination of both at relatively equal levels. Thus, the explicit and implicit applications in this study have potential realistic implications for ELF-related pedagogical practices to be implemented in EFL classrooms.

Participants' Opinions About Their Projects

The participants not only implemented but also evaluated their ELF-aware teaching practices, following both peer teaching and practicum. At the end of each teaching session, the lesson was evaluated by the teachers and their colleagues through in-class discussions. The pre-service teachers were also asked to assess the teaching sessions in the interviews. The pre-service teachers reported in the interviews that overall, they were content with the teaching projects of the course. According to the reports, they gave them a chance to try to apply the lesson plan they had prepared, evaluate its feasibility, and see different ELF-related lesson plan samples, which gave them inspiration for their future practices and thus broadened their horizons for teaching in real life.

The participants also favored incorporating video watching, reading, listening, discussion, reflection, and communicative tasks and lectures on ELF and related issues into an ELF syllabus. While explicit ways were thought to provide a fast and straightforward introduction to ELF, implicit ways were deemed to be useful in complementing explicit ways through covert implementations. It was suggested by some teachers that in a real syllabus, the ELF-related content could be extended to the whole school term, touching upon ELF step by step to raise the learners' awareness. According to these suggestions, the flow of the ELF syllabus can be from the implicit to the explicit or from the explicit to the implicit, and since these two approaches are complementary, they should be integrated at some point. According to the participants' comments, in an ELF syllabus, if the implicit approach were to be applied before the explicit one, it would serve the purpose of helping a smooth transition by setting the grounds with its potential effects on the subconscious. If the implicit approach follows the explicit, the former would support strengthening of the ELF concept.

Another theme that was commonly discussed about ELF-aware teaching projects was the difficulty of correcting intelligible deviations from standard norms. Most pre-service teachers said at first they understood ELF use as *anything goes* without giving the issue a real thought. Then through reflection and discussion, they said they started to think about what to correct and what not to correct, and it was hard to decide, as there is no clear set of criteria for intelligibility. Some said corpora studies would give them an idea about the correction criteria. Also some participants said students' needs and the goals of learning English would affect their correction decisions. Also a decision commonly reached by the participants in discussions was that a set of SE norms should be taught up to a certain level of proficiency like the intermediate or the upper-intermediate, and corrections should be made accordingly. Then following the intermediate or the upper-intermediate levels, students' intelligible deviations from SE can be tolerated. This was thought to be necessary because the students would be in need of standard norms at least to a moderate level to convey their messages accurately, to feel safe under the pressure of this EFL-dominant system, and to pass the high stakes exams. However, as some participants recommended, awareness-raising activities about ELF use, like showing videos of different NNS accents and talking about them, should begin before the intermediate level to mitigate a possible student resistance to ELF at higher levels.

The practicum experience of the pre-service teachers was their first official real-life teaching experience in an actual classroom. Engaging with their community through project work, they had an impactful experience. Although the pre-service teachers felt this experience was precious in helping them get accustomed to the job, the limitations coming from the practicum experience itself made most of them feel "restricted." This limitedness was especially experienced in private schools and derived from the prescriptions of mentor teachers, the practicum school policy itself bound with native norms, and parental pressure. So in this restricted setting, the autonomy of the pre-service teachers was undermined, and this prevented or limited the integration of ELF into the classes as well. However, there were some pre-service teachers whose school settings or mentor teachers were more supportive about ELF-related issues, like emphasis on learners' cultures and multiculturalism and the use of L1 in the classroom. This was seen especially in state schools. Overall, despite the factors inhibiting ELF-aware pedagogy in practicum schools, almost all the pre-service teachers were observed to make efforts at integrating ELF-related elements into their lessons, and the experience was found to be useful and providing personal satisfaction to the participant teachers as they tried to put what they learnt for the whole term into genuine practice for the first time via meaningful ways of engaging with their own community.

Participants' Opinions About the Project-Based Course

The results have shown that the participants' overall satisfaction with the project-based ELF-aware education course has been high. That is, a great majority of participants have been satisfied with the theory-research- and practice-based format of the course targeting self-initiated, collectively assessed, real-life-based ELF-aware teaching projects. Integration of ELF into ELT was practiced as project work in the form of peer teaching and practicum, which was also highly appreciated by the participants. The teacher candidates said they presented, participated in, and evaluated concrete samples of ELF-aware lessons through peer teaching, got ready for real-life practice, and also experienced trying to apply ELF-aware pedagogy in real-life settings through practicum. Although practicum was a hard experience for most teachers because of the external conditions like native-governed school policies, parental pressure, and the attitudes of mentor teachers and supervisors favoring being nativelike, they were still observed to be motivated and made strong efforts to include ELF in their lessons. The projects being multifaceted with the components of research, creativity, interaction, and multilingual and multicultural diversity was also deemed to be a positive aspect contributing to teachers' development by a great majority. However, some participants also complained about the heavy course load with a great number of duties regarding not only ELF in theory but also ELF in practice and suggested reducing the number or the contents of the assignments. The participant teachers were highly content with the in-class discussions where they evaluated their ELF-aware practices. They said they were able to witness different ELF-aware practices and discussed the ways to improve them. It was also stated that there was a sense of ELF community among the class members in the second term, as the class members had internalized the ELF perspective and developed a sense of ownership. Thus another goal of project work was achieved well through this course (i.e., the student-teachers managed to build a community of practice regarding ELF pedagogy before moving into the in-service teacher community).

All the pre-service teachers also confirmed that this course affected their attitudes as an ELF user. All of them stated they had become more tolerant to variations and more confident in speaking. As stated by most teachers, they were not afraid of making mistakes so they were now more motivated, more comfortable, and more fluent and agile in speaking. Many of them also said they now focused more on negotiation of meaning in their interactions. One pre-service teacher also said ELF-aware pedagogy removed the distances between herself and English, and one said she now sees the English-speaking people as a whole. Yet, some teachers also said few people are aware of ELF, so they still feel under the pressure of those people adopting a native-oriented approach. However, most of the participant teachers reported that they informed people around themselves about ELF. Thus, they became more concerned with ELF-related issues in their community. As they stated, they became critical about approaches and people defending a native-bound paradigm. Lastly, all the pre-service teachers exposed to this project-based ELF-aware pre-service teacher education course stated that they were planning to integrate ELF-aware pedagogy in their future teaching practices.

A final point worth mentioning is the assessment of project-based learning in this course, which is based on performance. We think this assessment method with its process-based structure marked with step-by-step performance analyses made by multiple agents, namely the instructor, the peers, the mentor teachers as community partners in their practicum schools, and the pre-service teachers themselves has a high potential to contribute to the student-teachers' understanding and implementation of teaching. The student-teachers were asked about this aspect, and they were all in favor of being assessed on their performance through a process-oriented project-based system involving multiple tasks. Although the process was found to be demanding by most pre-service teachers, all the participants agreed that it was a valuable experience. Thus our project-based and ELF aware pre-service teacher education model can also serve as a sample assessment model for teacher education programs. Since the course was project-based, each and every step – developing ELF-aware lesson plans, implementing them, and evaluating them – had its place in the overall course assessment of each student-teacher with clear rubrics specific to each step. The student-teachers were assessed on the basis of their performance in research and creativity in developing ELF-aware lesson plans, their ELF-aware teaching, and their critical reflections on their lesson plans and implementations as well as their participation in the reflective interactions. Also a great variety of assessment techniques have been applied, which might have contributed to the self-improvement of the teachers in dynamic ways. That is, the assessment was product- and process-based with lesson plans and their implementations were made by multiple agents (i.e., the course instructor, the peer teachers, the mentor teachers in their practicum schools, and the pre-service teachers themselves). It was also centered on the authentic performance of each and every teacher. The teachers were able to see several samples of ELF-aware pedagogy and receive feedback about the steps – namely their plans, practices, and evaluations – from several sources, their instructor, their peers, and themselves. Also, there was continuous and constructive feedback highlighting the strengths and the points to be improved. As a result, in this course, there were no standard tests putting strain on the pre-service teachers to memorize and convey "certain" facts. The student-teachers were encouraged to discover and construct their own reality in their own varying ways and through continuous reflective interactions with their instructor, peers, and community partners and assessed upon their own performance. Thus, the approach we have adopted in our teacher education and teacher assessment model was social constructivist, created space for variability and flexibility, and gave teachers a sense of responsibility, community, and belongingness, all focusing on the ELF reality.

Conclusion

The project-based ELF-aware pre-service teacher education model proposed and explored in this study can serve as an efficient means to gain deeper insights into ELF and ELF-aware pedagogy, discover and experience one's own applications of ELF-aware pedagogy in real-life-based contexts, and assess the ELF-related teaching practices in a collective and supportive manner. This was evidenced by the participants' growing awareness of ELF and ELF pedagogy, their great range of ELF-aware practices reflecting their independent problem-solving skills implemented and evaluated comprehensively, and their sound evaluations of their teaching projects. By being engaged with their community, the pre-service teachers had meaningful and purposeful opportunities to test how ELF can be incorporated into the English classrooms in their local settings and witness different stances their community partners (i.e., the students, the in-service teachers, and the school administrators) may take on native and non-native speakers and related ELF-specific issues. Thanks to project work, they were also able to see and experience ELF-aware pedagogy on the stage as inexperienced practitioners. Thus project work gave them the chance of becoming aware of their own ELF-related potential and the potential of linguistic and cultural diversity with the real English classrooms in their communities, making use of such types of potential in creative ways, and in the end, evaluating the big picture in multivariate ways.

Herein, the participants have been exposed to a novel pedagogy (i.e., ELF pedagogy) that embraces multilingual and multicultural diversity and whose methodology is still in the process of being defined. Besides, this pedagogy is one which they themselves have not experienced consciously and systematically as learners. Thus, their contributions to its definition in the form of ELF-aware teaching projects integrating research, application, and evaluation are noteworthy in the way that they have the potential to not only clarify and enrich the ELF pedagogy but also broaden the teachers' own repertoire with regard to novel applications suiting the non-native speaker reality and the great diversity of multilingual and multicultural interactions in this modern age.

It is essential that this model or models like this one be incorporated into teacher education programs so that prospective teachers can assume these ELF-aware roles. In fact, individual courses are not enough on their own. For a complete mind-set orientation, the whole English language pre-service teacher program must be designed in an ELF-aware manner with diverse courses on sociolinguistics, methodology, materials development, bilingualism, and practicum highlighting ELF and related issues through different forms of training with intensive critical reflection, personal experimentations, and reflective interactions.

However, in order that these ELF-focused changes can happen, a transformative change is also necessary in pre-service teacher education programs in Turkey. Studies on pre-service teachers' perceptions about teacher education programs report problems like i) very limited teaching experience offered in the teacher education programs; ii) lack of variety in the school teaching experience with respect to mentor teachers, proficiency levels of students, and school settings; c) non-integration of theory with practice; and d) inadequate critical reflection practices (Akcan 59; Seferoglu 376–377; Tezgiden-Cakcak 275–278).

Hence, for effective integration of ELF-aware teacher education models into pre-service English language teacher education programs, the goals and practices in these programs should be toward encouraging teachers to become reflective practitioners and even transformative intellectuals in Tezgiden-Cakcak's terms (129–135). In doing so, there should be a balance between theory and practice. The extent of practicum and peer teaching should be increased, and they should always be synthesized with versatile teaching projects integrating research, creativity, and interaction. Moreover, teacher education students should start practicum not in their senior year but much earlier, for instance in their sophomore year, with increasing levels of observation, instruction, and critical reflection throughout their education program and with sound collaboration of pre-service teachers, mentor teachers, and practicum supervisors based on effective and continuous feedback. If these changes are applied, ELF in theory and practice can be integrated more extensively and effectively into the teacher education programs and the prospective teachers can establish their own ELF-related perspectives through more intensive forms of reflection and action.

Lastly, if this project-based ELF-aware pre-service teacher education model can be transcended to teacher education programs worldwide, this can pave the way for more egalitarian and humanistic learning contexts, where multilingual and multicultural diversity in and out of the class is acknowledged, valued, and utilized for meaningful purposes. Teachers are the key agents of such a change, and we should heavily, enthusiastically, and collaboratively invest in them and engage them with the community with mind-broadening, real-life-based projects. Only through such efforts can we become aware of, question, and possibly change the established native- and Standard English–bound viewpoints in ELT.

References

Akcan, Sumru. "Novice Non-native English Teachers' Reflections on Their Teacher Education Programmes and Their First Years of Teaching." *PROFILE Issues in Teachers' Professional Development*, vol. 8, no. 1, 2016, pp. 55–70.

Baird, Robert, et al. "The Complexity of ELF." *Journal of English as a Lingua Franca*, vol. 3, no. 1, 2014, pp. 171–196.

Bandy, Joe. "What Is Service Learning or Community Engagement?" wp0.vanderbilt.edu/cft/guides-sub-pages/teaching-through-community-engagement/. Accessed 20 March 2019.

Bayyurt, Yasemin, and Nicos C. Sifakis. "Developing an ELF-Aware Pedagogy: Insights From a Self-Education Programme." *New Frontiers in Teaching and Learning English*, edited by Paola Vettorel. Cambridge Scholars Publishing, 2015a, pp. 55–76.

———. "ELF-Aware In-Service Teacher Education: A Transformative Perspective." *International Perspectives on Teaching English as a Lingua Franca*, edited by Hugo Bowles and Alessia Cogo. Palgrave Macmillan, 2015b, pp. 117–135.

———. "Foundations of an EIL-Aware Teacher Education." *Preparing Teachers to Teach English as an International Language*, edited by Aya Matsuda. Multilingual Matters, 2017, pp. 3–18.

Fried-Booth, Diana L. *Project Work*. Oxford University Press, 2002.

Holst, Janet K. "Implementing Project-Based Learning in Pre-Service Teacher Education." citeseerx.ist.psu.edu/viewdoc/download?doi=10.1.1.111.5998&rep=rep1&type=pdf. Accessed 16 March 2019.

Jenkins, Jennifer. "Repositioning English and Multilingualism in English as Lingua Franca." *Englishes in Practice*, vol. 2, no. 3, 2015, pp. 49–85.

Kemaloglu-Er, Elif. "Project-Aided Language Learning: Gains, Problems, Solutions." *Proceedings of the 1st Conference on the Issues & Problems of Foreign Language Education Departments*, edited by Mustafa Kinsiz, Ayalp Talun Ince, and Kemal Demir. Mugla University, 2008, pp. 205–219.

———. *Integrating ELF Awareness into Pre-Service Teacher Education: Insights From Theoretical and Practical Experience*. PhD dissertation, Bogazici University, 2017.

———, and Yasemin Bayyurt. "ELF-Aware Teacher Education with Pre-Service Teachers: A Transformative and Technology Enhanced Case from Turkey."

ELF: Pedagogical and Interdisciplinary Perspectives, edited by Natasha Tsantila, Jane Mandalios, and Melpomeni Ilkos. Deree – The American College of Greece, 2016, pp. 261–267.

———. "ELF-Awareness in Teaching and Teacher Education: Explicit and Implicit Ways of Integrating ELF into the English Language Classroom." *English as a Lingua Franca for EFL Contexts*, edited by Nicos C. Sifakis and Natasha Tsantila. Multilingual Matters, 2018, pp. 147–163.

McLeod, Aida Koçi. "Service Learning and Community Engagement for English Classes." americanenglish.state.gov/files/ae/resource_files/etf_55_3_pg20–27.pdf. Accessed 19 March 2019.

Orlova, Natalia. "Incorporating Project Work in ESL Teacher Training." March 2008. www.tesol.org/read-and-publish/journals/other-serial-publications/compleat-links/compleat-links-volume-5-issue-1-(march-2008)/incorporating-project-work-in-efl-teacher-training. Accessed 17 March 2019.

Power, Anne. "Community Learning as Authentic Learning With Reflection." *Issues in Educational Research*, vol. 20, no. 1, 2010, pp. 57–63.

Seferoğlu, Golge. "Teacher Candidates' Reflections on Some Components of a Pre-Service English Teacher Education Programme in Turkey." *Journal of Education for Teaching*, vol. 32, 2006, pp. 369–378.

Sheppard, Ken, and Fredricka L. Stoller. "Guidelines for the Integration of Student Projects in ESP Classrooms." *English Teaching Forum*, vol. 33, no. 2, 1995, pp. 10–15.

Sifakis, Nicos C. "ELF Awareness as an Opportunity for Change: A Transformative Perspective for ESOL Teacher Education." *Journal of English as a Lingua Franca*, vol. 3, no. 2, 2014, pp. 317–335.

———. "ELF Awareness in English Language Teaching: Principles and Processes." *Journal of Applied Linguistics*, vol. 40, no. 2, 2019, pp. 288–306.

———, and Yasemin Bayyurt. "Insights From ELF and WE in Teacher Training in Greece and Turkey." *World Englishes*, vol. 34, no. 3, 2015, pp. 471–484.

———. "ELF-Aware Teacher Education and Transformative Learning. Comments on Éva Illés." *Journal of English as a Lingua Franca*, vol. 5, no. 1, 2016, pp. 147–153.

———. "ELF-Aware Teacher Learning and Development." *Handbook of English as a Lingua Franca*, edited by Will Baker, Jennifer Jenkins, and Martin Dewey. Routledge, 2017, pp. 456–467.

Stoller, Fredricka L. "Project Work: A Means to Promote Language and Content." *Methodology in Language Teaching: An Anthology of Current Practice*, edited by Jack A. Richards and Willy A. Renandya. Cambridge University Press, 2001, pp. 107–119.

Tezgiden-Cakcak, Yasemin. *Preparing Teacher Candidates as Passive Technicians, Reflective Practitioners or Transformative Intellectuals?* PhD dissertation, Middle East Technical University, 2015.

———. "A Critical Review of Teacher Education Models." *International Journal of Educational Policies*, vol. 10, no. 2, 2016, pp. 121–140.

Part III

Immersion and the International

6 Social Activism Italian Style

Building a Community of Practice Through Language Immersion and Civic Engagement While Studying Abroad

Bruno Grazioli

Language development is an interactional rather than unilateral process, that is, language learners participate as agents in the formation of their own linguistic competence, as much as others they interact with. This approach resonates with Ochs and Schiefflin's idea (although applied to children's language development) that learning is fundamentally "collaborative and development is a dynamic outcome of (learners') involvement in activities with others who guide their participation" (Ochs and Schiefflin 6). This is especially true when learners are placed in the context of the country where the foreign language is spoken, that is, in a context where students must function in the foreign language in order to achieve specific goals.

As learners progress and become better communicators, they also become members of communities as their communicative efficacy "depends upon their grasp of shifting and enduring perspectives that give meaning to an array of relationships, institutions, moral worlds, and knowledge domains" (7). In the present article, I use the concept of community of practice as a conceptual framework for language acquisition, and social justice participation as a lens for creating a common goal in a community of practice, where project-based learning methodology represents the link between the two components. This approach relies on the belief that the success of language learning in a study-abroad context cannot be isolated from the growth and development of learners' identity while abroad and must be situated in the larger community context. By expanding students' capacity to incorporate and practice the Italian language away from the classroom setting – that is, away from the traditional teaching-assessment cycle – and by facilitating cooperative work toward a shared interest, the academic course in which such an approach was adopted supported students' spontaneous interaction with locals in the target language and promoted the intercultural growth of the students.

Internationalization: A 21st-Century Skill

As the world turns increasingly multicultural and interconnected, becoming a global citizen is presented to US-based undergraduate students as a 21st-century skill to acquire not only to address the need for graduates to be competitive in a global workplace but also as a way for them to develop and practice soft skills, such as communication, the ability to work with others, problem-solving, adaptability, flexibility, independence, open-mindedness, motivation, and self-awareness. This is in line with the Liberal Education and America's Promise initiative's demand for "high-quality, hands-on learning that prepares students to deal with complexity, diversity, and change" ("LEAP Employer-Educator Compact" 2013). It also aligns with the NAFSA Association of International Education's recognition for career advancement as one of the seven benefits of studying abroad.

Especially in the last decade, North American higher-education institutions have undergone a process of internationalization so as to raise their profile on a global scale and attract foreign students. Sending students abroad for periods of time that vary from two weeks to two semesters has become a consolidated practice for American higher-education institutions. Based on the most recent *Open Doors* report funded by the Department of State's Bureau of Educational and Cultural Affairs, published on November 13, 2018, studying abroad as an academic practice saw an increase of 2.3% during the academic year 2016/2017 in comparison to the previous year. More than 300,000 students spent a portion of their academic year in a foreign country, and about 55% of them chose Europe as their destination. In regard to studying abroad in Italy, which this paper is primarily preoccupied with, another interesting data point *Open Doors* provides is the fact that Italy is the first non-English-speaking country (second only to the United Kingdom) chosen as a study-abroad destination and welcomes almost 11% of the entire flow of American students.

Language Learning in a Study-Abroad Context

Embarking on a study-abroad experience naturally raises the issue of foreign language preparation, a learning objective that seems to have disappeared from the forefront of the educational mission of several US-based higher-education institutions. According to a recent report from the MLA (Modern Language Association), despite the internationalization efforts of these institutions, foreign language enrollments at a graduate and undergraduate level are on the decline (Looney and Lusin 2018). For those that still integrate an advanced language component in their curriculum, especially at the post-beginning level, the progress of students' language competence represents an ongoing point of discussion mostly revolving around simple questions such as "Do students become better language speakers while abroad?", "How does studying abroad impact on students' language competence?", and so on. These are the same questions that contemporary research on language learning in study abroad have attempted to answer.[1]

The benefits that studying and living abroad have for the acquisition of linguistic and sociolinguistic competence have long been noted (Regan 61–91). These studies have concluded that language learning in a study-abroad context is more effective when fostered through observation, participation, and reflection. This implies that a more comprehensive approach to language learning than classroom-based instruction – that is, an approach based on participation rather than acquisition – should have a more powerful effect on language and cultural competencies (Swain and Deters 820–836). Interaction with individuals speaking the foreign language is central to the social processes of second language acquisition (SLA) and is related to where the learners are learning and how much contact and feedback they get from native speakers in the speech community in which they are living temporarily. However, research around SLA in a foreign country seems lacking in substantial studies about the way language learning is informed and enriched by other – that is, non-linguistic – components.

Isabelli-Garcia and colleagues highlight the complexity of study abroad research and of language development in a study-abroad context because of the ramifications these two fields have with other domains, such as international student mobility, higher education policy, and also intercultural competence (Isabelli-García et al. 441–442). Additionally, the study abroad context has often been treated as a black box or as a categorical label comparing learners in a study abroad program to others in a domestic, more formal and traditional instructional context, with the result that specific features of study abroad such as exposure, social contact, and cultural experiences were all "consolidated into this physical context, i.e., black box as opposed to a glass box, without any internal components available for inspection" (Taguchi 128). Too often, evaluations of the effects studying abroad has on learners take a binary form, effective or not effective, which eschews the understanding of what actually goes on in a study abroad context (128). In light of this, some have claimed that SLA is, or at least has been, dominated by US-based studies so much so as to exhibit a strong commitment to utilitarianism, that is to prove the direct correlation between the development of students' language skills and their study-abroad experience (Kinginger, *Measuring* 29–30).

Recent studies have finally begun to ask new and different questions, such as how can we better explore the relationship between in-class teaching and learning while studying abroad and out-of-class experience and engagement? And also, what role does learner self-regulation play in shaping an individual's experience abroad? (Isabelli-García et al. 471). The need for a greater understanding of how international education impacts on one's proficiency in a foreign language has encouraged the development of new interests and approaches that take into consideration the close connection between the outcomes of individuals' language learning process and the development of their own identities as language speakers.

Community of Practice and Second Language Acquisition

Learning does not take place in isolation.[2] Learning is naturally a collaborative endeavor situated in a specific context where individuals in a community strive to negotiate meaning. This is one of the principles at the basis of Etienne Wengers and Jean Lave's formulation of the concept of community of practice (CoP). Their publication entitled *Situated Learning: Legitimate Peripheral Participation* (1991) and Wengers' further elaboration of the concept in the book *Community of Practice* (1998) introduced the CoP theoretical framework in academic research, including Second Language Acquisition (Hourdequin 14). Their notion of a community of practice defines a situation in which people are associated on the basis of a common and shared interest and improve their skills by working alongside each other. The community is, then, the place, or else the context, where so-called newcomers can learn from more experienced members of the same community in a process of constant progress. As a result, learning is intrinsic to the concept of a community of practice, and language learning, especially in the context of the country where the foreign language is spoken, is really a natural extension of such concepts, as it relies on the ability of non-native speakers to learn from native ones.

The application of Wengers and Lave's framework to SLA research dates back to the late 1990s, and it has been used to further the understanding of the way language acquisition works.[3] One of the advantages of employing the community of practice theoretical model in the context of language learning is that it places greater emphasis on the social situatedness of learning, that is in relation to a particular community. Learners must think of themselves and must be seen as participating legitimately in those communities in order to fully access their resources (Swain and Deters 824). In turn, rather than reproducing an existing community, "the participation of newcomers also entails changes and transformation of the community" (825). The fundamental assumption behind the community of practice model is that people interact in specific circles in order to achieve shared goals, and the work they do as well the ideas they share constitute their practice.

Embedding Community Engagement in the Dickinson Italian Studies Curriculum in Italy

Community-engaged learning at the academic level can broadly be defined as an educational experience built into an academic course that allows students to earn credit. During this experience, students participate in activities organized within the community that meet not only identifiable goals outlined as part of the course learning objectives but also the needs of the community itself. Community work must take into consideration the growth of learners as well as of the community they interact with (Cone and Harris 28). While learners get involved within the community where they volunteer their time, they also engage in a process of reflective thinking in order to gain better understanding of the course content, as well as their active participation and presence in the society.

The combination of academic content with practical work in community-based organizations supported by critical reflection aims at enhancing learners' sense of civic responsibility while working for the greater good of the community. Community-engaged learning is a valuable agent of change both for the wider society we live in and for learners themselves, who, besides meeting specific academic expectations, also benefit from this experience on a personal level. Exposure to diversity, in whatever forms it presents itself within the community of choice (age, race, sexual orientation, religion, disability, and so on), impacts on learners' identity development and cultural understanding. While researchers have investigated this, there is still a paucity of studies about the integration of sustainable community engagement in a study-abroad curriculum and, even more so, about the development of learners' language proficiency as a practical outcome of community work and personal reflection.

The Community-Engaged Learning course entitled "Forms of Social Activism in Italy" was offered as part of the course offering for the Dickinson College Italian Studies Program in Bologna (Italy). Fifteen out of the 16 students who were part of the Italian Studies program attended the course on Italian activism during the fall semester 2018. Upon arriving in Bologna, all students had already completed three or four semesters studying the Italian language. The course was composed of an in-class and an out-of-class portion: the former consisted of discussion-based meetings exploring the notion of Italian activism, and the latter consisted of a civic engagement program to be completed at different times during each week. Both components were conducted solely in Italian.

The course aimed at introducing students to the concept of activism in Italian culture by examining how citizens, individually and collectively, have achieved social change in post-unification Italy and more specifically over the last 50 years. This approach was intended to help students gain understanding of the progress of the Italian society in the last century through the study of its social movements. In the course, students firstly discussed what activism is by describing it as it has emerged in their own culture and place of origin. They learned that the term *activism* does not quite translate directly to the Italian *attivismo* but, rather, to a variety of expressions highlighting different notions of this phenomenon (*impegno*, *militanza*, *partecipazione sociale*, *cittadinanza attiva*, *volontariato*). The specific focus on Italy also offered them the opportunity to identify differences/similarities between European and American examples of activism. Week after week, the course explored various forms of Italian activism: civil rights (women's, LGBTQ, immigrants', and so on), pedagogical, environmental, and food activism, *artivism*, and music activism. Each form of activism was associated with, and exemplified by, key figures in Italian culture (for instance, Maria Montessori and Loris Malaguzzi represented pedagogical activism; Mario Mieli and Porpora Marcasciano, LGBTQ activism; Carlo Petrini and Massimo Bottura, food activism) following a chronological order and focusing on case study analysis. In the end, students grew to appreciate how social change often results from individuals' determination in defiance of adverse social and political conditions, and they also acquired a historical framework by means of which they were able to contextualize seminal facts and events in contemporary Italian history and society.

Classes were structured around a combination of class discussion and empirical observation. While building upon students' community engagement experience, class time was initially devoted to exploring various concepts of activism, as well as analyzing specific types of activism and how they operate (Occupy Movement, social media, hacktivism, strikes, boycotts, demonstrations, gate-crashing, culture jamming, and so on). Students also learned by means of direct observation and by experiencing the spaces in Bologna that bear the historical mark of civic protests (the Bologna 1977 uprising), acts of terrorism (the 1980 train station bombing), and the role of collective memory in constructing historical and cultural identity (the museum for the memory of Ustica).

Most important, the course was built around a solid Community-Engaged Learning (CEL) component in which students actively participated in community work in three civic organizations operating in the areas of diversity and social justice (civil rights such as women's, LGBTQ, immigrants', and so on; pedagogical, environmental, and food activism; *artivism*; and music activism) in local associations with which Dickinson in Bologna partnered for the specific purposes of the course. By integrating community involvement and community engagement with academic coursework and reflective thinking, students gained a deeper and more practical grasp of the course content, as well as a broader appreciation for their host community, its culture, and its people.

Project-Based Learning as Civic Engagement

Students volunteered in the following three civic organizations: Mondo Donna Onlus, Antoniano Onlus, and Cassero.[4] Service was conducted in Italian, and students kept a reflective journal, where they were asked not only to record what would happen during their hours of service but also how their experience was evolving over the course of the semester. The initial expectation was for all students to complete a minimum of two hours of volunteer work per week over the course of a ten-week period (total of 20 hours minimum), which everyone successfully managed to do, at times making up for missed service hours by working double time in a given week.

Mondo Donna: Mondo Donna provides assistance to women and minors and also to refugee men and women and those who are economically disadvantaged. It operates in various areas by offering, for example, temporary accommodation to migrants, home-schooling services, educational services for minors, and a counseling center for women and much more. Dickinson students volunteered in two different ways:

1. They offered support to teachers during Italian classes that guests at Mondo Donna attend for as long as they are accommodated in one of the houses managed by the organization.
2. They tended to the children of those guests who were in class by organizing educational and recreational activities, feeding them, and so on.

Dickinson students at Mondo Donna always worked in collaboration with an instructor/mentor and with other volunteers, all Italian-natives either from Bologna or long-term residents in the city.

Antoniano Onlus: This is a Franciscan-inspired institution operating many volunteer programs (soup kitchens, assistance to refugees, medical and rehabilitation centers for children with disabilities). Dickinson students in Bologna volunteered at Social Tables Antoniano (*Mensa Padre Ernesto*), opened to expand the activities of an existing community kitchen in Bologna, which employs a very successful approach to addressing urban sustainability and food insecurity. It serves nutritious meals cooked with surplus ingredients obtained from local food banks or factories to families in situations of social vulnerability. Some students worked during one weekly lunch shift, which mostly accommodates single individuals, who are served not "restaurant style" (sitting at a table), but directly at the counter.

Other students worked during the only weekly dinner shift available, which caters to families. Guests (parents and their children) sat at family tables and were served by Dickinson students (together with other volunteers), who also connected with them on a personal level and tried to make them feel welcomed. The dinner service at Mensa Padre Ernesto is part of Food for Soul non-profit organization founded by chef Massimo Bottura and Lara Gilmore. By involving chefs, food suppliers, artists, and designers, Social Tables empower local communities to fight food waste through social inclusion and create a more civically conscious society.[5]

During their service, students also helped setting up tables before lunch or dinner and cleaning up afterward. In the end, they had their meal with the rest of the volunteers, after guests had left. Whereas volunteers were mostly Italian natives (with the exception of a couple who had been living in Italy for several years), guests were from a variety of ethnic backgrounds, but all had a good level of conversational Italian and naturally interacted in Italian with students.

Cassero: Cassero is the first nationally-recognized LGBTQ organization. It was founded in Italy over 30 years ago. As one of the leading institutions of the Italian LGBT movement, Cassero works to promote awareness around the LGBTQ community in the city and nationwide, to improve the quality of life of LGBTQ people, by advocating for social and political equality, and by addressing discrimination issues on national and international levels. At Cassero, Dickinson students worked in different capacities and participated in the activities of one of the following four groups according to their individual skills and interests:

1. **La Falla**: This is the official publication of the organization built around a real pressroom where volunteers discussed themes to research and articles to be published in the next issue. Dickinson students also contributed by writing an article that was published on La Falla's online blog.[6]
2. **Documentation Center**: This is both a library (containing 14,000 books, 6,000 videos, and so on) that is part of the national system of Italian libraries and a center of research and study for the university of Bologna students and scholars. Student volunteers helped out at the circulation desk but also participated in meetings with school groups that the Documentation Center organized to promote discussion around practical topics like gender identities, safe sexual behavior, and reproductive health.
3. **PeopAll**: This is the most political of all the four options that were offered to students. The mission of this sub-group of Cassero is to celebrate and educate the Bologna community at large about important LGBTQ-related events and commemorations, and also to organize gatherings, social events, campaigns on social media, and so on. Students took part in the organizational process, strategic planning, and preparation of events organized during the fall of 2018 (i.e., Coming Out Day in October, International Day for the Elimination of Violence against Women in November).
4. **Gender Bender Festival**: This is the cultural organization of Cassero, responsible for the programming of the series of cultural events during the fall and spring terms. *Gender Bender* is an international Festival (cinema, theater, dance, visual arts, music, and so on) built around the theme of gender identities, sexual orientations, and body representations in contemporary culture.[7] Students both participated in the series of organizational meetings leading up to the festival and also contributed by working as ushers during evening events.

Introduced in the SLA discipline in the late 1980s, the PBL methodology offers a pragmatic means through which course goals can be achieved (Beckett and Miller 3–14). PBL is not a course objective in and of itself, and it does not replace other teaching methods. The PBL opportunities that these community-engagement projects offered Dickinson students were to be immersed in real-life communication in the target language, in a context where students had to actively work, surrounded by people who were either natives of Bologna or had chosen this city as their home. While designing the course to integrate a PBL component as a critical aspect of students' experience abroad, I kept a few important principles in mind, which align with the three key factors Wengers identifies in a community of practice: mutual engagement, joint enterprise, and shared repertoire (Li et al. 2009). PBL

1. Has to be in line with the interests of students and fulfill their need to gain new experiences and be responsible for their work
2. Comes from concrete and real-life situations and is not restricted by school premises
3. Is interdisciplinary
4. Is above all an enterprise for each student but is carried out in groups
5. Supports the integration of academic coursework into the broader society and real life

(Kalabzová 4)

Differently from more traditional ways in which PBL has been used as a course component – that is, by presenting students with a problem or a question and having them work on solving or answering the initial input by working in groups – the course had one single starting problem/question (*How can you make a difference in the Bologna community?*), and students formed collaborative relationships not only among themselves but with locals as well, thus shaping and contributing to unique communities of practice.

Reflection and Journaling

As noted earlier, an integral part of the course and of the community-engaged service was to have students begin a process of reflective thinking by way of weekly journaling. Reflection is understood as the "intentional consideration of an experience in light of particular learning objectives" (Hatcher and Bringle 153). Whereas community service may not in itself produce learning, reflection constitutes the connecting bridge between activities learners are involved in and the content of the course. It is through a process of reflection and writing that students produce new notions of their participation in community work. The very act of articulating one's experience in a coherent verbal form produces new interpretations and meanings as it shapes personal experience into something others comprehend and can relate to.

Out of the several existing types of reflection, I selected the arguably most traditional one, journaling, of which various types exist as well (Eyler et al. 113). Slightly veering off from the model that Eyler, Giles, and Schmiede propose, for the purpose of this course, I asked students to keep a three-part journal in Italian, in which they had to address three different aspects of their service work and participation in the course in every journal entry. The three aspects I chose were a) an account of what had happened during their work in the respective civic organizations, which required students to carry out a simple observation of the people present and a description of tasks they had completed; b) a description of anything that might have been different from the previous week's service and/or that might have surprised, puzzled, or confused them – in other words, an event or occurrence they could not fully interpret, not so much in linguistic terms, but rather in terms of cultural differences; and c) a reference, whenever possible, to how course content related to their experience in the organizations or helped them understand events to possibly guide them in the future.

Students received the following indications as to how journal entries should be kept:

1. You will keep/write a journal about your service experience and observations.
    a. The aim of the journals is for you to reflect on your experience/observations and to integrate them into the course.
    b. Journals are not graded for what you write in them, but for how you connect experience/observations with the course content.
2. You will write a journal entry after every visit to the association you have chosen.
    a. Each journal entry should be approximately 200 words long and in Italian.
    b. You should identify an overarching theme and structure your entry around it.
    c. You will give each journal entry a short title.
    d. You may decide to incorporate images/photos in your entries. This will not affect the required word count indicated above.
    e. If you take photos during your service work hours, make sure to be sensitive and respectful towards people and always ask for permission.
3. Service work will take place on weekdays (Mon–Fri). You will submit journals by Friday.

a. Keep your journals online (in a folder, clearly dated) and share them with me.
b. You should develop the habit of writing an entry as soon as you have completed your weekly service work. Do not write entries all at once, as this will defeat the purpose of engaging in reflection and increased learning.
c. Your journal will have to be of high quality in order to get full credit. Journals lacking effort/integration/quality will receive only partial credit, if any.

A clarification is needed here about course content and how students were expected to connect with it in their diaries. As outlined, the course aimed at providing students with cultural and historical notions about the progress of Italian society in the last century particularly since the 1960s by using the lens of civic activism. The course was rooted in Italian culture, not in the theory of social movements, and, against Cone and Harris's recommendation, the course did not provide students with "pre-service training and theoretical concepts that the student will be expected to apply and understand in the community" (Cone and Harris 29–30). Instead, in this course, students worked toward expanding their capacity to define the concept of activism in Italian culture by analyzing various ways in which it has manifested itself, and, rather organically, worked in civic organizations that exemplified some of those manifestations. For example, in class, students were introduced to Mario Mieli and Porpora Marcasciano and learned about when and how these two key LGBTQ figures contributed to the advancement of the movement. In so doing, students who worked at Cassero could see their role within the organization as being part of a larger mission and, especially, of a consolidated tradition of Italian LGBTQ activism. Another example is food activism. In class, students learned about the birth of the Slow Food movement, embodied in the figure of the movement's founder Carlo Petrini, and about chef Massimo Bottura's philosophy, according to which cooking is a call to act, and a meal is an act of inclusion. Students volunteering at Mensa Padre Ernesto Social Table were not only made part of the organization's larger effort toward including individuals in social and economic need, but they also had the chance to understand where salvaged or donated food comes from and observe how it can still represent a source of livelihood for the disadvantaged pockets of our community.

Another important aspect of students' journaling process during the semester was my role as course instructor, especially as facilitator of students' reflection and learning. All journal entries students wrote each week were reviewed by me with the primary goal to offer them a platform where they could express their ideas, report observations, and record changes about themselves in relation to their service. In other words, I utilized the means of diaries to ensure that students could be heard, and as a result, it held them accountable for the quality of the content of their journal entries. Cone and Harris aptly describe the role of an instructor in relation to students' reflection process when they say that, as learners are engaged in a cycle in which work in community forms the basis for written reflection, "under the guidance of an instructor, reflective work is used to form abstract concepts and hypotheses are generated which then get cycled back into further concrete experiences" (29). In reflective thinking, instructors do not evaluate or assess but rather guide students in a process that is essentially personal because it informs the perception of themselves in relation to the community of people they interact with as part of their service, and, therefore, it informs their identity.

Language Learning and Intercultural Gains

In assessing students' language learning, it is difficult to tease out the contribution of the volunteer work in the community from other aspects of the students' study abroad experience, since no specific quantitative assessment was carried out on what aspects of students' ability to communicate in Italian actually improved (this was outside of the scope of the course, but it may actually constitute the starting point for further research in the future). However, it is possible to extract useful qualitative feedback about students' language progress, as well as about their intercultural growth, as a result of their interaction outside the classroom with a wide variety of people, all speaking Italian (at different levels and with different varieties, people from different regions but also non-native speakers) from the diaries and from end-of-semester course evaluations.

In general, diaries provide interesting data about what skills students felt were improving at a noticeable pace. In particular, the majority of students commented positively on the fact that their listening skills had progressed significantly as a result of their sustained interactions during community service hours. Another aspect that emerges almost universally from diaries is that students felt that Italians they met and spoke with as part of their volunteer work helped them improve. Whereas this is not a direct sign of language progression, it nonetheless suggests that students were operating in a context where they felt comfortable enough to speak, make mistakes, and receive feedback in a very different way than the kind of professional feedback they were used to receiving in the classroom (and by people who were not professionals in the field of language teaching). Therefore, even if I did not formally assess linguistic improvement linked to their work in the community, it is clear that students developed a unique openness to using Italian in their communications when their emotional filter (fear of making mistakes, fear of being judged, and so on) naturally lowered as a result of the inclusive atmosphere within the organizations. In addition, through PBL activities in the form of community work, students received an exceptional training in intercultural competence, and they actively practiced and acquired skills, such as personal and social responsibility, nonjudgmental attitudes, tolerance for ambiguity, and so on.

As for course evaluations, students generally commented on their participation in the community-engagement program as a whole, with little to no direct reference to the use of the Italian language. For instance, here are three different comments students made:

- "I feel as if I have improved, volunteering at the soup kitchen really helps and makes me feel good. I also get more comfortable with the people there and therefore can speak Italian better and more comfortably with them as opposed to a random Italian in Bologna."
- "The Civic Engaged Learning course . . . is vital to life, and especially to a liberal arts and science education; more CEL courses should be offered at Dickinson in Carlisle."
- "Social Activism – volunteer-work and reflection journals presented a new way of learning for me; this was challenging and opened my mind to new ways of learning both in and outside of the classroom."

Interestingly, whereas students tended not to comment directly on their perceived language progress, I believe this is evidence of the successful integration of service-learning into the course. Italian was the primary means of communication in and especially outside of class, and consistent use of the Italian language was essential to their successfully completing the course and the service-learning project. I also believe that we cannot separate the way students' speaking abilities in Italian improved from the way they matured as individuals while abroad. In this regard, students' diaries provide plenty of interesting examples.

In one case, a student defined her role at Mondo Donna as a "grain of rice." In her volunteer work, she completed mostly baby-sitting duties, which presented some challenges. Not only were children's communicative abilities rather low or non-existent in Italian (or English), but the student at times had to juggle several children on her own. In her diaries, the student initially expressed confusion and concern about her job, which, in her mind, was not in any way a form of activism. As a matter of fact, she explained in detail how, at the beginning of the course, her notion of the concept of activism was mostly based on the idea of protests, marches, and picketing and not on being a babysitter. As weeks went by, she became more familiar with the history of Mondo Donna and especially with its mission, which is to accompany immigrants on a path toward economic and linguistic independence in their new host country, Italy. Parents, especially mothers, of the children the Dickinson student tended to, were encouraged to attend Italian language classes where they acquired practical language skills to function in Italian on a daily basis.

When the student realized that had she not volunteered her time to look after the children, their parents might not have wanted to learn Italian, she also realized that her contribution, as little as it was, just like a grain of rice, was very valuable and necessary. Similarly, another student who also worked at Mondo Donna wrote several of her diaries around the theme of learning as power. She discussed how learning to speak Italian in order to live autonomously in the country stimulated those individuals to improve themselves and empowered them to aspire to a better living situation for their families. This also struck a personal chord with the student, as, in turn, she realized how important her own language progress in Italian was and how that made a difference in her experience as a foreigner in Italy.

A couple of students who volunteered at the soup kitchen within the Antoniano Onlus organization specifically commented on the fact that, despite the presence of a language barrier (arguably, I would add, a higher one in a context like the soup kitchen frequented by people who might not have received a formal education and whose ability to communicate might be driven by more urgent needs, such as to obtain food), they managed to connect with others on a deeper level thanks to their own ethnic backgrounds. One of them, whose mother is of Indian origin, reported being surprised when he found out that a guest was not only from India but also knew of the village where the student's mother had lived. At one point, he commented, saying that he believed that could not be a coincidence and that such an encounter gave his community service a new and different meaning. The other student was of Italian heritage; he had never met his grandmother, who was from Italy. He observed with attention the way salvaged or donated food was used by kitchen staff to make creative meals. He also noted how food became a metaphor in the context of the soup kitchen, that is a means of communication, a sign of inclusion, the meeting point between two communities, the one of the guests and the one of the volunteers. In a very personal and nostalgic way, he also compared that dynamic to the one in his own Italian-American family, where Italian traditions were, and probably still are, felt and important. Although he never had the chance to meet his grandmother, he said he felt he could connect with her by way of the powerful symbolic meaning that food had in a place like Mensa Padre Antonio.

Conclusion

The community of practice model lends itself perfectly to be used as a framework for second language acquisition in a study-abroad situation, where students, especially those coming from the same institutional background, like the ones on the Dickinson College Italian Studies Program, in Bologna, naturally exhibit the tendency to act as a group, have received homogenous instruction during the two years prior to their starting the program abroad, and share common or at least similar goals (academic and social). This paper has discussed the combination of the community of practice framework with a PBL-inspired methodology applied to a consistent process of civic-engagement service in local organizations in order to gain a better understanding of students' language learning practices, group dynamics, and changes in their identity.

I believe that foreign language study in a study-abroad context needs to be integrated fully into students' life experience in the foreign country. A similar approach can effectively, and easily, be applied to other foreign language classes but also to culture-based ones, precisely because it relies on the gains that are produced when communities meet and interact. The course Dickinson students attended while in Bologna was designed not simply around assignments and objective-driven tasks but rather around a process of regular and independent engagement with people outside and away from the safe institutional context of the college. The course required students to act, interact, negotiate, and communicate in Italian, which empowered them as agents of their own language learning progress, but it also encouraged them to find a new meaning for the role they had within the community of people where they were volunteering their time.

Notes

1. For a concise review of the main research trends in this field, see Celeste Kinginger "Enhancing Language Learning."
2. See Wengers and Lave, or Wenger.
3. See, for example, Toohey or Haneda.
4. www.mondodonna-onlus.it/, www.onlus.antoniano.it/, www.cassero.it/
5. "What We Do – Social Tables," www.foodforsoul.it/what-we-do/social-tables/
6. lafalla.cassero.it/
7. www.genderbender.it/en/

References

AACU. "Association of American Colleges and Universities, LEAP Employer-Educator Compact: Making Quality a Priority as Americans Go to College." 2013. www.aacu.org/sites/default/files/files/LEAP/compact.pdf. Accessed 19 January 2019.

Beckett, Gulbahar H., and Paul Chamness Miller. "Project-Based Second and Foreign Language Education: Present, Past, and Future." *Project-Based Second and Foreign Language Education: Past, Present, and Future*, edited by Gulbahar H. Beckett and Paul Chamness Miller. Information Age Publishing, 2006, pp. 3–14.

Cone, Dick, and Susan Harris. "Service-Learning Practice: Developing a Theoretical Framework." *Michigan Journal of Community Service Learning*, vol. 3, no. 1, 1996, pp. 27–39.

Eyler, Janet, Dwight E. Giles, and Angela Schmiede. *A Practitioner's Guide to Reflection in Service-Learning: Student Voices and Reflections*. Vanderbilt University, 1996.

Haneda, Mari. "Second Language Learning in a 'Community of Practice': A Case Study of Adult Japanese Learners." *Canadian Modern Language Review*, vol. 54, no. 1, 1997, pp. 11–27.

Hatcher, Julie A., and Robert G. Bringle. "Reflections: Bridging the Gap Between Service and Learning." *Journal of College Teaching*, vol. 45, 1997, pp. 83–89.

Hourdequin, Peter. "A Communities of Practice Perspective on Foreign Language Extensive Reading." *Extensive Reading in Japan: The Journal of the Extensive Reading SIG of the Japan Association for Language Teaching*, vol. 4, no. 1, 2011, pp. 13–17.

IIE. "Open Doors 2018." www.iie.org/en/Research-and-Insights/Open-Doors/Data. Accessed 19 January 2019.

Isabelli-García, Christina, et al. "Language Learning and Study Abroad." *Language Teaching*, vol. 51, no. 4, 2018, pp. 439–484.

Kalabzová, Milena. *The Application of Project Based Learning in the English Classroom*. PhD dissertation, University of West Bohemia, 2015.

Kinginger, Celeste. "Measuring Language Acquisition." *Language Learning and Study Abroad: A Critical Reading of Research*. Palgrave Macmillan UK, 2009.

———. "Enhancing Language Learning in Study Abroad." *Annual Review of Applied Linguistics*, vol. 31, 2011, pp. 58–73.

Li, Linda C., et al. "Evolution of Wenger's Concept of Community of Practice." *Implementation Science*, vol. 4, no. 11, 2009.

Looney, Dennis, and Natalia Lusin. "Enrollments in Languages Other Than English in United States Institutions of Higher Education, Summer 2016 and Fall 2016: Preliminary Report." *The Modern Language Association of America*, February 2018. www.mla.org/content/download/83540/2197676/2016-Enrollments-Short-Report.pdf. Accessed 19 January 2019.

NAFSA. "The Seven Cardinal Virtues of Study Abroad." www.nafsa.org/2016/05/12/the-seven-cardinal-virtues-of-study-abroad/. Accessed 19 January 2019.

Ochs, Elinor, and Bambi B. Schiefflin. "The Theory of Language Socialization." *The Handbook of Language Socialization*. Blackwell Publishing Ltd., 2011.

Regan, Vera. "Sociolinguistics and Language Learning in a Study Abroad Context." *Frontiers: The Interdisciplinary Journal of Study Abroad*, vol. 4, 1998, pp. 61–91.

Swain, Merrill, and Ping Deters. "'New' Mainstream SLA Theory: Expanded and Enriched." *The Modern Language Journal*, vol. 91, 2007, pp. 820–836.

Taguchi, Naoko. "Contexts and Pragmatics Learning: Problems and Opportunities of the Study Abroad Research." *Language Teaching* 51, no. 1, 2018, pp. 124–137.

Toohey, Kelleen. "Learning English as a Second Language in Kindergarten: A Community of Practice Perspective." *The Canadian Modern Language Review*, vol. 52, 1996, pp. 549–576.

Wengers, Etienne. *Communities of Practice: Learning, Meaning and Identify*. Cambridge University Press, 1998.

———., and Jean Lave. *Situated Learning: Legitimate Peripheral Participation*. Cambridge University Press, 1991.

7 Investigating Environmental Sustainability in an English Writing Course for International Students

PBL as an On-Ramp to Academic Belonging

Susan Huss-Lederman, Prajukti (juk) Bhattacharyya, and Brianna Deering

Increasingly, youth have taken on the mantle to champion environmental sustainability. Swedish teen Greta Thunberg inspired world-wide school walkouts for climate action (Yeginsu 2019). Sisters Melati and Isabel Wisjen started a ban on plastic bags in Bali that developed into a world-wide movement to eliminate them everywhere (Sullivan 2019). Such actions have raised global awareness of the importance of treating the environment with respect. This movement has gained recognition in language pedagogy, where materials have been made available for integrating sustainability topics into language instruction. For example, Alan Maley and Nik Peachey (2017) have edited a resource book for the British Council, offering creative ideas and plans to help teachers use the Sustainable Development Goals (SDGs) as topics for language courses. In the past few years, UNESCO and UNICEF, along with other international organizations, have provided the World's Largest Lesson, a web-based resource bank of multilingual materials and project ideas to enable youth to better understand the SDGs. If ever there were a global topic to connect students across cultures, environmental sustainability is it.

The work described here details how a college composition course for lower-division international students included three project-based learning (PBL) experiences on the topic of environmental sustainability. The ideas for the projects resulted from collaboration between English as a Second Language (ESL) faculty members Susan Huss-Lederman and Brianna Deering and geology faculty member Prajukti (juk) Bhattacharyya. These three projects – collaborating with domestic peers to prepare a science blog post for the general public, presenting posters on campus Sustainability Day, and filming public service announcements for campus social media – provided an on-ramp for international students to develop academic English to communicate beyond the composition course about topics that were personally meaningful. Furthermore, this process allowed students to make their mark in premier university programs, supported successful peer-to-peer interaction, and connected them to faculty who care about student success. All of these actions resulted in what student engagement researcher Terrell Strayhorn calls *belonging* (2019), students' understanding that they personally matter as members of the campus community and that the community has a stake in their success. PBL offered lower-division international students the opportunity to collaborate across disciplines and cultures with students enrolled in a 300-level environmental geology course for non-majors. Participating in these projects took lower-division international students out of the traditional composition classroom and into the mainstream of the university.

Project-Based Learning for STEM

Typically, courses in the STEM fields (science, technology, engineering, and mathematics) are ripe for project-based learning methodologies. Such approaches are in line with the development of 21st-century skills, as described in the National Research Council's 2012 report, *Education for Life and Work: Developing Transferable Knowledge and Skills in the 21st Century*. In their analysis of US K–12 education across STEM and English language arts disciplines, the authors noted that cultivating 21st-century skills requires students to solve open-ended problems, to make difficult decisions based on careful examination of evidence open to interpretation, and to communicate effectively, often asynchronously, through digital media. Furthermore, Liberal Education and America's Promise (LEAP), an initiative of the American Association of Colleges and Universities (2011), promotes high-impact practices in the examination of real-world issues, in all of their complexity, as part of their vision of high-quality education. PBL, an active learning approach, is such a practice.

Freeman and others (2014) conducted a comprehensive meta-analysis to demonstrate the positive impact of participating in active learning in STEM courses on student performances, especially for students from underserved populations. Similar findings have been reported by other authors (e.g. Aji and Khan 2019; Capri et al. 2017). PBL, in which teams of students examine an open-ended, complex problem, is an excellent way to incorporate active learning in any college-level course. It is possible to take this approach and apply it to courses in which students use the connection between scientific inquiry and civic engagement to examine a societal problem (Burns 2002). SENCER, Science Education for New Civic Engagement and Responsibilities, is the key initiative of the National Center for Science and Civic Engagement. In a SENCER approach, students deeply examine the connection between science and civic, or social, issues. Carefully examining the many dimensions of such a concern, detecting possible benefits or problems posed by a practice, concept, or idea, is an important element in developing critical thinking, a desired outcome for students obtaining higher education in the United States (The LEAP Vision for Learning 2011). In educating for sustainability, the development of 21st-century skills through SENCER finds a natural home.

The use of PBL, where students combine content knowledge with real-life community issues and citizenship action is a common practice in environmental education (e.g., Mordock and Krasny 2001, and the references therein). Eilam and Tropp (2010) argue that there are four essential pedagogical components of education for sustainable development (ESD). They describe those components to start from a (a) teacher-centered, lecture-based traditional academic learning, which they describe as "non-natural" learning, followed by (b) multidisciplinary learning, where students learn the subject from different perspectives and through the lens of different disciplines; (c) multidimensional learning, where students explore the subject matter in the context of space and time by actively participating in the learning process; and ultimately, (d), emotional learning, where students incorporate ethics and values in context of the course topic. They argue that co-implementation of all four components is necessary for student-centered, hands-on, minds-on learning and active participation, which is essential for promoting environmental literacy. Furthermore, environmental science educator Victor Nolet (2016) has noted that a focus on educating for environmental sustainability enables learners to think flexibly and critically by challenging assumptions and developing the ability to reason analytically. Students also gain a deeper understanding of how ecosystems work (108). *Project-based learning* differs from *doing projects* in that doing a project can be a repetitive, teacher-fronted exercise, focused purely on the product, while project-based learning issues from the students' inquiry and desire to learn ("The Difference between Projects and Project-Based Learning"). Because of the subject matter, university science courses provide a fit for the problem-based pedagogy that supports the development of 21st-century skills.

PBL for Academic Writing

Over the past years, the freshman research paper, an extended essay that integrates sources into an expository or argumentative framework, has come under scrutiny as the major writing product in first-year university composition courses. Rhetoric and composition researchers Rebecca Moore Howard and Sandra Jamieson (2014) have described problems that arise when novice academic writers attempt the research paper. These often include a conflict in the attitude about the purpose of the essay. For students, such an essay is a long paper that includes quotations from sources, while for teachers, the writing of a research paper is a journey along a path of critical reading, writing, and the synthesis of ideas. The struggle to integrate novel source ideas into an argument requires understanding that comes from deep knowledge of a topic and how authors use discipline-specific language. This poses a dilemma for the novice writer. Often, in an attempt to paraphrase or to summarize ideas that they are struggling to understand, such student writers engage in "patchwriting," which, according to Howard, occurs when "students produce something that looks like paraphrase, [when] they are actually drawing too heavily on the words of the source rather than rendering the ideas in 'original language'" (qtd. in Jamieson 2016, 504). For novice writers engaged in the research writing process for the first time, the demands of narrowing down a research question; conducting bibliographic research; selecting valid, reliable, academic sources; writing summaries; and crafting a documented essay in response to the research question are daunting tasks, compounded if students struggle with reading source materials. For novice writers preparing academic papers through a second language, the challenge of summarizing and paraphrasing is made even more difficult for several reasons. In a review and analysis of research studies of second language writing from sources, Liu and colleagues (2016) note that factors such as cultural differences regarding intellectual property, vocabulary knowledge, and overall language proficiency make the process of reading sources, summarizing them, and incorporating paraphrases into new work all the more difficult. The authors categorize recommended remedies to support students' command of English writing conventions, as used in Western academic contexts. Instructors are encouraged to clarify what constitutes appropriate use and attribution of sources and to be explicit about cultural differences in writing conventions.

In an analysis of Chinese students studying at a US university, Hirvala and Du (2013) note that English instruction in China does not emphasize academic writing and that Chinese academic writing conventions differ significantly from those expected in Anglophone educational contexts. Simply encouraging second language learners to paraphrase by substituting synonyms rather than as an engaged writing practice in which students construct meaning through interaction with a text is a mechanical exercise that does little to help a writer develop. In contrast, the projects presented here offered students many opportunities to discuss their research questions with classmates, faculty experts, writing partners, and members of the university community. Through this, students recycled and built upon language for meaningful communication that they commanded. In the projects reported on here, the dialogic nature of the PBL process mitigated many of the concerns encountered by novice writers managing research writing for the first time in a second language.

Stoller (2002) and Stoller and Myers (this volume) have noted the value that PBL offers content-based language instruction. The process naturally requires the integration of language skills and an understanding of genre, although students emphasize different linguistic skills at certain points in the process, as tasks differ in complexity. Projects may also be experiential, including contact assignments (Calvert 2015). Likewise, in the ESL composition classroom, students can wrestle with open-ended questions while using discipline-specific discourse in completing a project as they locate resources, share ideas, and maintain responsibility for project development in anticipation of presenting products to an identified audience.

In a composition course with a PBL emphasis, students still identify a problem that they want to address. Students search for and read academic sources to learn more about an issue and are responsible for crafting a text that critically examines it, just as they would for a research paper. The difference is that project-based learning is collaborative and often includes public presentation of work. For learners of English as a Second Language, the opportunity to collaborate with others to produce a text for an identified audience is valuable. Students have multiple opportunities to discuss what they are learning. For each project, students received templates to facilitate the organization of texts. Thus, students were less concerned about format and more concerned about the content of their work.

College Writing in ESL: Guiding International Students to Academic Engagement

College Writing in ESL has existed in the University of Wisconsin-Whitewater curriculum since 1965. Historically, any international student or domestic student who has been accepted into the university but still wishes to be in an ESL learning environment has had the option to enroll in this four-credit course, which partially satisfies the university's communication competency, required for the bachelor's degree. College Writing in ESL provides a culturally sensitive introduction to US university academics in a class of ten to 18 students. For first-year students whose first experience of independence and international travel is to study at a US university, such an atmosphere of the ESL course is a welcome one. Instructors orient, guide, and support students in seeking academic opportunities in the wider university while providing writing instruction.

To prepare students for the demands of academic writing in the university curriculum, the course goals are for students to become confident in structuring academic arguments in writing and to improve information literacy. The structure and pace of the course is modified to suit the needs of the English learners. The course objectives were for students to

1. Compose thesis-driven arguments
2. Develop a genuine research question

3. Select and evaluate reliable sources in the research process
4. Develop and apply rhetorical understanding to written work
5. Use appropriate structural and stylistic conventions (APA) in research writing
6. Prepare and deliver an oral presentation

During the spring 2017 semester, students met these objectives by writing two short essays (cause/effect and problem/solution) at the beginning of the semester and by completing three projects:

1. Collaborating in writing a blog post for the KQED *Do Now U* project
2. Preparing an academic poster for the campus Sustainability Day event
3. Composing and recording public service announcements related to sustainability practices within the community

At the time of this project, the English composition course met Monday through Thursday in 75-minute sessions, team-taught by two instructors and supported by a peer mentor, an upper-division student completing a major in education and a minor in teaching ESL. Thirteen students, representing six countries, enrolled in the course.

Students Become Researchers

To prepare for research projects, students' first formal assignments were to write two short essays – cause/effect and problem/solution, formats chosen because they would give students practice with the discourse structures for the *Do Now U* and poster projects. Essays included information on their own lifestyle or on the health of their home country, based on what they learned from information from the Global Footprint Network and the Happy Planet Index (New Economics Foundation n.d.). For a week, university reference librarians taught international students how to use online search tools and to evaluate sources for bias, reliability, and suitability in responding to a research question. At this time, students also practiced summarizing sources, quoting, and paraphrasing source material. They also attended the campus fall undergraduate research day event, where they interviewed upper-division undergraduate researchers about their projects, examining how research fit into their education and career goals. Once the English students had some practice with writing from sources and hearing undergraduate researchers discuss their work, they were ready to begin their projects.

Project 1: Collaborating on Do Now U[1]

Do Now U was a US-based project of the National Center for Science and Civic Engagement (NCSCE), headquartered in Washington, DC, and KQED Public Media, located in San Francisco, California. In fall 2016, KQED Public Media invited instructors in higher education to incorporate blogging about a topic related to science and society in their coursework. Each participating institution would have one blog post selected to appear on the *Do Now U* website. KQED staff provided a template for blog posts and a schedule for institutions to follow.

On the University of Wisconsin-Whitewater campus, Bhattacharyya, a professor of geology, proposed collaborating in the *Do Now U* project to Huss-Lederman and Deering, instructors of College Writing in English as a Second Language. This cross-disciplinary relationship is a longstanding one. As a former international student, Bhattacharyya has often collaborated with instructors offering ESL courses, guiding students into the undergraduate research program. Bhattacharyya was interested in fostering both the LEAP competencies and 21st-century skills that *Do Now U* offered the students in the geology course. English instructors Huss-Lederman and Deering were eager to offer international students the opportunity to collaborate with US domestic students and to challenge them to contribute to a group writing project on a contemporary social issue related to environmental sustainability. For students enrolled in both courses, the intercultural exchange was an attractive element of the assignment. As instructors, we realized that all students would gain strength in participating in the project.

Instructors introduced the blog project to students in both courses, explaining that it would take about three weeks to complete. Collaborating on a public writing assignment was a new venture for students in both courses. In the geology course, the *Do Now U* project was a minor course assignment that enabled students to research an environmental topic and write something brief about it for a general audience. For the international students, the *Do Now U* project was an important assignment that served as a springboard to a more sophisticated research writing project as students developed and applied their bibliographic research skills.

Instructors established groups, made the Google Doc blog template and assignment instructions available to students, and supported students throughout the project. Since there were 13 international students and 48 geology students, not every collaborative group could include international students, so international students partnered to participate in some of the groups. Students brainstormed possible topics and suggested resources for background information, entering their ideas and links to web-based supporting resources onto a shared Google Doc. Students took on specific team roles in writing, researching, and editing the blog post, with a team captain who made sure that the working group met deadlines. Whenever possible, English students wrote opposing viewpoints or counterarguments, a challenging aspect of argumentative writing. For example, in examining the effect of rising sea levels on tourism around the world, the international student on the team explained that although in the short term rising sea levels might increase revenue in countries where income relies on seaside tourism, in the long run, the prospect of flooding could outweigh any benefits.

For the geology students, *Do Now U* was largely an out-of-class assignment. However, the English students worked on their parts of the assignment in the writing lab during class time. In this way, English instructors could offer support in locating resources and in assisting the students in completing their part of the blog posting assignment. Participating in the project required all students to use digital communication in collaborative writing; however, students asked to meet face-to-face, too. Because the courses met at different times, instructors held collaboration sessions for students to work in the campus library outside of class. Domestic students in groups with international students appreciated the opportunity to work across cultures, both online and face-to-face. First-year international students, often hesitant about group work with domestic students, appreciated the opportunity to do so in an environment where everyone practiced 21st-century skills.

Even though KQED personnel could choose only one post for the *Do Now U* blog and it was not one from a team with international students, the international students were still glad to have participated in the project. When surveyed on their perceived academic language competence, international students indicated that they were now able to locate and evaluate academic resources, summarize them, and prepare counterarguments. They were confident that their academic vocabulary was developing. These skills were further practiced in the second project, in which students researched, prepared, and presented academic posters, conference-style.

Domestic students enrolled in the environmental geology course appreciated the opportunity to collaborate on a public writing project, commenting that although getting started was challenging, once team members started working, the process was engaging. One student commented, "I have never really worked with international students who didn't speak the same language as me. I think this was a good experience and it will benefit my career down the road where I may be working with people who also speak different languages than I do." Another noted, "This project helped me learn how it is to work with other people from another country and collaborate on a topic that is changing around the world." In sum, both the experience to work across cultures and to construct knowledge through that cross-cultural experience, benefitted the international and the domestic students.

Project 2: Sustainability Day Posters

Campus Sustainability Day is organized by the campus student government sustainability officer and the campus sustainability coordinator, who is responsible for promoting and monitoring green practices throughout the campus community. This is a way to mark Earth Day with exhibits and information sessions on improving sustainability practices. Students in the English composition course prepared academic posters using the undergraduate research template (a special, large-dimension PowerPoint slide that is color-printed on a wide-format printer). Just as in a traditional documented essay, students were required to summarize, paraphrase, and effectively quote from academic sources. However, unlike most traditional documented essay assignments (but typical of academic posters), students included graphic images, such as photographs, which also required appropriate attribution. Bhattacharyya continued involvement with the international students, providing the template for posters and arranging their printing.

Similar to the blog template furnished by KQED for the *Do Now U* project, the format for undergraduate research posters served as an academic writing organizer for the students. By converting the PowerPoint to Google Slide format, Huss-Lederman and Deering were able to easily provide written feedback to students. Students could work with a partner or on their own, and through file sharing, students could easily collaborate on their poster. While some students continued working with the topic that they had chosen for *Do Now U*, others chose topics specific to their home countries. Topics included overpopulation, desertification, deforestation, ozone depletion, and ocean pollution, among others. Once posters were completed, students practiced explaining their work and responding to questions. Then, during the morning session of Sustainability Day, students took questions from people who attended the campus event. Because the posters included images, Students and attendees alike used these as visual scaffolds as they engaged in academic discussion.

Project 3: Public Service Announcements for Social Media

The third project emerged organically during the Sustainability Day event. The campus sustainability coordinator offered the international students the opportunity to develop and record 30-second public service announcements related to green topics relevant to the campus community. For this assignment, students could work individually or with a partner. The class first viewed professional PSAs to gain an understanding of effective formats. They then storyboarded their own PSAs, locating effective graphics and determining the narration and any audio effects. Topics included recycling plastic and aluminum, cutting down on food waste in the dining halls, community gardening, the campus bike-share program, and enjoying local parks. The campus technology library lent cameras, camcorders, and tripods to any students who wished to use them. The class visited the instructional video production studio for those who wished to record their announcement using the green screen. The student social media coordinator for sustainability chose a few of the videos for use on campus.

Discussion

For novice writers, perhaps the most frustrating parts of writing from sources include having limited opportunity to share work beyond a peer or a teacher and struggling to express ideas, newly learned in the second language, in their own voice. For the international students in this composition course, there were many opportunities to share what they were learning and to discuss it during project development and when presenting final products. In the process of completing assignments, international students met all writing and presentation objectives for the composition course. Furthermore, working on the blog post, followed by preparing research posters, offered students several opportunities to use and re-use new language in specific academic contexts. Collaborating on the blog post required students to use all language skills and to communicate effectively with upper-division students who were native speakers of English. The enjoyment of cross-cultural collaboration was mutual; the students enrolled in the geology course enjoyed the opportunity to work with international students on their teams, too.

Investigating important environmental issues from multiple perspectives (both pros and cons) raised students' awareness and knowledge of environmental issues, as well as their critical thinking and analytical skills. As (Short 2009) pointed out, this can potentially lead to increased self-efficacy for the students and confidence in their skills to be able to bring real behavioral change, which is one of the major goals of environmental education. Students were allowed to choose their own projects, instead of being assigned a project by the instructors. Therefore, they had complete ownership of the materials they created while the instructors took on the roles of facilitators. These research projects made societally relevant environmental issues more concrete and imbued them with personal meanings for students.

With the second project, preparing the academic poster, students built upon knowledge gained in collaborating on the blog post. International students applied their conceptual knowledge and academic language to further examine a societal issue that they cared about, either in the US or pertaining to their home country, and to present their findings in an academic poster. Because students had researched, discussed, and written about a topic close to their hearts, they were now ready to further their knowledge and to publish their work in a new format. On Sustainability Day, they spoke with confidence to members of the university community about their work. Students used the same poster template that participants in the university undergraduate research program use. Thus, the poster itself served as a scaffold for the oral presentation of information. In addition, the international students learned of opportunities to participate in the university undergraduate research program, a signature academic offering of the university. The experience thus opened students' eyes to programs of study beyond those that they had chosen with their parents before enrolling at the University of Wisconsin-Whitewater.

Second language learners benefit from reflecting on how their language competence develops through doing projects. Research conducted by Beckett and Slater (2005) on project-based learning in academic ESL contexts found that English learners need to see how engaging in project-based learning helps them to develop proficiency in the target language. In the activities reported here, student assessment of each project indicated that international students, overall, enjoyed the project-based approach. They could see that their command of English improved throughout the semester. The opportunity to share what they were learning and producing with a wider audience, beyond the students and teachers in the composition course, motivated students while they sharpened essential academic communication skills. Throughout the semester, Huss-Lederman and Deering required students to reflect upon their experience with each project and to share their observations in class. Upon completion of the first project, the blog post for consideration by *Do Now U*, students evaluated the project through an anonymous, online survey. Although only six international students completed the survey, all indicated that they had improved their academic proficiency in writing and command of vocabulary. In the final course evaluation, all students overwhelmingly indicated that they enjoyed doing projects related to writing that required conducting research and creating products that they could do and share outside of the classroom.

Although this was a college composition course, students gained experience not only in the process of academic writing from sources, but also in collaborating with each other and with domestic students on writing. They wrestled with open-ended questions concerning environmental sustainability. Furthermore, they observed more advanced peers discussing research posters at the undergraduate research day and then were able to take on that process themselves on Sustainability Day. In each case, the students engaged in the 21st-century skills of critical thinking and communicating effectively in diverse groups. Finally, in preparing and recording public service announcements, students used different forms of professional-grade, digital video technology in a campus recording studio. In effect, the composition course served as a gateway to academic expression to the wider community. These international students were not flies on the wall, observing domestic students "doing college"; they were engaged scholars, sharing expertise first with classmates and then with members of the blogosphere and the campus community. They belonged and mattered.

For instructors, the keys to success were communication and organization. All instructors were committed to working as a team. English instructors Huss-Lederman and Deering enjoyed the opportunity to enhance their knowledge of scientific inquiry and to use the discourse of science in their teaching. Geology instructor Bhattacharyya appreciated the expertise of English composition instructors in integrating a collaborative writing assignment into the geology course. The projects offered students at different stages of academic English proficiency a way to personalize the writing process.

Conclusion

As one international student recently commented to Huss-Lederman and Deering, writing is not just about writing. It is a form of expression to share ideas, and what one has written does not exist just to be read. For the international students in this composition course, there were many opportunities to share what they were learning and to discuss it during project development and when presenting final products. In each of these efforts, students had many opportunities to talk about what they were writing and to present their work orally and visually. Because of the results of efforts reported here, PBL is now the focus of this writing course.

PBL is a long-standing staple for college-level STEM courses and, specifically, for environmental education. Such an approach gives students ownership of their learning instead of making them passive recipients of knowledge. In the work reported here, the *Do Now U* project required international students to collaborate with domestic students on high-interest topics of their own choosing. They explored multiple perspectives of current environmental issues, such as deforestation, ocean acidification, sea level rising, and ozone depletion. In developing counterarguments, international students thought critically about available information, took media bias into account, approached topics from multiple perspectives, and, most important, listened to people who might hold a view different from their own. Students' curiosity and passion motivated them to learn. In turn, students were motivated to master the language to communicate their views with people they did not know. In this, they stepped out of their comfort zone. Finally, in creating public service announcements, the international students contributed to the well-being of their campus community. Each academic action situated students, not as outsiders or visitors to US culture, but as university students in an interactive academic context in which their participation was valuable.

Finally, it should be noted that whether university students are from the region or from another part of the state, from the US or from another country, a sense of belonging is fundamental for their success (Strayhorn 2019). Part of that belonging lies within social ties, but an important element also originates in student engagement with faculty. In working on these projects, the international students made important connections with faculty outside of the program in English as a Second Language. Some considered pursuing majors in disciplines they are passionate about instead of the ones they originally chose with their parents. In sum, through project-based learning, these students realized that they had more agency in their own future career goals than they had originally thought. In this case, project-based learning in this English composition course not only supported students in learning a second language but also helped them to learn about themselves and to determine their own educational pathways.

Acknowledgments

Thanks to Rossitza Ivanova for comments on an earlier draft of this chapter and to Wes Enterline for drawing international students into campus sustainability efforts.

Note

1. See Bhattacharyya et al. (2018) for a detailed description of this project.

References

Aji, Chadia A., and M. Javed Khan. "The Impact of Active Learning on Students' Academic Performance." *Open Journal of Social Sciences*, vol. 7, 2019, pp. 204–211.

Beckett, Gulbahar H., and Tammy Slater. "The Project Framework: A Tool for Language, Content, and Skills Integration." *ELT Journal*, vol. 59, no. 2, 2005, pp. 108–116.

Bhattacharyya, Prajukti, et al. "Using the SENCER Approach in Collaborating Across Disciplines: Participating in Do Now U." *Science Education and Civic Engagement: An International Journal*, vol. 10, no. 2, 2018, pp. 5–10.

Burns, William David. "Knowledge to Make Our Democracy." *Liberal Education*, vol. 88, no. 4, 2002, pp. 20–27.

Calvert, Kelly. "The Ecology of English: Real-World Experiences in Sustainability and Language Learning." *Language Learning Beyond the Classroom*, edited by David Nunan and Jack Richards. Routledge, 2015, pp. 202–212.

Carpi, Anthony, et al. "Cultivating Minority Scientists: Undergraduate Research Increases Self-Efficacy and Career Ambitions for Underrepresented Students in STEM." *Journal of Research in Science Teaching*, vol. 54, no. 2, 2017, pp. 169–194.

"The Difference Between Projects and Project-Based Learning." *TeachThought*, 2 August 2018. www.teachthought.com/project-based-learning/difference-between-projects-and-project-based-learning/. Accessed 30 March 2019.

Eilam, Efrat, and Tamar Tropp. "ESD Pedagogy: A Guide for the Perplexed." *Journal of Environmental Education*, vol. 42, no. 1, 2010, pp. 43–64.

Freeman, Scott, et al. "Active Learning Increases Student Performance in Science, Engineering, and Mathematics." *Proceedings of the National Academy of Sciences*, vol. 111, no. 23, 2014, pp. 8410–8415.

Global Footprint Network. www.footprintnetwork.org/. Accessed 17 February 2018.

Hirvala, Alan, and Qian Du. "'Why Am I Paraphrasing?': Undergraduate ESL Writers' Engagement With Source-Based Academic Writing and Reading," *Journal of English for Academic Purposes*, vol. 12, June 2013, pp. 87–98.

Howard, Rebecca Moore, and Sandra Jamieson. "Researched Writing." *A Guide to Composition Pedagogies*, edited by Gary Tate, et al., 2nd ed. Oxford University Press, 2014, pp. 231–247.

Jamieson, Sandra. "Is It Plagiarism or Patchwriting? Toward a Nuanced Definition." *Handbook of Academic Integrity*, edited by Tracey Bretag. Springer, 2016, pp. 503–518.

"The LEAP Vision for Learning: Outcomes, Practices, Impact, and Employers' Views." *Association of American Colleges and Universities*, March 2011. www.aacu.org/sites/default/files/files/LEAP/leap_vision_summary.pdf. Accessed 13 November 2017.

Lehtomäki, Elina, et al. "Global Connectedness in Higher Education: Student Voices on the Value of Cross-Cultural Learning Dialogue." *Studies in Higher Education*, vol. 41, no. 11, 2016, pp. 2011–2027.

Liu, Gi-Zen, et al. "Best Practices in L2 English Source Use Pedagogy: A Thematic Review and Synthesis of Empirical Studies," *Educational Research Review*, vol. 19, November 2016, pp. 36–57.

Maley, Alan, and Nik Peachey, editors. *Integrating Global Issues in the Creative English Language Classroom: With Reference to the United Nations Sustainable Development Goals*. British Council, London, 2017.

Mordock, Kaylay, and Marianne E. Krasny. "Participatory Action Research: A Theoretical and Practical Framework for EE." *Journal of Environmental Education*, vol. 32, no. 3, 2001, pp. 15–20.

National Research Council. *Education for Life and Work: Developing Transferable Knowledge and Skills in the 21st Century*. The National Academies Press.

New Economics Foundation. "Happy Planet Index." http://happyplanetindex.org/. Accessed 17 February 2018.

Nolet, Victor. *Educating for Sustainability: Principles and Practices for Teachers*. Routledge, 2016.

Short, Philip C. "Responsible Environmental Action: Its Role and Status in Environmental Education and Environmental Quality." *Journal of Environmental Education*, vol. 41, no. 1, 2009, pp. 7–21.

Stoller, Fredricka L. "Project Work: A Means to Promote Language and Content." *Methodology in Language Teaching*, edited by Jack C. Richards and Willy A. Renandya. Cambridge University Press, 2002, pp. 107–119.

———, and CeAnn C. Myers. "Project-Based Learning: A Five-Stage Framework to Guide Language Teachers." *Project-Based Learning in Second Language*

Acquisition: Building Communities of Practice in Higher Education, edited by Adrián Gras-Velázquez. Routledge, forthcoming.

Strayhorn, Terrell L. *College Students' Sense of Belonging: A Key to Educational Success for All Students*. 2nd ed. Routledge, 2019.

Sullivan, Michael. "How Teenage Sisters Pushed Bali to Say 'Bye-Bye' to Plastic Bags." *National Public Radio*, 26 January 2019. www.npr.org/sections/goatsandsoda/2019/01/26/688168838/how-teenage-sisters-pushed-bali-to-say-bye-bye-to-plastic-bags. Accessed 30 March 2019.

Yeginsu, Ceylan. "Skipping School to Save the Earth." *New York Times*, 14 February 2019. www.nytimes.com/2019/02/14/world/europe/uk-climate-change-student-protest.html. Accessed 30 March 2019.

Part IV

Heritage Learning and Language

8 Project-Based Learning in the Context of Teaching Heritage Language Learners

Maria Carreira, Claire Hitchins Chik, and Shushan Karapetian

This chapter considers project-based learning (PBL) in the context of teaching heritage language learners (HLLs). According to the Buck Institute for Education, PBL involves students working for a prolonged period of time on a task that is complex and addresses a real-world challenge or need. While the instructor sets the general parameters for topic selection, students have a say in choosing a specific angle on which to work. In this way, engagement is promoted and sustained over the course of defining a problem, collecting information, processing or analyzing the resulting data, and producing a final product that reports on the outcome. This could take many forms: a pamphlet, poster, webpage, written report, oral presentation, or even video. Regardless of the form, however, all products are developed for a real-world audience. Progressing from topic selection to product completion is carefully structured by the instructor: The process is broken down into manageable steps with clear rubrics at each stage, and opportunities are provided to study models of the final product in the target language, present/discuss the project "so far," and receive ongoing, in-depth feedback throughout the unit, including on early drafts of the final product. Each step aims to give students opportunities to work with authentic input and produce high quality output.

The term *heritage language learner* is used to describe two groups of learners: those with some linguistic knowledge of the HL and those with "familial or ancestral ties to a particular language" (Hornberger and Wang 27) but no measureable proficiency in it. In terms of the latter, the language may not have been spoken in the family for generations, but an emotional connection remains through family history (e.g., Fishman). By contrast, Valdés defines a HLL as someone who is "raised in a home where a non-English language is spoken, who speaks or at least understands the language, and who is to some degree bilingual in that language and English" (38). In this case, learners are either born in the US to immigrant parents or arrive during childhood and, despite becoming English dominant once mainstream schooling starts, maintain some proficiency in the HL. Polinsky and Kagan describe HLLs with knowledge of the language as "narrow" definition HLLs, and those with a familial/emotional connection, but no linguistic knowledge, as "broad" definition HLLs. Regardless of differences in linguistic profile, affective connections to the associated culture and community are typical of both groups of learners.

In terms of language teaching, broad definition HLLs have language needs similar to those of second language learners (L2Ls). By this, we mean that they may need the kind of comprehensive instruction on grammar and vocabulary given to L2 learners. At the same time, it is important to acknowledge their connection to the target language through classroom activities and the selection of course themes. Such acknowledgment is key to recognizing them as legitimate members of the heritage culture with something to contribute to the class. By contrast, narrow definition HLLs, who are the focus of this chapter, present a unique challenge for instructors because they arrive in our classrooms with some knowledge of the HL, but what that knowledge consists of varies greatly from student to student. The first issue may be acknowledging the spectrum of varieties of the HL students bring to the classroom. Pluricentric languages (like Spanish and Armenian) consist of multiple codified standard varieties, and what the students speak at home may not always correspond to what is taught in a particular classroom. Diglossic languages, like Arabic and Eastern Armenian, are defined by the complementary distribution of the literary and vernacular codes, often leading to a sharp contrast between the student's exposure to the vernacular at home and formal instruction in the literary code at school. The second issue to acknowledge is that, unlike L2Ls, for whom the classroom is the primary setting of L2 learning, HLLs acquire their HL in the home, where language-use patterns can vary widely along dimensions such as the exclusive use of the HL versus a mix of the HL and the dominant societal language, or the presence/absence of monolingual relatives. Exposure to the HL is also influenced by the uneven availability of contexts beyond the family in which the language can be heard and spoken; for instance, access to a wider local community of HL speakers, opportunities to participate in community organizations, such as churches or after-school HL programs, or travel to the country in which the HL is spoken. Immigration history will also have an impact: Those who arrive in the US as early or late teens will have more exposure to the language than those who arrived before adolescence or are born in the US. Different family backgrounds and experiences produce learners with a wide variety of strengths and weaknesses in the HL, making it essential to follow a pedagogy specifically tailored to this population.

Heritage Language Pedagogy, Project-Based Instruction, and the Community

Taking the factors just discussed into account, best practices in HL pedagogy seek to 1) build on and expand the home-based abilities that HLLs bring to the classroom; 2) respond to HLLs' life experiences and motivations for studying their HL; and 3) differentiate instruction in order to manage different levels of proficiency and ensure meaningful and valuable learning opportunities for all students. Each of these points will be explored further.

Building on HLL abilities involves using what Kagan and Dillon call a "macro-based" pedagogy (also referred to as a "top-down" approach), where instruction is centered on authentic materials and tasks from the very beginning. Students listen to, view, or read carefully selected materials that have been created by and for native speakers, examples being songs, videos of presentations on any number of topics, or newspaper articles. Students approach and interact with the content at the level of "big picture" ideas or interpretations. Form-focused activities that center on discreet language items are introduced later in the teaching process, targeting specific knowledge gaps as they become relevant for understanding main ideas, answering questions, or completing tasks. In other words, effective HL teaching is selective with regard to language instruction. L2Ls, in contrast, require a reverse sequence, i.e., a "micro" or "bottom-up" approach, especially at the lower levels. A comprehensive coverage of language topics is typical, with scaffolding in the form of vocabulary sets and grammatical structures provided so that content can be accessed by these students. HLLs would be bored by such an approach, while an initial focus on content acknowledges their HL skills and for this reason enhances engagement.

Engagement is also enhanced by responding to HLLs' bilingual and bicultural experiences and to their motivations. Respondents to a survey conducted by Carreira and Kagan gave the following top two reasons for enrolling in HL classes: firstly, wanting to learn about their cultural and linguistic roots (almost 60%) and secondly, wanting to communicate better with family and friends in the US (57.5%). Cantonese-, Japanese-, Mandarin-, and Spanish-speaking respondents placed professional goals above these personal ones. Good HL teaching, we can conclude, seeks to build on and expand HL students' all-round linguistic repertoires so as to equip them to better communicate in both the "insider" contexts of home and the HL community, as well as in the wider society, in particular within the professions. A focus on issues of identity is also a hallmark of good HL teaching, with the strategic choice of topics or project themes helping HLLs explore "their cultural and linguistic roots" as well as the challenges and rewards of straddling two cultures and languages.

Differentiated instruction enables teachers to respond to points 1) and 2) by providing strategies that address the variations in language proficiency that HLLs present in the classroom and also probe individual differences in terms of life experiences, issues of identity and belonging, and motivations, all of which occupy a central role in HL learning. Research can only paint a very general picture of a group in relation to these topics; individual HLLs will vary in unique ways, and the tools of differentiated instruction, in particular formative assessment, provide instructors with the means to uncover idiosyncrasies as a first step to addressing them.

How does PBL respond to our three points? In keeping with the best practices of HL teaching, PBL begins with a real-world problem that requires students to interact with authentic materials, engage in complex tasks such as analyzing or synthesizing, and create a product for public consumption. HLLs initially use their home-acquired skills to approach the work, adding vocabulary, grammatical structures, and functional skills as dictated by the requirements of the assignment in relation to their proficiency levels at the start of the course. In other words, differentiation is "built into" the process, as is the stipulation to selectively target language items, both of which occur naturally as students proceed with their projects.

In terms of our second point, projects that are community-based or involve service learning are ideal vehicles for building on HLLs' closeness to the HL community and their stated desire of communicating better with members of this community as well as their family. Speaking to this goal, the first project we examine, the Armenian Service Learning Project (ASLP), has students interview a group of HL-speaking seniors. The second project, the Professions Project (PP), answers the long-term aim that many HLLs express of using their HL for professional purposes. The PP explores this theme within the context of the academic community. Connections are made with relevant personnel in schools of business, engineering, journalism, medicine, and more. Students then conduct interviews and the information received is subsequently used to inform the design of their project. Interdisciplinary collaboration such as this proves particularly useful in developing the necessary skills for professional growth of the HL.

At the heart of both of these projects is the notion of community, which occupies a central role in language learning. One of the "5Cs" in the *World Readiness Standards for Learning Languages* (National Standards Collaborative Board), *Communities* calls for learners to use the target language to interact and collaborate in local and global communities, both "real" and virtual. This goal applies at all levels of instruction, for all languages and learners, heritage and non-heritage alike. In HL teaching, this construct has additional significance in that, as noted earlier, for many learners connecting with HL-speaking communities is one of the primary impetuses for studying the HL (Carreira and Kagan). More than that, recent research suggests that communities may be an essential feature of HL learning. In Helmer's study of a Spanish HL class in a Southwest charter high school, learners rejected activities that they perceived as serving no other purpose than to practice grammar. Appropriately titled, "*It's not real, it's just a story to learn Spanish*," this study underscores the importance of "meaningful activity and authentic materials that connect the curriculum to students' linguistic strengths, target-culture knowledge, and the communities from which they came" (186). In this view, the role of communities is to provide authentic venues in which to apply language beyond the classroom, allowing instructors to replace language-focused instruction that fails to motivate HLLs with opportunities for realistic engagement.

The projects we discuss fulfill this imperative but at the same time go beyond it. Both the ASLP and the PP allow students to grow as the HL is extended into new and challenging contexts and is used for novel purposes; however, in addition to novel linguistic engagement, these projects also take advantage of the diversity found in academic and local communities to broaden students' experiences and worldviews. The ASLP taps into the diversity found in the Glendale community in Los Angeles County, while the PP takes advantage of an academic community that is diverse in terms of both multiculturalism and disciplinary expertise. As we can see, the term *community* can cover many different entities. In the ASLP project, the community in focus is not the HL community as a whole, but a sub-group, namely seniors attending a particular care facility, while in the PP, it refers to personnel within various academic departments and, within these, specific sub-fields relevant to the project. By exposing students to environments that are generally unfamiliar, interactions and perspectives that are not typically part of their everyday world are introduced.

Beyond benefiting learners, these kinds of projects are also valuable from a societal standpoint. As noted in a recent report by the American Academy of Arts and Sciences, the US has a pressing need for individuals who can provide social and legal services to immigrant communities in their languages, to say nothing of the need for a bilingual workforce in the international realms of diplomacy, business, research collaboration, and more. Also underscoring the role of community in language learning, this report recommends greater involvement of and collaboration between local, non-English language communities and the educational system as a way of improving language education. The ASLP, in particular, answers this call.

The Armenian Service Learning Project

The community site chosen for the ASLP project is an Adult Day Health Care (ADHC)/Community-Based Adult Services (CBAS) center in the city of Glendale whose participants are mostly, if not entirely, composed of Armenian elderly. An ADHC/CBAS is a licensed community-based day-care program providing a variety of health, therapeutic, and social services to those at risk of being placed in a nursing home, including: "professional nursing services; physical, occupational, and speech therapies; mental health services; therapeutic activities; social services;

personal care; hot meals and nutritional counseling; and transportation to and from the participant's residence" (California Department of Aging). The daily program runs from eight in the morning to one in the afternoon.

Currently, over 300 centers exist in many urban and rural areas in the state of California. In the city of Glendale, there are five such centers with an overwhelming Armenian majority. The average number of daily participants ranges from 60 to 100 elderly who are typically anywhere from their late 50s to their early 90s. As is the case with the general Armenian population in Glendale, the participants in the ADHC/CBAS program are of varying backgrounds, including those from the Republic of Armenia, Iran, Iraq, Lebanon, Syria, and other diasporic communities.

Description of the Project

The heart of the project involves students of an advanced Armenian course at UCLA, taught by co-author Shushan Karapetian, forming partnerships with the elderly at an ADHC/CBAS center in Glendale. The logistics involved in arranging these partnerships are taken care of by the instructor. At every stage, students produce reflection journals that trace their experiences, learning development, and growth both in linguistic abilities and overall sociocultural knowledge and skills. Students are required to meet at least seven times for one hour per meeting with their partner and produce reflection journals for every encounter, in addition to pre-service and post-service entries. The service-learning component counts for 15% of the final grade and is fully integrated into the course: In the meetings, students discuss culturally relevant material that is presented in class through diverse media, such as readings, literary works, movies, songs, stories, and autobiographies. In addition to this, meetings will necessitate utilizing concrete linguistic skills that are developed and enhanced in class, such as the use of the formal register, the aorist tense, or the subjunctive. The reflections are divided into two parts, linguistic and sociocultural, in order to display the parallel development in both areas. The ongoing reflections culminate in a final presentation and paper that outline the students' growth and change from the beginning of the quarter to the termination of the service-learning partnership.

Before moving on to detailed instructions for the first three meetings with the ADHC/CBAS partners and subsequent student reflections, it is useful to consider the characteristics of the project in light of effective service-learning components as outlined by Eyler and Giles. The authors define five characteristics that lead to positive outcomes: placement quality, application, reflection, diversity, and community voice. Each of these will be considered.

Placement quality poses the issue of reciprocal benefit. How is this project both productive to students and useful for the community?

From the students' perspective, opportunities are presented to interact with native speakers of Armenian who have little or no knowledge of English and cannot join in the frequent code switching or reliance on English typical of HLLs. Students use discussion topics covered in class as springboards for their meetings with the elderly, in the process improving and honing their speaking abilities and enriching their understanding of the topics. Moreover, the use of reflective journals provides an opportunity to develop writing skills. Although it may seem that benefit accrues more to the students, the elderly will also receive a very valuable service, that of company and interest. The value of such a service should not be underestimated in a culture that traditionally honors the elderly as the most powerful and respected members of society. Many of the participants in ADHC/CBAS centers have lost their prestigious role in the context of a new country and truly revel in the idea of having someone, especially a younger member, show interest in their life, their stories, and their opinions. They receive a sense of pride and satisfaction in being able to pass on their perspectives and wisdom to a young Armenian.

The second of Eyler and Giles's characteristics is *application*, as in how students can relate what they learn in the classroom to what they do in the community and vice versa. In this project, the service-learning component is intricately connected to the course material. The cultural topics taught in class form the core themes for the meetings with the elderly. Then in a cyclical manner, the responses and interactions that result from the meetings serve as resources for discussions in class. In addition, the elderly are a rich, vibrant, and authentic source of cultural and historical knowledge. Elements of Armenian heritage and culture that are introduced in the course can be expanded during the meetings with additional validation, commentary, and explanations from the elderly. In terms of linguistic topics, the specific grammatical features learned in class are used in authentic conversations with a native speaker.

Reflection is the third essential characteristic of an effective service-learning program. How are students being thoughtful about their experiences? As mentioned earlier, and exemplified here, students will be reflecting in multiple modes (written, oral), at all stages of the process, and in a cyclical manner. This process is nurtured by classroom activities and the meetings, which in turn feed back into the course material.

The fourth aspect needed to create a strong service-learning program is *diversity*. How does the experience lead to tolerance and understanding? Diversity does not have to be solely limited to racial-, sexual-, or gender-related issues. It can also be based on age, dialectal differences, and geographical variations. There is inherent diversity in the Armenian population based on its historically diasporic nature. Students will associate with Armenians from diverse geographical backgrounds, with different sociolinguistic and sociocultural repertoires, varied life experiences, and from an older generation. The same is true for the elderly, with "younger" replacing "older."

The final feature of an effective service-learning program is described as *community-voice*. Are the concerns of the community being met? This partnership aims to ease the loneliness and isolation of the Armenian elderly, creating relationships between the participants and students that are unique and special for the senior community at the participating ADHC/CBAS center. In cases where their own family members may be too distant, busy, or linguistically incapable of forming the desired bonds or demonstrating acceptable norms of honor and respect, the elderly may benefit immensely from partnerships with students who not only have meeting time built into their course schedule but also the cultural and linguistic tools that are needed for the interaction.

Course Organization

In this section, we provide an outline of classroom topics/themes as well as guidelines for students in their first three meetings with their ADHC/CBAS partners.

1) *First Meeting:* Formal Introductions

    - The class will review
        - making formal introductions
        - speaking about themselves, family, childhood, academic activities.
    - The formal register will be introduced/reviewed in conducting the above activities.
    - Students will practice in pairs and perform sample interviews with each other.

    Guidelines

    - Meet elderly partner.
    - Introduce yourself using everything we have learned.
    - Ask them to introduce themselves – i.e., family, work, hobbies – whatever they want to talk about.

    Reflection #1

    Sociocultural: How did the meeting go overall? What was your impression of your partner? What was his/her reaction to you? What did s/he think about your studies? What did s/he think about you studying Armenian? What did s/he tell you about themselves? What does this tell you about the person? What did s/he want to talk about?

Linguistic: Was it difficult to carry on a conversation in the formal register for so long? Did you ever slip into the informal? If yes, were you reprimanded or corrected? At any point, did you have difficulty coming up with certain words or phrases in Armenian? What were they? What happened when this type of difficulty occurred? Did your partner help, or did you provide an explanation or perhaps attempt to give the English word? Did you have trouble understanding your partner? If yes, what did you do to aid comprehension?

Quotation: Write down one phrase, sentence, or thought your partner said which you liked, connected with, or reflected on.

2) *Second Meeting*: Life in the Past

- The aorist tense will be covered, as many heritage students have trouble conjugating verbs in the simple past because many are irregular.
- Students will also review question words and appropriate ways of using questions in a formal conversation.
- Students will read factual texts about Armenian immigration patterns from the time of the Genocide to the present.
- They will read literary representations, such as poems and short stories.
- They will watch a video clip of a famous author talking about his past.

Guidelines

- Students ask their partners about his/her childhood and what it was like to grow up in Soviet Armenia/Iran/Iraq/Lebanon.
- What were the major events in his/her life that shaped his/her worldview?
- How did s/he end up in America? Why did s/he come? Willingly/unwillingly?

Reflection #2

Sociocultural: Were you surprised by his/her story? What information was new for you about his/her immigration experience? Did s/he talk about any of the events we covered in class? What were the major events that shaped his/her life? Was your partner's experience similar to your family's experience? Why or why not?

Linguistic: Were there any communication gaps in the conversation during which either you or your partner did not understand each other? If yes, how was this resolved? Were there any verbs you had difficulty with in the aorist? Which ones?

Which verbs did you use most often? Why? Were there any vocabulary words you were unfamiliar with or learned from your partner? Write down five and make sentences with them.

Quotation: Write down one phrase, sentence, or thought your partner said which you liked, connected with, or reflected on.

3) *Third Meeting*: What It Means to Be Armenian

- Students will review the future tense/subjunctive.
- Students will talk about identity in class.
- They will read poems, short stories, and newspaper articles dealing with issues of how identity is constructed in a diasporic community.
- They will discuss how people deal with multiple identities. In the Armenian case – Armenianness within Armenian society/community and being Armenian in a host country.
- They will learn philosophical vocabulary, such as *acculturation, assimilation, bicultural, bilingual, construction, ethnicity, globalization, identity, majority, minority*.

Guidelines

- What does it mean to be Armenian?
- How do you define Armenianness?
- What does it mean to be a good Armenian?
- What will happen to the Armenian people?
- What will happen to the Armenian diaspora?
- What will happen to the Armenian language?
- What advice would you give to a young Armenian in America?
- What role does the Armenian language play in preserving Armenian identity?

Reflection #3

Sociocultural: Were your partner's responses surprising in regard to what it means to be Armenian? What makes a good Armenian in your partner's opinion? Were his/her responses similar or different to yours? Do you agree with his/her predictions about the future of the Armenian people and the Armenian language? Please explain. Do you consider his/her advice valuable? Why/why not?

Linguistic: Did you encounter any difficulty in posing questions about identity? Did your partner understand/use the same philosophical terminology as you did? What new words did he/she use? Please list them.

Quotation: Write down one phrase, sentence, or thought your partner said which you liked, connected with, or reflected on.

In sum, the ASLP project targets the particular needs of HLLs by focusing on issues of identity and belonging and embodies all the characteristics of effective service-learning. The built-in dimension of community allows for both linguistic and socio-cultural themes introduced in the course to be explored in contexts beyond the classroom, adding a richness and authenticity to the material.

The Professions Project

The PP project is part of *Spanish for the Professions*, a 300-level college class at California State University, Long Beach (CSULB), taught by co-author Maria Carreira. The class is the first in a sequence of five courses leading to a certificate in professional Spanish awarded to heritage students by the Spanish Program at CSULB. A required course for all students seeking the certificate, *Spanish for the Professions* aims to acquaint students with general professional-level language and the vocabulary of their field of study or intended career, as well as skills that support independent language learning. Some of the certificate courses that follow offer more field-specific preparation, for example, Spanish for Business, Spanish for the Health Professions, Spanish for Legal Interpretation, and Spanish for Bilingual Teachers. Other courses for the certificate are part of the curriculum for the Spanish major, including linguistics, culture, and literature courses. Upon completing all of the coursework for the certificate, students take a proficiency examination given by a company that specializes in evaluating functional proficiency. Their score becomes part of their certificate portfolio, along with some of the materials produced in this and other courses. By and large, students in this class have fairly strong communicative skills; they fall in the range of the Intermediate-High to Advanced-Low levels of the ACTFL oral proficiency guidelines (American Council on the Teaching of Foreign Languages 2012). As is typically the case with HLLs, their reading and writing skills are lower: Intermediate-Mid to High.

The class meets two days a week, for 90 minutes at a time. Tuesdays are designated days for project work, leaving Thursdays for more traditional language learning activities, such as reviewing particular grammar points or the rules of orthography. In this way, *Spanish for the Professions* blends traditional language instruction with PBL.

Description of the Project

During the first week of the semester, students group by their field of study or intended career, according to their preference. Typically these comprise six general categories, representing the most common fields where speaking Spanish is an advantage or a must: health care, business, education, translation/interpretation, communications/media, and the law. Ideally, groups consist of four students with common interests, though sometimes it is necessary to form slightly smaller or larger groups. The professional categories are general enough that they can accommodate the formation of several groups with foci on different sub-specialties, if needed. For example, within the general field of health care one group may focus on medical interpretation and another on health initiatives for US Latinos. Also during this week, the rules of group work are specified and agreed to by every student, and some training is provided on common problems surrounding collaborative learning, such as what to do with students who are not pulling their weight or when the expectations and procedures for group work are unclear (Gibbes and Carson; Notari et al.). However, it is important to note that the challenges of group work are such that they cannot be adequately dealt with in a one-time training session but require ongoing attention by the instructor and students.

With these preliminaries in place, the next step is finding a project. In keeping with the tenets of PBL, the project must address a real-world problem with some level of complexity, not one whose solution can be arrived at through group work in the span of a class or two, as typically happens with task-based learning. This is not an easy undertaking in light of time constraints: Each group must present a proposal to the class, revise it per the feedback they receive, and get it approved by the instructor by the end of the fourth week of the semester. This gives students three weeks (i.e., the second through the fourth week of the semester) to research their project and come up with a work plan, which must include 1) a description of the real-word problem being addressed; 2) the type of product that will address this problem (e.g., a video, a pamphlet) and the technical (non-linguistic) skills needed to create this product (being able to make a video or design a pamphlet); and 3) key sources of information on the problem as well as the technical skills needed to produce a high-quality product. This process involves the groups in brainstorming about real-world needs in their field, settling on one of these, and doing some research to hone their understanding of the problem and what is involved in crafting a solution. Instructor guidance is crucial throughout this process and may include helping students find a project or fine-tune their own project idea, as well as helping them find critical resources, including people to talk to in relevant departments and beyond academia. The following projects were undertaken by two different groups, each composed of students with shared professional interests. These groups are referred to as the "communications and journalism group" and the "education group."

The Communications and Journalism Group: A Promotional Video

The original goal of this project was to advertise a journalism course in Spanish – the first of its kind taught at CSULB – that was being offered the following semester in the Department of Journalism and Public Relations (JPR). Over the course of time, the goal expanded to include creating a video that could serve to promote an option in Spanish-language journalism that was additionally being created for journalism students. To this end, students in the communications and journalism group prepared a 10-minute video in Spanish that highlighted the enormous reach and power of the Spanish-media in the US and described what the JPR was doing to prepare students to take advantage of the career opportunities that present themselves within this market. The video, which was posted on the JPR's webpage, included interviews with JPR professors, professional journalists, and graduates of the program, as well as a virtual tour of the department's top-of-the-line facilities and equipment.

In terms of technical know-how, the students in this group were able to draw on the academic training of some members who were media studies majors, specifically their video-making, interviewing, and script-writing skills, to produce their final product. The main challenge for them came in the form of producing advanced-level oral language. To address this challenge, the students read articles on the US Spanish-language media and perused websites of journalism departments in universities in Spanish-speaking countries, taking note of vocabulary and expressions that they could use in their video. Similarly, to prepare for the interviews, they watched a number of Spanish-language interviews and studied the use of questions, transitions, and other cohesive devices.

The Education Group: An Informational Poster

The education group focused on the Single Subject Credential for those seeking to be K–12 teachers of Spanish, an area that straddles the Spanish Program and the College of Education. The group began by interviewing the Single Subject Credential specialist in the Spanish Program and learned that many students neglected to follow the complicated sequence of steps needed to obtain the Single Subject Teaching Credential in Spanish. This often resulted in unnecessary delays for students and an increased workload for the specialist. To address this problem, the education group created a poster in Spanish that featured a flowchart of the relevant steps and corresponding sources of information for fulfilling these steps.

Consisting of short phrases (i.e., language that is characteristic of the Intermediate Level), the end product would seem to be too easy for students at the Advanced level. However, this project presented students with the considerable challenge of working out how to deal with concepts that do not exist in the Spanish-speaking world and for which there are no straightforward terms that can be looked up, such as "single subject," "the Clear Credential," and "K–12." In this sense, the project was harder than the one done by the communications and journalism group, which involved collecting language from authentic Spanish-language products and applying it to the creation of the video. Of course, students in the education group had to familiarize themselves with the general properties of the poster format, in particular its most common grammatical structures, which are significantly different from those typically used in English posters. This involved collecting and studying authentic posters from the Spanish-speaking world.

The poster was beautifully designed to look like a blackboard with a teacher's handwriting flowing over it, which made it visually well suited for displaying at the entrance to the office of the Single Subject Credential specialist, where it now resides.

Different Projects, Shared Processes

The preceding projects differ from each other by content (the material being learned) and product (how students demonstrate their learning). In this way, the projects are differentiated according to students' professional interests and goals. At the same time, all projects follow a sequence common to PBL involving information collecting, processing, and producing.

This common sequence serves three important purposes. First, it ensures that all projects engage students in practices that promote language learning and train students to become independent language learners. These include (a) getting input in the target language (in PBL, this happens primarily at the information-collecting stage); (b) making form-meaning connections, which is associated with the information processing stage; and (c) creating output, which happens primarily at the information producing stage. Second, this approach ensures that all students receive extensive exposure to and work with language that is specific to their intended professional field. Third, the framework of information collecting, processing, and producing provides a uniform structure for organizing instruction such that all students are on the same page with regard to the type of work being done at any point in time. This is essential for imbuing the class with a sense of community and common purpose, as well as for making the workload manageable for the instructor. Thus, for six class meetings (i.e., six weeks), all groups gather and process essential pieces of information and materials that they need to create their intended product. A typical class for the communications and journalism group during this stage might involve collecting articles on the US Spanish media and annotating them for content and language. The students working on the poster learned about the Single Subject Credential, read documents in Spanish from teacher-training programs abroad to acquaint themselves with the relevant language, and studied posters in Spanish to familiarize themselves with this format. Crucially, regardless of the specifics of their project, all groups are engaged in finding authentic products to model and, from this process, compile the language and information that is critical to the creation of the product (e.g., vocabulary, formatting conventions, content knowledge). In terms of accountability, all students in a group take turns finding authentic materials and leading a discussion of how this material can contribute to the creation of their product.

The final three weeks of the semester are spent creating the product. The notion of "audience" takes center stage at this point, as the groups consider how to optimize communication. In some cases, this may involve using non-standard Spanish vocabulary or even some English words. With this in mind, all groups create and edit different pieces of their product, availing themselves of the information they have collected and going through cycles of feedback and revision. Thus, the work is both differentiated – a necessary feature of HL teaching in general and this course in particular, where students have different professional goals for Spanish – as well as unified – a necessary feature to ensure that all students meet the larger instructional objectives of the course and are adequately prepared for the next level of instruction in the certificate program. In this way, PBL provides both content flexibility and procedural rigor.

All in all, students are involved in multiple disciplines and partnering with other academic departments in the course of completing their projects. The type of crossing of disciplinary and linguistic boundaries that takes place in the process proves essential to developing language for real-world use in the professional fields.

Assessment

Following best practices in PBL, the projects described in this chapter are evaluated from the perspective of performance-based assessment (Hibbard), which is to say that they are assessed in terms of how successfully they tackle the real world problem that they were designed to address. Accordingly, in *Spanish for the Professions*, the promotional video is evaluated in terms of whether it serves to promote Spanish-language journalism and for the information poster, whether it adequately conveys information about the credential process to prospective candidates. For the Armenian project, the relevant question is whether the classroom activities, meetings with the community members, and the reflection pieces exemplify the five characteristics posited by Eyler and Giles, namely, placement quality, application, reflection, diversity, and community voice.

In each case, assessment is premised on criteria with relevance in the real world, beyond the classroom, which is an important feature of performance-based assessment. This makes for integrated assessment, where all elements of a product matter, namely the quality and relevance of the information and the format or means used to convey that information, as well as, of course, language. Crucially, language is never tested in isolation, as often happens with traditional testing. Rather, it is embedded in a real-world context and serves a real-world purpose. Also, in contrast with traditional testing, which focuses on what students know, performance-based assessment looks at what students can do with what they know (i.e., how well they apply their knowledge and skills to a task, see Hibbard).

In this framework, assessment and the project work itself are interconnected. Project work is broken down into steps, each of which follows a cycle of product creation, feedback, and revision, all of which are laid out in a detailed work plan/course calendar at the beginning of the class. Taking the information poster by way of example, an early step in the process involves selecting the information or content to be included in the poster. Students receive feedback, revise in accordance with this feedback, and receive a grade on their efforts before proceeding to the next step. Thus, the project is broken into steps, each of which is assessed for purposes of giving students the opportunity to improve on their work. The more sources of feedback, or formative assessment, the better – the instructor, peers, and, whenever possible, a real-world audience. This use of ongoing, low-stakes assessment proves essential for scaffolding the successful completion of complex projects and enables students to build the foundation for a good grade.

Authentic models play a particularly important role in the process. In *Spanish for the Professions*, students collect many authentic models of the target product, study their properties, and actively model their work after them. These models are also used by the students to co-construct rubrics through a process that involves identifying the features of good as well as bad products. In this way, learning, product creation, and performance-based assessment are all part of the same process.

Summary and Conclusions

As illustrated in this chapter and summarized here, PBL that incorporates a community-based and interdisciplinary dimension makes it possible to instantiate key principles of HL teaching:

1) Build on and expand the home-based abilities that HLLs bring to the classroom through macro-based, authentic instruction.

In the ASLP and PP, leaners are exposed to and use the HL in real-world contexts created by diverse communities of speakers/writers. Both projects go beyond the typical use of the textbook as the primary source of language and content knowledge, allowing "authenticity" to be shaped and defined in terms of local HL-speaking communities. Given that HLLs acquire the HL primarily through naturalistic interaction in the home setting rather than through education, connecting the classroom with real-world environments of language use is particularly important for this population.

2) Respond to HL learners' bilingual and bicultural experiences.

HLLs' experiences are rooted in the community, and for many HLLs, motivations for studying the language and future professional plans connect back to the community. Forging these connections within the context of an academic course increases engagement and meaning for these learners.

3) Differentiate instruction in order to manage different levels of proficiency as well as different needs, interests, and goals vis-à-vis the HL.

PBL facilitates differentiation in terms of language learning in that home-acquired skills are supplemented by additional vocabulary, grammatical structures, and functional skills as the need for these arises while completing the project. This is particularly evident during the course of interacting with community members or relevant professional personnel. Additionally, PBL allows for different content to be pursued by learners within the overall theme of the unit. In the PP, content is differentiated in terms of learners' goals vis-à-vis areas connected to an academic field and its associated community. In the ASLP, learners explore and expand on class topics that interest them in the course of interviewing HL-speaking seniors. In both cases, connections to community expose students to content in meaningful ways.

To the focus of this volume, PBL creates a bridge between language education and language use in the real world. As the American Academy of Arts and Sciences report reminds us, the need for this connection and its potential benefits is particularly relevant where HL teaching is concerned.

References

American Academy of Arts and Sciences. *America's Languages: Investing in Language Education for the 21st Century*. Author, 2017.

American Council on the Teaching of Foreign Languages. "ACTFL Proficiency Guidelines 2012." 2012. www.actfl.org/publications/guidelines-and-manuals/actfl-proficiency-guidelines-2012. Accessed 12 November 2018

Buck Institute for Education. "Buck Institute for Education." n.d. https://studentsatthecenterhub.org/resource/buck-institute-for-education-bie/ Accessed 16 February 2019

California Department of Aging. "Program Overview." 2015. www.aging.ca.gov/ProgramsProviders/ADHC-CBAS/Program_Overview.aspx. Accessed 1 October 2019.

Carreira, Maria, and Olga Kagan. "The Results of the National Heritage Language Survey: Implications for Teaching, Curriculum Design, and Professional Development." *Foreign Language Annals*, vol. 44, no. 1, 2011, pp. 40–64.

Eyler, Janet, and Dwight E. Giles Jr. "Where's the Learning in Service-Learning?" Jossey-Bass Higher and Adult Education Series. San Francisco, CA, 1999

Fishman, Joshua A. "Three Hundred-Plus Years of Heritage Language Education in the United States." *Heritage Languages in America: Preserving a National Resource*, edited by Joy K. Peyton, Donald A. Ranard, and Scott McGinnis. McHenry, 2001, pp. 81–97.

Gibbes, Marina, and Lorna Carson. "Project-Based Language Learning: An Activity Theory Analysis." *Innovation in Language Learning and Teaching*, vol. 8, no. 2, 2013, pp. 171–189.

Helmer, Kimberley. "'It's Not Real, It's Just a Story to Learn Spanish': Understanding Spanish Heritage-Language Student Resistance in a Southwest Charter High School." *Heritage Language Journal*, vol. 11, no. 3, 2014, pp. 186–206.

Hibbard, Michael K. "A Teacher's Guide to Performance-Based Learning and Assessment." *Association for Supervision and Curriculum Development (US) (ASCD)*. Alexandria, 1996.

Hornberger, Nancy H., and Shuhan C. Wang. "Who Are Our Heritage Language Learners? Identity and Biliteracy in Heritage Language Education in the United States." *Heritage Language Education: A New Field Emerging*, edited by Donna M. Brinton, Olga Kagan, and Susan Bauckus. Routledge, 2008, pp. 3–35.

Kagan, Olga, and Kathleen Dillon. "A New Perspective on Teaching Russian: Focus on the Heritage Learner." *The Slavic and East European Journal*, vol. 45, no. 3, 2001, pp. 507–518.

National Standards Collaborative Board. "World Readiness Standards for Learning Languages." National Standards in Foreign Language Education Project, Alexandria, VA, 2015.

Notari, Michele., Adrian Baumgartner, and Walter Herzog. "Social Skills as Predictors of Communication, Performance and Quality of Collaboration in Project-based Learning." *Journal of Computer Assisted Learning*, vol. 30, no. 2, 2014, pp. 132–147.

Polinsky, Maria, and Olga Kagan. "Heritage Languages: In the 'Wild' and in the Classroom." *Language and Linguistics Compass*, vol. 1, no. 5, 2007, pp. 368–395.

Valdés, Guadalupe. "Heritage Language Students: Profiles and Possibilities." *Heritage Languages in America: Preserving a National Resource*, edited by Joy K. Peyton, Donald A. Ranard, and Scott McGinnis. McHenry, 2001, pp. 37–77.

9 *Círculo Juvenil de Cultura*

A 10-Year Experiment in Service Learning and Community Engagement

Mariana Achugar, Kenya C. Dworkin y Méndez, and Felipe Gómez

The *Círculo Juvenil de Cultura* Program at Carnegie Mellon University is a Hispanic Heritage language and cultures program for community children of Latinx origin and university students that began in 2007. Throughout the past decade, *Círculo* strived to enhance the opportunities to maintain and develop the communication skills and appreciation for Latinx cultures through a project-based multidisciplinary curriculum that integrated Spanish language use with cultural and content learning. The program functioned as meeting space to generate social networks among Latinx adults, university students, and children in a medium-size city with a small density of Hispanic residents. We also intended to develop awareness in the larger community about the richness, diversity, and contributions of Latinx cultures and peoples at the local, national, and international level.

The creation of *Círculo* was a response to local needs and research-based issues that foregrounded the importance of providing strong and dense social networks, positive representations, and opportunities for minority language use to ensure language maintenance and positive identity development for immigrants. In terms of their language maintenance and cultural integration, differences between the first, second, and third generations of immigrants have shown that by the third generation, most Latinx immigrants are not able to speak Spanish (Valdés et al.). The US context, because of dominant monolingual language ideologies and anti-immigration policies directed at Hispanics, constrains the process of Spanish heritage language acquisition, use, and loss (Fishman). As research on ethnolinguistic vitality has shown (Giles et al.; Dailey et al.), the number of members in a community and its socio-economic status are important contextual factors that impact language attitudes and maintenance. Also, having clearly delimited spaces for heritage language use supports its maintenance (Gibbons and Ramirez). Developing minority language resources requires a strong social network, opportunities for use, and positive attitudes toward the groups that use it. Studies in the US like Rumbaut and Portes's showed that the intergenerational transmission of social and cultural capital is an important aspect of positive integration and identity development.

In our case in Pittsburgh, Pennsylvania, we did not have a context of strong ethnolinguistic vitality, but neither was there stigmatization of Spanish, as in other regions of the country. This offered challenges and possibilities in terms of designing a program to support the maintenance and development of Spanish and Latinx cultures. How could we support and strengthen the chances of maintaining and appreciating Latinx language and cultures in this particular socio-historical and regional context? Our response was to design a space in which local residents and university students would have opportunities to use Spanish and engage in cultural and service activities while connecting to resources in the greater Pittsburgh community.

Program Design Features

Círculo Juvenil de Cultura draws on community-based and service-learning traditions as well as on cultural historical activity theory (Cole). From this perspective, educational programs design learning and socialization processes that are part of culturally organized activities connecting to the local community. The experiences of bilingual and bicultural after-school programs like *La Clase Mágica* at UCSD, led by Olga Vázquez, that integrated work with Latinx children in the community with the education of university students, served as a model for our initiative.

In 2007, we created the *Círculo Juvenil de Cultura*, a program with the dual purpose of serving Latinx students on campus as well as Latinx families and children in the community. Its primary goals have been to 1) to promote Spanish-language maintenance and acquisition and foster dual-language linguistic and cultural competency; 2) establish a network of community partners including the children's families and educational, artistic, technological, and philanthropic individuals and institutions; and 3) promote native/heritage speaker and L2 learner college student engagement with the community through the various roles they play within the program, e.g., as volunteers, teachers' aides, and instructors.

The program building work began by conducting a survey of the community to identify its needs and interest in a heritage language and culture program. The survey revealed there was community interest among Latinx parents in it, as well as institutional support for us to engage in this project. This positive environment encouraged us (a group of Hispanic Studies faculty in the Department of Modern Languages, with the assistance and support of two colleagues from the History Department) to volunteer our time and join efforts to design the program. We decided to offer the program as a workshop on 10 consecutive weekend days every semester in order to be able to integrate the work with children, university students, and institutional resources. These workshops were designed as projects that had a concrete outcome (e.g., a play, a stop motion film, a radio program, a computer game, and so on) resulting from participants' collaboration to create a product or event that would be shared with the larger community (Figure 9.1).

The program included three levels of activity in which the various stakeholders (i.e., children, university students, families, and community organizations) interacted. The first level targeted direct work with children via a project-based curriculum integrating arts, technology, and language learning. The second level was directed to the work with university students who volunteered in the program mentoring children, directing classroom activities, and providing individualized attention. The third level integrated the work with the families and the community-based organizations, including them directly in the project work with the children. In the following sections, we detail the work at each of these levels illustrating the principles and characteristics of the model with examples from various workshops.

Why a Círculo Juvenil de Cultura?

The Hispanic population in the Pittsburgh area is estimated in 2006 to be 12,234 according to the US Census. However, more informal surveys have found a growing presence, about 25,000 strong, of Latinos/Hispanics in the community. These changes in the local population also represent demands of services geared towards fulfilling their particular needs. For example, the Pittsburgh Diocese has a growing need for Spanish speaking priests. St. Hyacinth Church and St. Regis Church, in Oakland, regularly offer services in Spanish given by Rev. Dan Vallecorsa. Local banks, like PNC, are starting to advertise in Spanish as seen in the ads on Forbes Avenue and also on Route 19. There is also a Pittsburgh Metropolitan Area Hispanic Chamber of Commerce that gathers over 33 Hispanic professionals and supports local Hispanic business, and a health services initiative, the Salud children's program organized by Doctor Diego Chaves. There are also several organizations that focus on serving the work and cultural needs of this community, the Hispanic Center and the Latin American Cultural Union. However, there are no special educational programs to support language maintenance and development for this group. A Spanish heritage language program for children would fulfill one of the needs of this growing population, offering children from Hispanic descent an opportunity to develop literacy in Spanish and enrich their knowledge of the heritage culture.

Once children begin school they start to switch to English and become immersed in the dominant English language culture. Since the Hispanic community in Pittsburgh is not centralized in one area there are not many opportunities for children to establish Spanish-speaking social networks or to learn about their heritage. Being able to maintain their heritage language and culture provides these children with an opportunity to become bilingual and bicultural. Expanding the linguistic and cultural resources they have allows them to develop a positive sense of self and to have access to more opportunities in the future. Parents also need to have a group of peers to share strategies and ideas on how to support their children's language and heritage outside of the home. The main goal of the program is to create a space for families and children to support and reinforce their Spanish language abilities and stimulate their interest for the Hispanic/Latin American culture.

Mariana Achugar
machugar@andrew.cmu.edu
412-268-1895

Kenya C. Dworkin
kdworkin@andrew.cmu.edu
412-268-8052

Figure 9.1 Our very first workshop, in 2007, culminated with a play whose script, costumes, and scenery were created by the children, their parents, two community facilitators, undergraduate and graduate students, and faculty. "La Gran Aventura del Viaje por América" involved problem-solving, travel, and learning from each other about different cultures

First Level of Activity: Work With Children

Project-based learning approaches the design of learning environments around key questions exploring authentic situated problems through collaborative activities scaffolded with tools or expert others resulting in a product shared with the larger community (Blumenfeld et al.). The project-based curriculum allowed us to have an outcome-based lesson organization. Additionally, it enabled us to address our students' multi-level and multi-age needs. Because of the small number of child participants in the program (an average of 12 to 25 per workshop), we were not able to offer differentiated instruction to them. However, integrating ages and proficiency levels provided us with an opportunity to incorporate cooperative learning and group work as ways to support individual differences and challenge all students. Each session was organized with a combination of whole-group activities (e.g., social chat, describing pictures, collaborative writing, brainstorming, and TPR) beginning with a welcoming and finishing with a wrap-up that brought everyone together. During the development of each session, child participants had a chance to work in equal ability groups to engage in pattern practice, edit each other's work, and exchange ideas (e.g., info-gap activities). Cross-ability groups allowed participants to support each other through rehearsals, working on vocabulary, reading to each other, and producing collaborative visual arts products. Individual work allowed participants to push their meaning-making possibilities through writing, listening, and drawing. The assessment of group and individual work included evaluating the expansion of Spanish language resources, cultural knowledge, and community building. In the following subsection, we will provide examples of the types of assessment used that reveal the qualities of the children's learning in these three areas.

The workshop on stop motion film was designed to introduce students to filmmaking, expose them to contemporary stop motion short films from Latin America, and develop their narrative skills in Spanish. The workshop included beginning sessions where students watched stop motion films such as *Popol Vuh*, directed by Ana Maria Pavez (Chile 2006), and *Tikitiklip*, directed by Alejandra Egaña and Paz Puga (Chile 2005). These sessions included comprehension-checking activities and vocabulary building activities, doing vocabulary building activities, and analyzing story structure. To complement this experience, we organized and held a small children's film festival that was open to the larger community, showcased Latin American animation films, and provided the participants with more examples of the genre. Then, they worked in groups to craft their own script and design the film's puppets and scenery. Finally, they filmed the movie and edited it in the lab with assistance from a fine arts graduate student. The final product was a short film, *El Lobo, el elefante y el rey* [The Wolf, the Elephant, and the King], which was shown to the larger community at two venues, the university and the main local public library, as well as at events organized by and for the local Spanish-speaking community, such as the "Feria al Servicio de la Comunidad" Latin American festival, held at the University of Pittsburgh.

To assess students' language and culture learning during this workshop, the participants' Spanish-language proficiency was assessed using the Peabody Vocabulary Test and a diagnostic narrative writing task. These measures were compared to their productions and oral explanations of their own film (The Wolf, the Elephant, and the King). Findings suggested that all students increased their vocabulary knowledge of specialized terms and were competent in the narrative genre. However, there were individual differences based on their language trajectories and levels of participation in the task.

Second Level of Activity: Work With University Students

The program relied from the start on recruiting volunteers from the college student population and surrounding community to promote their engagement through the various roles they could play and to help us work toward the fulfillment of our stated mission. Most of these volunteers have been undergraduate students at the Carnegie Mellon and neighboring University of Pittsburgh campuses who are either native/heritage speakers or L2 learners with at least low-intermediate-level Spanish skills. Volunteers can assume several roles for the functioning and success of the program – as student volunteers, aides, and sometimes as instructors/facilitators – the primary role being acting as mentors while giving the child participants in the program support and accompaniment as they work toward the completion of small tasks within a larger overarching term project. In addition, students have also reported that they enjoyed and benefited from their participation in the program because of the experience of working with children, learning about the diverse cultures of the Spanish-speaking world, and connecting and networking with fellow students and other members of the local community.

Student volunteers go through an orientation meeting before being directed to obtain university and state required clearances for working with children, a process that became more complex and time-consuming particularly in Pennsylvania over the recent years but for which the institution's Leonard Gelfand Center for Service Learning and Outreach offered valuable guidance and support to the degree their budget and staff limitations allowed. Once students filed their clearances, they began working with the program. Most chose to work directly with the children, leading small groups toward the completion of tasks, facilitating group dynamics, explaining/rephrasing instructions, or summarizing and synthesizing results for sharing with other members of the group or the community. The growth that comes from these interactions (mainly with the children but also with instructors, organizers, families, and other student volunteers and members of the community involved in the program) is not limited to linguistic ability but extends into cultural proficiency, an area that students in the program tend to acknowledge and value highly.

In end-of-workshop anonymous evaluations, student volunteers often mentioned benefitting highly from exposure to, and learning about, Latinx culture, as well as from opportunities to interact and speak Spanish with native and heritage speakers, including children and their families and other volunteers. Some described the work with children as a new experience that provided them with learning opportunities and life skills, both in terms of language and cultural knowledge and, more generally, in terms of developing resources to help them use Spanish and to interact with this type of population. A few of the respondents commented on the (at least) two-way street involved in the experience, one adding with respect to the children: "I feel I learn more from them than they do from me" ["*Siento que aprendo más de ellos que ellos de mí*"]. Several respondents demonstrated further awareness of the impact on the lives and skills of the children in a friendly space outside of regular school as a major reason to continue participating as volunteers, along with it being an empowering experience that made them feel they were substantially contributing to the community.

At the time of their participation, some of the students were working toward majors or minors in Hispanic studies or had attended our courses. Volunteer work also helped these students sustain or increase their motivation and interest, as evidenced by those who later moved on to become Hispanic studies minors or majors or continued to seek opportunities to contribute locally to the community through student groups and clubs, organizing alternative spring break trips to Guatemala, Nicaragua, and other countries or working with local Spanish-speaking refugees or immigrants.

While student volunteers had additional and concrete opportunities like those described here to interact with Spanish speakers in the program, these were not always limited to the development of linguistic skills. In certain cases, it was possible to create an ideal touch point between content, language, and culture. For instance, students in a fourth-year topics course examining representations of monsters in Latin American art, literature, and film were asked to create a puppet show based on a short story by Horacio Quiroga and present it to child participants in the program. In another example, students in a course on community radio in Latin America were instrumental in the development and implementation of a radio workshop we called "Radiociclón." In this workshop, children decided what they wanted the different sections of their radio program to be and recorded themselves narrating cultural news briefs, telling jokes, participating in a riddle contest, or creating audio commercials for their favorite toys and books. In sum, while these opportunities were beneficial to the development of the *Círculo Juvenil* workshops and offered ways for student volunteers to provide the children with assistance on specific tasks toward the particular aim of a term project, they were also opportunities for them to strengthen their understanding of content matter and apply it with a real, defined, concrete audience in mind – all within the framework of a project-based curriculum.

Graduate students in our MA and PhD in Second Language Acquisition programs also played an important role in the program. Given their dramatically increasing expertise in the area of language acquisition, research skills, and the fact that some of them had previous teaching experience, these students often performed the functions of a teacher/facilitator or a leader among the student volunteer group. The aforementioned stop motion film workshop was led by one of these PhD students in collaboration with an MFA student from the College of Fine Arts. After a series of meetings designed to familiarize her, as primary facilitator, with the program's mission, composition, and logistics and then to develop a week-by-week plan toward the culmination of the semester-long project by the children, she identified a list of necessary materials and short films that could be used throughout the semester for the participants to have models. This was so they could progress in terms of vocabulary and their familiarity with the structural and visual elements of a narrative. The activities she designed in collaboration with one of us included, for example, the use of finger puppets for children to engage in role plays and narrative exercises. This contributed to the children's exploration and definition of choices for creating and representing characters and developing the story they would eventually be telling through the short stop-motion film. Moreover, she also developed a survey for the families to elicit from them more information about the types of activities they engaged in using the Spanish language at home and their awareness of other resources in the community to help their children maintain and develop their Latinx language and culture skills.

In a subsequent semester, this same PhD student also directed a workshop on journalism and newspapers. Using the methodology from her previous experience as a framework, she developed weekly activities for the children to work toward the creation of three issues of a digital newspaper. In this case, the children collaborated – in teams formed according to their ages, linguistic competence in Spanish, and literacy levels – to create visual and textual materials for sections, such as cartoons and jokes, sports and entertainment, arts, and one about their schools and communities. The tasks included brainstorming, designing, writing, illustrating, editing, and publishing with help from student volunteers.

Another instance of this kind of interaction was developed in the spring of 2013, with support from the University of Pittsburgh's Center for Health Equity. One of our MA students in the SLA program worked as co-facilitator for a food-themed workshop called "Nuestra comida/ Our Food." The objectives were for the children to familiarize themselves with, prepare, and enjoy different foods from the Spanish-speaking world. They also created original recipes using ingredients native to the corresponding parts of the world from which the recipes came. As a final project, they included their creations in a community recipe book along with photographs, descriptions of culinary experiences, and traditional recipes passed down from their families and cultures. The workshop was structured around the idea that children and their families would participate (e.g., family members took turns sharing in the instruction, preparation, and enjoyment of these recipes). Other members of the community, such as local Latinx student groups (e.g., the Spanish and Latinx Student Association at CMU, SALSA, and the local CMU and University of Pittsburgh chapters of the Society of Hispanic Professional Engineers, SHPE) also participated, coming in to teach the children how to make simple foods such as *empanadas*. The MA student's role was to coordinate with the families and community groups and design adequate activities to prepare the children for each hands-on presentation. The planning and design of the activities was done in consultation with and under the supervision of one of the faculty co-coordinators and counted toward the student's MA degree requirements. In her reflection, the graduate student expresses, "*Círculo Juvenil* helped me distinguish different teaching methods and styles I could use with bilingual children. In the readings, we distinguished examples of families that [wanted] to preserve their language, and [aimed] to have second- and third-generations understand and speak it."[1]

In every one of our workshops, we paid great attention to being inclusive regarding the diversity found in Latinx cultures. For this workshop in particular, this included attention to certain principles, such as how to talk about bodies and not create or support certain stereotypes; exploring traditional foods and recipes consumed by Latinx people and the places where some of their ingredients originated; and variations in regional lexical terms to name and describe them. Additional supporting activities involved looking into nutrition principles, learning the basics of composting and growing our own food, and a visit to a local Latinx grocery store.

In a final example, one of the MA students who volunteered for the program led a study on parents' understanding of the program. This study later became part of her dissertation research when she moved on to a doctoral program in education at a neighboring institution (Abarca). Her research questions focused on what the parents understood as the role of the program, if they thought individual and community needs they identified were being met or addressed by it, and what they did to support their children's linguistic and cultural learning beyond bringing them to our program.

Third Level of Activity: The Meaningful Core of Working With Community-Universities, Families, Community Organizations, and Funders

For *Círculo*, "community" has many definitions: each one describes people or groups important to our all-around potential for success. This has meant working continuously to foster and sustain connections and in-kind or financial support from our home department and institution, without which our program would not have been possible. Our department head and staff (and especially one particular faculty member), as well as our college and several university offices and programs have served as steadfast partners from the beginning. Other CMU supporters include the CMU Modern Languages Resource Center, Gelfand Center for Service Learning and Outreach, School of Music, Center for Arts in Society, WRCT 88.3 FM radio station, our students (undergraduates and graduates), students at other local universities, community teaching artists, amateur sports coaches and organizations, funding and community development agencies, and public health initiatives (e.g., the Carnegie Libraries, Sprout Fund, ReMaking Learning Council, Vibrant Pittsburgh, the Greater Jewish Federation of Pittsburgh, and University of Pittsburgh Center for Health Equity).

One could represent the structure of the *Círculo*-partners relationship as a series of extending, concentric circles with the child participants, student volunteers, and facilitators at the core. These circles represent connections to different layers of partners (e.g., parents and families; the Modern Languages department and other CMU offices; other educational institutions; community-serving organizations, non-profit organizations, and public health initiatives; and funding agencies. As a whole, the model represents individual growth for all involved at its core and expanding collaboration or partnering with each expanding circle, each one bringing to bear its influence on the contiguous inner ones and ultimately, on the core. Roberts and Coghlan conducted a study on community healthcare partnerships, establishing a direct correlation between the potential success at the core circle and the contributions of the expanding circles. Despite the difference in field, findings apply just as well to describe *Círculo*'s situation with in-kind donations of time and talent and material, financial, or professional support and working with the children, student volunteers, and facilitators.

Parents, other immediate and extended family members, and friends have proved crucial to our mission, not only because it is they who send their children to our program and often provide some of the instructional support but also because they are instrumental in spreading news of our program to other parents in their networks. We also have had a high rate of returning students and younger siblings, as well as child participants growing into tweens and teens and becoming *Círculo* volunteers. We have learned over the years that for the primary demographic we would like to attract, word-of-mouth works best, although we reach others through our and other cultural and educational organizations' social media and e-blasts. There is a unique advantage to holding all of our *Círculo* sessions on campus: we have access to rooms, a computer lab with word processing stations, and other university and departmental resources (e.g., free parking, Internet, WiFi, a printer, a copy machine, paper, projectors with sound systems, and even percussion instruments). This is a great plus for our heritage-language and L2 undergraduates because instead of having to seek volunteer, internship, or service-learning opportunities off-campus in the community, which is not always easy for them because of class schedules and transportation issues and the limited number of Spanish-speaking opportunities in Pittsburgh, *Círculo* brings the community – families and varied artistic and other career professionals – to them. We provide our students an in-house experience. A number of practitioners and researchers mention as a frequent challenge the identification of off-campus, service-learning sites and partners. However, this advantage is not without drawbacks (e.g., when one is trying to attract children and families lacking the material resources to travel to our campus in Oakland, one of several drawbacks we will discuss in the Challenges and Future Directions section of this chapter).

Community and other sorts of partnerships are also essential for potentially successful university collaborations focused on education and community building. Sigmon, cited in Jacoby et al., expressed that university-community partnerships should be "organic, complex, and interdependent systems" (XIV). The network of community partner organizations *Círculo* has fostered and continues to build on provides the students who help facilitate our program not only valuable linguistic and cultural contact and content, as noted in the preceding section but also real-world experience via different sorts of collaborations with community members, agencies, organizations, and institutions, which, in turn, expands their spheres of reference and gives them insight into a broad definition of the "working world" and the place Spanish and Latinx culture has in it. As Shaffer, cited in Tang and Logonnathan explains, "they gain in self-esteem as they participate in the act of being helpful to others" (214), to which Weiler and colleagues, cited in Billig, in referring to high school students, add, "they develop communication and social skills as they work with adults in service situations. They get to experience a sense of belonging as they work in the context of a meaningful activity that is making a difference in the community" (17).

An advantage of seeking *Círculo* partners in Pittsburgh – a resource rich, mid-sized city – is that it is home to numerous universities and colleges, cultural institutions, entrepreneurs, community development organizations, and small funding initiatives. Collaboration amongst them is common and encouraged. Given its modest size and fairly progressive politics and policies, working with social, cultural, and even funding networks in Pittsburgh is much easier than it might be in a larger city. This is even more the case within the growing Latino community, e.g., the growing and working relationships between Casa San José and the Pittsburgh Hispanic Development Corporation, Coro Latinoamericano and Vibrant Pittsburgh, the Metropolitan Area Hispanic Chamber of Commerce and the Latin American Cultural Union, and even the mayor's endorsement and support for the Latino Community Center. All these institutions have partnered with *Círculo* and with each other, as have other funding sources, such as Vibrant Pittsburgh, the Jewish Federation of Greater Pittsburgh, and the Sprout Fund, to mention a few. Fifteen years ago, Reddel, as well as Salamon, noted in their research the increasing interconnectedness of private, public sector, and non-profit organizations, due to their realization that true problem-solving required it, as different levels of stakeholders began to see that it could create a winning situation for all involved – especially communities. Universities today are putting that theory to the test and finding that they, their faculty, and their students, too, can have an enormous role to play in community revitalization (Martin et al.).

Definitions of Community and Community Building

Concomitant with our educational mission, and given our broad definition of "community," what is at the core of all our *Círculo* workshops is a horizontal view of community building and development, a form of social justice founded upon faculty/student-community engagement that is mutually beneficial to all sides. To make something Cortés describes as a "societal curriculum" operational in a service learning project, we should aim for situating community service-learning as "engaged practice – a practice that offers learning in situ through challenges to notions of power, identities, community and change" (Cooks and Scharrer 44–45).

A practice called asset mapping should be essential for projects initiated by faculty at universities to be grounded in this more egalitarian view of service learning. This is often accomplished via already established connections particular faculty members or campus groups have with outside organizations or communities through past engagement with them. The results of asset mapping promote the notion that all sides of the potential partnership can make substantial contributions to it, something Kretzmann and McKnight have called "asset building" (185) in which growth in the community is relationship driven, the relationships being with the other partners in the alliance, an educational institution, and, perhaps, even funders. This is important to be able to move away from any notion that there is some sort of inherit deficit in the community that educational and other institutions must address, as Collins and others would have us believe.

That is certainly the case with *Círculo*. For us and our students, our service learning activities are an opportunity to take our linguistic and cultural goals into real world experiences. We cannot replicate the situations provided by the service learning experience in our classrooms through textbooks. Community organizations and members take on roles as co-educators, thus highlighting the importance of reciprocity in community service learning relationships (Jacoby). In addition, it furthers not only our educational goals and the philanthropic goals of certain organizations but also encourages our student volunteers to discover and analyze some of the social inequalities often found in immigrant communities living in predominantly monolingual, English-speaking communities in the US. For our predominantly American or non-Hispanic, foreign-born students to learn Spanish and use it purposefully to both learn about and help a non-mainstream community can be seen as a political act (Mitchell). Research like Pompa's shows that early on in the recent history of college student community engagement through service learning, frequently, it expressed a patronizing attitude and was seen very uni-directionally as an experience in which there was clearly a benefactor and recipient and in which "service" was equated with "social justice" (Furco). Even prior to this, Yappa, cited in Jacoby et al., had already called into question the issue of seeing universities as the "domains of solutions" and communities as "domains of problems to be solved," a dichotomy that mirrors the first world–developing world paradigm (23).

Given this potentially uneven view of the relationship between universities and community partners, there have also been scholars who have asserted that university students gain far more than community partners not only when this view is taken but when the actual structure of the relationship is "transactional" (Gelmon et al.; Ferrari and Worrall). This means that project goals are met, but nothing else changes. There is no other plan; no promise of continued, sustained, and meaningful engagement; no substantial change in the partnering organization, its clientele, or the university-community partner relationship (Enos and Morton). Yet, when the relationship is "transformative," as the afore-cited authors define it, it is open to evolving and more sustained commitment. Student and faculty participants and their local groups' counterparts are more likely to begin to feel they are part of a community (Jacoby et al.).

Aspects of potential transformation vary according to the nature of participants. For many immigrant children and families participating in *Círculo*, just the fact that their language and culture is being valued can have an enormous impact on how they see themselves as members of the greater society and what their place in it is and can be. For parents, *Círculo* provides a particular and very validating kind of community-building experience. Spanish-speaking parents who are often too geographically or socioeconomically separated are given the opportunity to establish relationships with other parents who are experiencing similar issues with alienation, isolation, and a feeling of powerlessness due to their condition as minority members of a not very integrated society. Their children, too, who are often part of a public school cohort composed of only a handful and even fewer Spanish-speaking children and adolescents, will establish friendships with other *Círculo* children. Together, they not only see that there are other children like them but also that university students, instructors, and other community members serving as facilitators value and respect the language, culture, and values of their families. In addition, because the workshops occur in a university setting and they are interacting with students who are going out of their way to study their language and culture, they are receiving a quick introduction to an environment to which they may eventually feel ready and able to aspire. Finally, the student volunteers benefit in multiple ways. The experience itself impacts their academic and social learning. They achieve this through a real-world experience and by applying their language and culture skills, as well as those involving critical thinking and problem analysis and solution – all in a second language. On a personal level, they have the potential to grow in terms of their ability to be responsible, communicate interpersonally, and increase their communications skills. The experience may even influence them in a way that impacts their career choice or where they might want to live, as well as what they might want to do with some of their spare time or through their workplace. Finally, the student volunteers are able to build stronger relationships with the involved faculty and feel as though they are getting something more than just an "academic" education at their institution. This strong corollary between service learning, social justice, and transformation was not always the case, though.

Our fall 2014 *Círculo* workshop, ¡Cantemos!, is an example of culturally relevant education and critical pedagogy. It involved two local, partnering, non-profit funders, Vibrant Pittsburgh, whose mission it is to help new immigrants find their way in the city and feel welcome, and the Jewish Federation of Greater Pittsburgh. Both were interested in supporting innovative community building, but the collaboration also ended up including a local, bilingual-bicultural community choir; a foreign-trained, professional Latina music director; a senior choral group outside Allegheny County in a more monocultural, small-town setting; a small children's choir under that same choir's auspices; both Carnegie Mellon and the University of Pittsburgh; and a large number of Latino children and families. *Círculo* teamed up with Coro Latinoamericano and received funding for a proposal titled "It Takes a Family: The Círculo Outreach Program, Placemaking, and Community Building." In addition, the workshop involved 19 children, 15 families (parents from among them assisted with various aspects of the workshop), 17 student volunteers (several of them foreign born; two of them musicians), and the three *Círculo* co-directors.

The timing of the proposal made it so at the very least a major product of the project would be a December holiday concert presented by the group of children participating in the program and Coro Latinoamericano. Not satisfied with just reproducing Latino Christmas musical traditions, our team worked hard to make the workshop transcend "tradition" and take on new, community-building meaning for all involved. So, adult facilitators and student volunteers created materials ancillary to the actual music the children were learning to complement and actually partially refocus the holiday songs and help them engage with music and its lyrics more from a cultural and linguistic perspective than a faith-based one.

The "¡Cantemos!" group became a nurturing community of children, families, student volunteers, and adult facilitators for whom the process of community building took on more importance than the specific dogmatic exigencies of any particular holiday being acknowledged. If we were to help these new families integrate and find their place in their new city without sacrificing important traditions, this is what we, as a facilitating group, decided was important for our participants to be exposed to. This is, in fact, what the funding agencies themselves valued, which is why they supported our project.

Conclusion: Challenges and Future Directions

Any exploration of *Círculo*'s ten-year experiment must include discussion about past and future challenges to the program's existence and some consideration of how it might evolve to meet those challenges, given what we now know. For example, with many of its successes have come concomitant, problematic issues regarding teaching staff, faculty commitments, and even resources – institutional or other. These all can and do have a great impact on the sustainability of any project such as this.

First, there is the simple issue of teaching and research faculty who already bear the burden of work and research requirements and, as in *Círculo*'s case, have taken primary responsibility not only for the organization of each workshop – its design, scheduling, community partner and facilitator identification, student curriculum and training, and publicity – but also, and most significantly, its execution. This has frequently required one, two, or all three faculty co-directors to be present on campus – for up to three to four hours, on whatever weekend day – a Saturday or Sunday – was chosen for any particular ten-week session. Moreover, all the grant writing, curriculum planning, logistical work, and student training takes place during the work week, when faculty are already engaged in their other required activities. Incidentally, when one of us is gone for a conference, sabbatical, or other reason, this places an inordinate burden on the *Círculo* faculty members who are left. The issue of burnout is also an important consideration when thinking about what kind of sustained commitment one can expect from these individuals. The excessive load is also possibly a disincentive for other, especially younger or untenured, faculty to get involved.

Another challenge is being on a campus where the administration speaks highly of faculty who are deeply engaged in the community and involve their students but does not include this kind of teaching, service, and research among their promotion criteria. The school may rely very heavily on individual faculty members, or groups of them, to be sufficiently passionate about and driven by this work to not be dissuaded by the burden and take it on. It also may not truly commit to creating an institutional center for community engaged teaching, learning, and research to serve as a draw for potential community partners (Enos and Morton 20–41). The fact is that while we do have the Gelfand Center for Service Learning and Outreach, and it has been quite supportive of our mission, it is small, underfunded, and understaffed. It also does not include research on service learning as one of its foci, nor does it provide support for non-English activities in their own outreach programming. In addition, there is no School of Education on campus that could fill in this gap and also potentially provide financial and pedagogical support and faculty and graduate students interested in the topic. There are numerous, very successful service learning initiatives on campus, and while some of them take place in more resource-rich departments or schools, the fact is that their existence depends heavily on faculty passion and drive, their access to students, and their community connections.

There is also the issue of whether the service program will be, in essence, the main focus of a specific course, an integrated part of that or another course, or an activity independent of any course. Each one of these iterations has its pros and cons regarding time commitment, curriculum and pedagogy, practicality, and evaluation. Whereas in a relatively small language program, it is not always possible to have an ongoing, full-credit, service-learning offering, making an out-of-class, lower-credit service activity available to students places an undue burden on faculty because they will likely not be compensated in time or money for the extra work and may end up supervising enough individual students that they could have constituted a standing class on their own. These are all things one learns as one experiments with different service learning models, but the fact is that most institutions do not have a policy in place to redress the aforementioned problems.

In returning to an issue that was mentioned in a previous section regarding the possible negative consequences of always holding our workshops on campus, we have to acknowledge that there may be a flip side to what can be seen as an advantage for both the community and us. Always expecting Latinx families with children to be able to and comfortable with coming to Oakland and our campus, to an area of the city and an institution about which they may have negative perceptions due to lack of knowledge about it, from a social if not cultural point of view, may limit our ability to reach the very families and children who might most benefit from a partnership with our program and its resources. Conversely, we and our students are also deprived by not really having an opportunity to engage with and learn from interacting with members of a demographic we might otherwise not have access to. Finally, our funding and other community partners lose out because their investment may end up being used to help other groups less accessible for community building work and its rewards.

Connecting with the larger Latino community in areas farther away from the university and connecting to working-class and undocumented residents of the community is a huge challenge that can only be addressed by flipping the model and taking the workshops to them, which brings us back to the issue of the possibility of faculty and student availability and institutional commitment. For example, while we have more than reasonable access to public transportation, it is not always the most efficient way to take our work and meet the community where it lives. This is complicated by the fact that it is very difficult to procure campus transportation for this purpose, as our university does not own a fleet of vehicles for the purpose of student transportation. Renting vehicles and drivers is costly and often limits one because of issues like lack of funding and driver availability. And yet, taking *Círculo* to not just one but numerous communities needs to be our goal in the future, which will most likely require us to change our model.

We have indeed been thinking about how to change our model, and one of our conclusions is that we must rethink the program's structure in order to make the model more sustainable for the faculty members involved, better take advantage of community partners and resources, better reach the families who might most benefit from a partnership, and also most contribute to our desire to make the experience more transformative for our students and community members. Furthermore, research by Miron and Moely revealed that when community partners took a more active role in the service-learning projects, they reported more and better benefits to their organizations than those that did not.

One possible solution is to convert our original, ten-week workshop model into a series of self-contained, 1- to 3-day sessions (to be held on consecutive weekends) that can quite literally be taken off campus and on the road to different communities, e.g., Beechview, Brookline, Allentown, downtown, and a few other cities outside Allegheny County (e.g., Greensburg, Meadowlands, Cranberry, Allequippa) – all communities with what could be considered "substantial" Latinx communities, despite how small the group is overall.

Another challenge we have encountered through the years is to be able to document the children's bilingual and biliteracy development. The workshops' duration and the intermittent attendance of children make it difficult to impact language development. Individual differences and multilevel grouping have impeded us in designing creative, self-directed learning tasks as well as project-based activities that enable instructors and volunteers to provide children more individualized feedback and support. However, we are still trying to find ways to provide more systematic instruction to enhance language learning. In contrast, we have been able to observe culture learning and clear attitudinal shifts in terms of positive self-image and community appreciation. These positive outcomes encourage us to continue working on integrating language, culture, and content learning through meaningful project-based work centered in the community.

Note

1. This is the authors' translation of a fragment of the original Spanish-language report.

References

Abarca, Erika. "Parents' Understanding of a Heritage Language Program (HLP) for Children." *Third International Conference on Heritage/Community Languages*, National Heritage Language Research Center, UCLA, Los Angeles, CA, February 2018. Unpublished Conference Paper.

Billig, Shelley H. *Research on K-12 School-Based Service-Learning: The Evidence Builds*. RMC Research Corporation, 2000.

Blumenfeld, Phyllis, et al. "Motivating Project-Based Learning: Sustaining the Doing, Supporting the Learning." *Educational Psychologist*, vol. 26, no. 3&4, 1996, pp. 369–398.

Cole, Michael. *The Fifth Dimension: An After-School Program Built on Diversity.* Russell Sage Foundation, 2006.

Collins, James. "Language and Class in Minority Education." *Anthropology and Education Quarterly*, vol. 19, no. 4, 1988, pp. 299–326.

Cooks, Leda M., and Erica Scharrer. "Assessing Learning in Community Service Learning: A Social Approach." *Michigan Journal of Community Service Learning*, vol. 13, no. 1, 2006, pp. 44–45.

Cortés, María C. E. "Who Is Maria? Who Is Juan? Dilemmas of Analyzing the Chicano Image in U.S. Feature Films." *Chicanos in Film: Representations and Resistance*, edited by Chon Noriega. University of Minnesota Press, 1992, pp. 74–93.

Dailey, Rene M., et al. "Language Attitudes in an Anglo-Hispanic Context: The Role of the Linguistic Landscape." *Language and Communication*, vol. 25, no. 1, 2005, pp. 27–38.

Einfeld, Aaron, and Denise Collins. "The Relationships Between Service-Learning, Social Justice, Multicultural Competence, and Civic Engagement." *Journal of College Student Development*, vol. 49, no. 2, 2008, pp. 95–109.

Enos, Sandra, and Keith Morton. "Developing a Theory and Practice of Campus-Community Partnerships." *Building Partnerships for Service Learning*, edited by Barbara Jacoby, et al. Jossey-Bass, 2003, pp. 20–41.

Ferrari, Joseph R., and Lorie Worrall. "Assessments by Community Agencies: How the 'Other Side' sees Service-Learning." *Michigan Journal of Community Service Learning*, vol. 7, no. 1, 2000, pp. 35–40.

Fishman, Joshua A. "Three Hundred-plus Years of Heritage Language Education in the United States." *Handbook of Heritage, Community, and Native American Languages in the United States: Research, Policy, and Educational Practice*, edited by Terrence G. Wiley, et al. Routledge, 2014, pp. 36–44.

Furco, Andrew. "The Engaged Campus: Toward a Comprehensive Approach to Public Engagement." *British Journal of Educational Studies*, vol. 58, no. 4, 2010, pp. 375–390.

Gelmon, Sherril B., et al. "Community-University Partnerships for Mutual Learning." *Michigan Journal of Community Service Learning*, vol. 5, 1998, pp. 97–107.

Gibbons, John, and Elizabeth Ramirez. "Different Beliefs: Beliefs and the Maintenance of a Minority Language." *Journal of Language and Social Psychology*, vol. 23, no. 1, 2004, pp. 99–117. doi:10.1177/0261927X03260809.

Giles, Howard, et al. "Towards a Theory of Language in Ethnic Group Relations." *Language, Ethnicity and Intergroup Relations*, edited by Howard Giles. Academic Press, 1977, pp. 307–348.

Jacoby, Barbara. *Service Learning in Higher Education: Concepts and Practices*. Jossey-Bass, 1996.

———, et al. *Building Partnerships for Service-Learning*. Jossey-Bass, 2003.

Kretzman, John P., and John McKnight. *Building Communities From the Inside Out: A Path Toward Finding and Mobilizing a Community's Assets*. Asset-Based Community Development Institute, Institute for Policy Research, Northwestern University, 1993.

Martin, Lawrence, et al. "Bridging 'Town and Gown' Through Innovative University-Community Partnerships." *The Innovation Journal: The Public Sector Innovation Journal*, vol. 10, no. 2, 2005, pp. 2–16.

Miron, Devi, and Barbara E. Moely. "Community Agency Voice and Benefit in Service Learning." *Michigan Journal of Community Service Learning*, vol. 12, no. 2, 2006, pp. 27–37.

Mitchell, Tania D. "Traditional vs. Critical Service Learning: Engaging the Literature to Differentiate Two Models." *Michigan Journal of Community Service Learning*, vol. 14, no. 1, 2008, pp. 50–65.

Pompa, Lori. "Service-Learning as Crucible: Reflections on Immersion, Context, Power, and Transformation." *Michigan Journal of Community Service Learning*, vol. 9, no. 1, 2002, pp. 69–73.

Reddel, Tim. "Beyond Participation, Hierarchies, Management and Markets: 'New' Governance and Place Policies." *Australian Journal of Public Administration*, vol. 61, no. 1, 2002, pp. 50–63.

Roberts, Cynthia, and David Coghlan. "Concentric Collaboration: A Model of Leadership Development for Healthcare Organizations."*Action Learning Research and Practice*, vol. 8, no. 3, 2011, pp. 231–352.

Rumbaut, Rubén G., and Alejandro Portes. *Legacies: The Story of the Immigrant Second Generation*. University of California Press, 2001.

Salamon, Lester M. *The Tools of Government: A Guide to the New Governance*. Oxford University Press, 2002.

Shaffer, B. *Service-Learning: An Academic Methodology*. Stanford University Department of Education, 1993.

Sigmon, Robert L. "The Problem of Definition in Service Learning." *The Journey to Service-Learning*, edited by Robert Sigmon, et al. Council of Independent Colleges, 1996, pp. 22–44.

Simons, Lori, and Beverly Cleary. "The Influence of Service Learning on Students' Personal and Social Development." *College Teaching*, vol. 54, no. 4, 2010 [2006], pp. 307–319.

Tang, Siew Fun, and Loshinikarasi Logonnathan. *Assessment for Learning Within and Beyond the Classroom*. Springer, 2016.

Valdés, Guadalupe, et al. *Developing Minority Language Resources. The Case of Spanish in California*. Multilingual Matters, 2006.

Weiler, Daniel, et al. *An Evaluation of K-12 Service-Learning in California: Phase II Final Report*. RPP International and The Search Institute, 1998.

Yappa, Lakshman. "Service Learning and Social Justice." Pre-Conference Workshop, *National Society for Experiential Education*, San Diego, CA, 20 October 1999. Unpublished Comments.

Part V

Civic Partnerships

10 Multilingual Justice in the Streets and in the Classroom

Translating a Digital Time Line of US Domestic Worker Organizing

Michelle Joffroy

In early 2016, I became part of a small interdisciplinary team of scholars at Smith College, in Northampton, Massachusetts, that was seeking to build connections between activists of color and the Sophia Smith Archives, by putting the archives to work in support of current organizers and movement leaders. We believed that by creating access to materials that document the untold histories of working class women of color activists, contemporary organizers could work collaboratively with students and scholars to turn their "history into action." We proposed doing this through community-based partnerships that opened the archives to organizers and that put pedagogical practices in the service of feminist, immigrant, and worker organizations' goals. My colleague, Jennifer Guglielmo, and I were particularly interested in fortifying US domestic worker organizers' knowledge of their history and using it to strengthen contemporary campaigns, with a pedagogical model that centered knowledge production and communication within a larger social justice paradigm. As scholars of Latin American women's social movements and cultural production (Joffroy) and US immigrant women's labor history (Guglielmo), we recognized the transnational intimacies of domestic workers' experience and the urgent need for connecting activists to their movement ancestors. Ultimately, through a collaborative process that spanned the spring and fall semesters of 2016, we developed a digitally-based, multidisciplinary, and multilingual project that linked scholars and students across the curriculum via an intermediate-level Spanish language and cultural studies course and a history research seminar. Pedagogically designed using community-based research and learning frameworks (CBR) and invested in the pedagogical potential of new technologies, our courses put students and scholars in the service of domestic worker organizers beyond the campus through a partnership with the Boston-based Matahari Women Workers' Center.[1]

This chapter tells the story of my course *SPN 230: Doméstica, Precarious Subjects, and the Politics of Intimacy in Latin American Literature and Film* to illustrate how community-based partnerships and emerging digital technologies can drive pedagogical innovation in the second language acquisition classroom and meet both students' and partners' needs.[2] In the case of *Doméstica*, my students and I cultivated a community of practice in second language acquisition that centered our partner's commitment to language justice, which strives to reflect the collective, intersectional, transnational, and multilingual identities not only of contemporary social movements but also Spanish language communities. Our commitment to a language justice framework significantly reoriented and impacted our second language acquisition pedagogy and practice. Foremostly, it stimulated a deeper and metacritical engagement with Spanish as a living, dynamic, multifaceted, multisited, and political language for social change.

Like many other social justice organizations, our community partner was attuned to the potential for technology to play a meaningful role in movement-building. Seeking an innovative way to connect workers to their history, Matahari was interested in how technology could be used to turn the history of US domestic workers (which for the most part was confined to academic research and scholarly publications) into an accessible, portable and multilingual organizing tool for their members. In large measure, they were interested in exploring more robust uses of digital technology in their organizing to capitalize on the already active social media use of most of their members. Technology's role in higher education and specifically the language classroom is also a pressing pedagogical question, as well as a site of curricular experimentation, and that was certainly the case for *Doméstica*. Prior to the 2016 collaboration with Matahari, previous iterations of the course integrated digital technologies, such as WordPress sites, digital journals, and blogs, and collaborative writing assignments using Google Docs. Our and Matahari's shared interest in technology's potential led to the decision to experiment with building a digital time line of US domestic worker history. During the 2016 spring semester, students in the seminar *HST 383: U.S. Domestic Worker Organizing* (taught by Jennifer Guglielmo) developed content based on the existing scholarship on US domestic worker history. Using Knight Lab's user-friendly digital time line platform, Timeline JS, seminar students produced an organizing tool that was portable and smartphone-compatible and that literally put history in domestic workers' hands. The following semester, also using Timeline JS, *Doméstica* students collaborated with lead organizers at Matahari to curate and translate time line content for use by Spanish-speaking member organizers in a specific neighborhood-based campaign to mobilize primarily Spanish-speaking domestic workers in the greater-Boston area. Pedagogically, students in *Doméstica* had to focus deeply and intentionally on Spanish writing and communication skills to produce materials that would adhere to the conventions and constraints that this technology, and its users, required. Accordingly, the focus of our practice was to create concise *and accessible* Spanish-language narratives of domestic worker organizing history to be used in a non-academic setting, by and for predominantly immigrant, Spanish-speaking domestic workers.

Histories of Domestic Worker Organizing, Multilingual Justice Frameworks, and Community-Based Research

On November 29, 2010, New York State made history when it became the first state in the US to extend essential labor protections to domestic workers with the New York Domestic Workers Bill of Rights. Among the rights the law extended were protections from harassment based on sex, race, religion, and national origin – protections especially significant to a labor sector composed predominantly by immigrant women of color. The Domestic Workers Bill of Rights amended existing state labor laws to grant domestic workers many of the rights from which they had been historically excluded at the federal level. Some of these basic protections were the right to receive overtime pay, one day of rest per week (or overtime pay if they work on their day of rest), three days of paid time off after one year of employment, and eligibility for disability benefits for domestic workers who work fewer than 40 hours per week.[3] By drawing on historical protections granted to other sectors, domestic worker activists successfully harnessed existing New York State Human Rights Law, New York Labor Law, and New York Workers' Compensation Law to create equal protections for excluded domestic workers. Likewise, they drew on the legacies of movement ancestors like Dora Jones and the history of domestic worker organizations like the Domestic Workers Union that Jones helped to found in 1934. Alongside their legislative victory, activists and domestic worker movement leaders demonstrated the power of historical knowledge and the potential for using that knowledge to shape more just futures.

By the summer of 2012, activists in Massachusetts, including from the Matahari Women Workers' Center, had been mobilizing for several years to build political support for a state Domestic Workers Bill of Rights that would produce the kind of labor protections that New York had successfully enacted. The organizing work was hard for many reasons, not least of which was the commonly held belief that Massachusetts domestic workers had no historical state-level protections upon which to build their campaign. Lacking this history, they anticipated a long journey to articulate a basic set of rights and protections that both workers and politicians could mobilize around. Monique Nguyen, Executive Director of the Matahari Women Workers' Center, often reflects on this period as a time of real struggle for domestic workers, activists, and movement organizers who needed a substantive referent in the legislative history as well as a mobilizing narrative that could unify a diverse, dispersed, multilingual, and largely immigrant community of domestic workers. Almost miraculously, as Nguyen describes it, she discovered precisely what they needed. Her story goes something like this. While digging through Radcliffe College's Schlesinger Library archives, Nguyen came across an August 1970 letter written by Melnea Cass – who was at that time president of the Women's Service Club of Boston – and addressed to the governor of Massachusetts, Francis Sargent. Cass was well-respected as a community leader in the Boston area, especially for her grassroots organizing and civil rights activism in the predominantly African American South End and Roxbury neighborhoods. In her letter, she urged Sargent to sign House Bill #5797, which she described as "a product of the Women's Service Club's very diligent and consistent efforts," on behalf of black men and women "who for many years were relegated to household work . . . [and] exploited as you know." Emphasizing the exploitation of black household workers, Cass made clear the injustice of their exclusion from basic labor protections, writing, "We are determined that this shall pass away and that those forgotten workers will share in the benefits of all workers in their categories" (Cass). Sargent signed the bill, establishing the wage and overtime laws that have, in fact, applied to domestic workers in Massachusetts since the 1970s. To Nguyen's astonishment and joy, the letter was exactly the touchstone they needed: a historical referent affirming legislative precedent and existing labor protections, as well as proof of a local history of domestic worker activism and organizing by women of color. Nguyen sums up the personal significance of Cass's letter with a moving anecdote: since the day she discovered it, Nguyen has carried a copy of Melnea Cass's letter in her purse everywhere she goes. She often ends her story with an image of the many other domestic workers, activists, and Matahari organizers who have likewise copied and created multilingual translations of Cass's letter to carry and share as material proof of a history that all domestic workers are a part of. In July 2014, Governor Duval Patrick signed the Massachusetts Domestic Worker Bill of Rights, enacting what scholar Eileen Boris describes as "the most comprehensive regime of rights and enforcement, enhancing its inclusion of private household workers under its wage and hour, worker compensation, and collective bargaining laws from the 1970's" (2) – laws, as Boris emphasizes, that were a "product of the efforts of Melnea Cass and the other African American activists of the Women's Service Club of Boston" (2).

As a scholar who teaches about the cultural representation of domestic workers in Latin America, I am keenly aware of the historical resonances and transnational connections – cultural, linguistic, political – between US and Latin American domestic workers. *Home Economics: The Invisible and Unregulated World of Domestic Work*, a 2012 report produced by Linda Burnham and Nik Theodore for the National Domestic Workers Alliance, provides a useful window into such connections through its succinct exploration of the history of domestic work in the US. As summarized in the report, domestic work "has always been a feature of US life, beginning with the enslaved, indentured, and semi-free female laborers of colonial times" (3). The US colonial histories of labor exploitation cited in the study mirror similar origins of domestic labor in imperial Spanish America, where the so-called *casa poblada* (or patriarchal household), with its requisite pool of indentured indigenous women laborers, served as the primary unit of social and economic organization in the colonies (Kuznesof). During the 19th century, domestic work was a key source of employment in the US for "African American women in the South; for Mexican, Mexican American and Native American women in the West and Southwest; for Asian women and men in California and Hawaii; and for European immigrant women in the Northeast and Midwest" (Burnham and Theodore 4). Similar demographic trends shaped the history of domestic work in most Latin American nations during the 19th century: poor, rural, indigenous, and Afro-descendant women migrated in large numbers from agrarian communities to new national urban centers in search of work (Kuznesof). In the US, immigration patterns originating in the early 20th century have culminated in a current domestic worker sector that is predominantly immigrant-based and increasingly Latinx, producing a literal intersection of the labor and cultural histories of US and Latin American domestic workers (Burnham and Theodore). The US domestic workers' rights movement, accordingly, reflects these shifts. As we enter the second decade of the 21st century, Spanish and other non-English languages play a central role in the organizing and mobilization of domestic workers in their state- and federal-level campaigns for political rights and labor protections. This is most certainly the case for the Matahari Women Workers' Center, one of several organizations that played a key role in the passage of the 2014 Massachusetts Domestic Worker Bill of Rights. Matahari counts a high number of Latin American immigrants among its member-organizers and has made an explicit commitment to a multilingual justice framework for building the domestic workers movement. The collaboration between *Doméstica* and Matahari required that I, along with my students, do the same in our second language acquisition practices.

The concept of multilingual justice, also referred to in this essay as language justice, is necessarily expansive, but at its core – as numerous organizers, popular educators, activists, and community leaders attest – it affirms a commitment to building social movements by creating spaces where diverse communities "can communicate across languages" (Arguelles, Williams, Hemley-Bronstein i). As expressed by the creators of the *Language Justice Toolkit*, "the term 'language justice' is a powerful way to describe individuals' fundamental right to have their voices heard" (Arguelles, Williams, Hemley-Bronstein i). Extending this individual right to entire communities and cultures, language justice recognizes "the social and political dimensions of language and language access, while working to dismantle language barriers [and] equalize power dynamics" (Arguelles, Williams, Hemley-Bronstein i). Attentive to the historical and cultural barriers to movement building, as well as to unequal power dynamics within and between organizations, multilingual justice frameworks have played a central role in some of the most important transnational social movements of the past two decades. A key example is the first US Social Forum (USSF) convened in the summer of 2007 in Atlanta, Georgia, which structured the position of a Language Access Coordinator (LAC) into its planning and organization. Hilary Klein, who served as the LAC, describes how the Social Forum's organizing slogan "Another World Is Possible, Another US Is Necessary" transcended its discursive status by prioritizing "the participation of low-income communities of color and other marginalized groups" (77). This indeed created "another" kind of organizing space altogether, one in which "rather than academics or employees of non-profits analyzing their problems for them, oppressed communities were there speaking for themselves" (77). Such a non-hierarchical, horizontal approach posits knowledge and authority as always and already existing within communities of color and other marginalized groups. Extending the assumption further, not only can oppressed groups speak for themselves, but they can (and must) speak to each other from these locations of knowledge. Creating and modeling the conditions necessary to liberate and facilitate knowledge-sharing between communities was a significant outcome of the USSF and, according to Klein, "would not have been possible without [a] multi-lingual infrastructure" (77).

Understanding the ideological power dynamics of language in movement building, particularly the historical positioning of English as the language of knowledge and power, is key to achieving the social transformation that movements seek. English, as Ruben Solis, of the Southwest Workers Union, notes, "is used most of the time so it is positioned ideologically as superior to others" (Klein 78). Solis alludes not simply to a linguistic hierarchy that privileges English but to the authority and power that accrues to knowledge communicated through it. Multilingual justice commitments are, at their core, commitments to dismantling language hierarchies and cultivating the conditions for intercultural equality within movements so that everyone can "participate as equals regardless of the language spoken" (Klein 77–78). Klein cites Steve Williams, of People Organizing to Win Employment Rights (POWER), to underscore and emphasize the centrality of multilingual capacity to movement-building:

> the people who will lead a movement for social transformation in this country are multi-racial and multi-lingual . . . to build solidarity between these communities, we have to make sure that they have the tools to communicate with other organizers and activists.
>
> (78)

The member-organizers of Matahari Women Workers' Center not only agree with Klein's, Solis's, and Williams's assessments, they rehearse this social transformation through their practice of language justice in activities and multilingual capacity building at all levels of the organization. One particularly moving illustration of this took place during a 2017 workshop held in the aftermath of the successful campaign for a Massachusetts Domestic Worker Bill of Rights. A group of about ten domestic workers (members of Matahari), roughly half of them Spanish speakers, came together to reflect on and strategize about how they might win back some of the power that employers continued to hold over domestic workers' labor conditions. While preparing for the workshop, Executive Director Monique Nguyen found inspiration in historian Vanessa May's 2011 book *Unprotected Labor: Household Workers, Politics, and Middle-Class Reform in New York, 1870–1940*, particularly the story of the Domestic Workers Union (DWU) and its African American union president, Dora Jones. May's description of the late 1930s labor conditions for African American domestic workers echoed many of the conditions Matahari was facing in their diverse, immigrant-based organization. Similarly, the strategies that the DWU, Jones and their allies used to help domestic workers gain control over their workplace resonated strongly with Nguyen. She felt confident that a shared reading of this history could spark much-needed energy and motivation for Matahari members (Personal communication). Nguyen selected a short, three-page excerpt from the book for translation to Spanish (by a former *Doméstica* student) and structured an opening exercise for the workshop in which participants took turns reading out loud, in English and in Spanish, the selected text. Member-organizers listened to each other read, in their chosen languages, to the history of their shared movement ancestors in at least two of the current movement's primary languages. Nguyen often tells this story at public events as an example of what a multilingual justice commitment looks like, emphasizing the power of creating opportunities for participating, across languages and as equals, in the shared history of domestic workers. She reflected recently on this experience in response to my question about why a multilingual justice practice matters for Matahari:

> As a working women's organization that is multilingual-racial-cultural, we strive for inclusion . . . as through our practice of multilingual justice where we use the tools of language interpretation and translation to ensure that all persons in our space can engage, listen, speak, vision and dream in the language of their hearts and minds. If we did not necessitate and prioritize the translation . . . of the text, we are choosing to silence and invisibilize the people who speak the language, and put up barriers to those who could be part of our community fighting for justice.
>
> (Nguyen)

Nguyen's comments echo and affirm the shared goals of other multilingual justice advocates who prioritize equal access, equal representation, and the right to participate, hear, and be heard regardless of language or cultural identity in all social spaces. Though not enshrined in a single, static definition, language justice (including multilingual justice) frameworks can consistently be characterized by several key elements:

> Language justice is rooted in a *history of resistance* by communities and peoples whose voices and cultures have been suppressed for generations. Language justice is an alternative to that historical pattern of disenfranchisement and oppression. It affirms the fundamental rights of individuals and communities to language, culture, self-expression, and equal participation.
>
> Language justice is a *process of organizing and advocating* to win proactive policies that will help achieve equity and have meaningful impacts across race and language.
>
> Language justice offers a *vision of society* that honors language and culture as fundamental human rights, and which does not settle for providing more people with access to the status quo, but rather alters institutions to provide space for full democratic participation.
>
> (Arguelles, Williams, Hemley-Bronstein 2; emphasis mine)

The issue of language justice has also been a historical concern within non-governmental, international, and transnational justice institutions such as the United Nations. For example, the Universal Declaration of Linguistic Rights (UDLR), also known as the Barcelona Declaration, was created in 1996 to support linguistic rights, especially (but not limited to) those of endangered languages. Adopted at the conclusion of the World Conference on Linguistic Rights (June 6–9, 1996) in Barcelona, Spain, the Declaration was signed by the International PEN Club and numerous non-governmental organizations and presented at that time to the UNESCO director general (though it has not gained formal UNESCO approval). It is particularly relevant that the Declaration's authors conceived of it as a response to perceived gaps in the 1948 Universal Declaration of Human Rights (UDHR) ("Universal Declaration of Linguistic Rights"). Viewed in this context, the UDLR centers language justice within a larger concern for global human rights more broadly, underscoring a dimension of cultural protections that the generic "universal" did not account for specifically. Basically, the UDHR identifies language as one of several categories that merit equal rights protections, but it lacks specificity as regards to the form and nature of those rights. This human rights/language rights dialogue echoes some of what has emerged in the social justice / language justice relationship: both illuminate the evolution of communities' sense of vulnerability due to cultural-linguistic identity, even within existing rights frameworks that ostensibly offer broad protections. I would even argue that a version of this dynamic is what we see playing out in the labor rights / domestic workers' rights environment, further deepening the resonance between multilingual justice capacity-building and social movements.

Within the humanities and interdisciplinary studies, questions of linguistic justice have also gained some urgency in recent decades as a philosophical, cultural, and pedagogical concern, as well as a social justice issue. In the academic context, an anxiety over disappearing languages has centered loss and vulnerability as the dominant markers of linguistic identities in the 21st century.[4] This is both an echo of and an interesting counterpoint to social movement activists' emphasis on intercultural development, linguistic empowerment, and language as a key driver in the creation of alternative futures produced through multilingual justice-committed movements. A recent example of academia's response to language justice, Columbia University's 2017–19 Sawyer Seminar on "Global Language Justice" at the Institute for Comparative Literature and Society (ICLS) offers some key insights into the concerns shaping academic discourses about and responses to language justice. Funded over a two-year period by an Andrew W. Mellon Foundation grant, the initiative supported public lectures, workshops, and pre- and post-doctoral positions with the aim of creating "a unique and lasting legacy around . . . language justice by incubating new graduate and undergraduate courses and developing new research directions for the humanities and social sciences" ("Global Language Justice"). The range of entry points for participants to engage with the topic of language justice reflects a sensitivity to both pedagogy and research as sites of innovation within the academy. As described on the ICLS webpage, the initiative "takes language justice as the *humanistic equivalent* of environmental justice and responds with a sense of urgency to the simultaneity of the rapid dwindling of linguistic diversity and endangered biodiversity." Extending the analogy, then, one could argue that just as environmental justice movements have historically been generated from within poor communities of color, with policy and institutional change following the lead of popular social movements, language justice politics and practice might best be articulated by and within increasingly multilingual, multicultural grassroots social movements. One potential lesson to be drawn from the extended analogy is that language justice efforts that fail to study and follow the lead of social movements may result in new policy or institutional gains but at the cost of a true transformation at the community or societal level. Because it centers histories of resistance, advocacy, and an alternative vision of society, a multilingual justice framework demands pedagogical practices that cultivate similar critical approaches to language and cultural studies. In its most distilled form, a language justice–oriented second language acquisition pedagogy is driven by a critical inquiry into whose Spanish we value – i.e., Spanish from a particular social class or region, with particular vocabularies – as well as a heightened awareness of the heterogeneity of the language and its situatedness and a critical interrogation of why the study of Spanish in academic settings has excluded some registers and vocabularies and enforced others.

Assessing multilingual justice frameworks from these two vantage points – one that offers a view from the grassroots, the other a view from the so-called Ivory Tower – a CBR paradigm offers the second language acquisition classroom an opportunity to compare top-down vs. popular models of creating language justice both in the streets and in the classroom. Transferring the multilingual justice framework to the *Doméstica* Spanish language classroom, as a shared commitment between partners, was at the heart of imagining new and innovative practices to deepen and strengthen connections between academic spaces and communities beyond the campus. CBR models can vary depending on a range of factors from academic disciplines to partner institutional identities, but the core commonalities align pretty consistently along three characteristics, concisely defined by Strand and colleagues:

> 1. CBR is a *collaborative* enterprise between academic researchers (professors and students) and community members.
> 2. CBR seeks to *democratize knowledge* by validating multiple sources of knowledge and promoting the use of multiple methods of discovery and dissemination.
> 3. CBR has as its goal social action for the purpose of achieving *social change* and *social justice*.
>
> (6; emphasis mine)

Not surprisingly, community-based research and learning in a second language acquisition classroom posed exciting challenges, pedagogically and philosophically. The principle challenge in *Doméstica* was designing a curriculum that could respond to our community-partner's commitments and philosophy – in this case, attending to multilingual justice as a practical and metacritical dimension of language study – while meeting the conventional language learning needs of students through a collaborative process. In this regard, the collaboration imperative of CBR obliges scholars, teachers, and researchers to move beyond a community service model that hinges on ideologies of charity and philanthropy. Collaboration, far from simply "lending a hand" or transferring the wealth of well-resourced communities to marginalized, under-resourced ones, posits a working relationship between equal partners who have equally valid interests and authority. In fact, principles of best practices for community-based research affirm that

> the ideal CBR project is one . . . where community people work with professors and/or students at *every* stage of the research process: . . . This sort of collaboration . . . means that research roles

and relationships are very different from those characterizing conventional academic research.

(Strand, Marullo, Cutforth, Stoeker, Donohue, 6; emphasis mine)

In an academic context, collaborative partnerships include knowledge resources as well as knowledge production, accessed and generated through consultative practices. Collaborative knowledge-making can only occur with a commitment to reciprocity and cooperation, divested of individual, unidirectional authority. Understood this way, successful CBR projects depend on the commitment to non-hierarchical, dialogic, and equality-based relationships in pursuit of shared goals.

On a philosophical level – though one with practical implications for *Doméstica* – the curricular "authority" conventionally vested in the instructor was reframed in our course, shifting to a collaborative, consultative, democratic process in which our community partner, Matahari, would play a role in project design and evaluation. In this regard, notions of expertise and authoritative knowledge were core issues of the collaboration because, although our partners were not second language acquisition "trained professionals," they nevertheless were experts in successfully navigating complex multilingual environments, environments where regional, class, and ethnic identities also intersected with language. As emphasized by scholars in the field, CBR "values equally the knowledge that each [partner] brings to [the] process" (Strand, Marullo, Cutforth, Stoeker, Donohue 6). Extending the locations of knowledge beyond strict disciplinary and institutional limits liberates partners to seek "both experiential, or 'local,' community knowledge and the more specialized knowledge of faculty and students" (Strand, Marullo, Cutforth, Stoeker, Donohue 7). The cultural and linguistic diversity of the Matahari community, with member organizers from different Central and South American countries, regions, and socio-economic, racial, and ethnic backgrounds positioned Matahari members, in substantive ways, as holders of authoritative knowledge about Spanish. They were equally qualified as experts in translation and interpretation as social justice tools for dismantling barriers to communication. The collaboration with Matahari dismantled hierarchical values of knowledge, repositioning the community as a source of expertise and ultimately democratizing knowledge. Referring to a "demystification" effect, Strand and colleagues draw attention to what I consider the more radical, metacritical implications of democratizing knowledge, namely, that it challenges "some basic assumptions about knowledge itself: what constitutes valid knowledge, how it is best produced (and by whom), and who should control it" (7).

In fact, the control and dissemination of knowledge created within communities has long troubled community-based research partnerships. Historically, uneven power dynamics and hierarchies of prestige and institutional privilege resulted in extractivist practices that permitted researchers to mine knowledge from communities and then control and disseminate it for the benefit of their individual or institutional gain – primarily through academic journals and monographs. These sites of dissemination ultimately hold little social value or political benefit for community partners. Academic circuits of knowledge become sites of exclusion that prevent communities from accessing and deploying their own expertise for their benefit. Rather than a democratizing effect, these elite circuits of dissemination reinforce hierarchies of power. This analysis extends, as well, to the very ways in which knowledge is spoken and communicated. Jargon-laden, theoretical language, coupled with conventions of institutional discourse make illegible communities' own knowledge. In this regard, digital technologies have gained attention as sites of greater possibility both in the democratization of knowledge production as well as dissemination. For CBR projects, the promise of access, the potential space for a wider range of conventions of expression, and the lower barriers to dissemination make social media platforms and digital technologies an intriguing tool in the democratization of knowledge. In the *Doméstica*-Matahari collaboration, our shared interest in creating access to historical knowledge about and for domestic workers required a willingness to build on the strength of social media practices of domestic worker organizers, who in the majority were active users of smartphones. A Spanish-language digital time line, easily accessed on a smartphone made sense; it simultaneously required a commitment to a writing pedagogy that responded to the platform's constraints and the users' needs. In short, students in *Doméstica* were obliged to shift away from an academic-writing model and develop writing skills rooted in community-organizing practices that value concise and accessible writing over complex, theoretical, and jargon-heavy academic discourse.

Rehearsing Language Justice / Reimagining a Community of Practice in the Second Language Acquisition Classroom

The *Doméstica*-Matahari collaboration illustrates some of the ways that CBR pedagogies can drive curricular innovation and transform classroom spaces by prioritizing social action and, in many cases, social justice as curricular goals. In what follows, I review some on-the-ground CBR practices and their impacts in my second language acquisition classroom. The sixteen students enrolled in *Doméstica* worked with Matahari organizers to curate the timeline of US domestic worker organizing for a local campaign that would use key historical episodes and the stories of movement ancestors to achieve local organizing goals. One priority was to connect domestic workers in the Boston area to a broader history that would allow them to see themselves as part of both an earlier and an ongoing struggle. Another objective was to illustrate the strategies that previous domestic workers had used under similar conditions, in other regions of the country. Finally, because many of Matahari's member-organizers have limited historical connections to the Boston area, a key goal of the curation process was selecting examples that could connect organizers to local history and to places and people who had been involved in the struggle for domestic worker labor rights before them. Once the time line was curated to a selection of 25 slides, *Doméstica* students prepared for their translation project by immersing themselves in this history of predominantly African American women's activism, much of it unfolding in the US South. This exercise connected very local stories to national ones and, ultimately, to international histories of domestic worker organizing. It also illuminated in concrete ways some of the core themes we were exploring in the course material through Latin American films, fiction, and visual art. Studying the resonances as well as differences between US and Latin American domestic workers' realities, students were able to critically engage with key concepts of race and white supremacy, experiences of in-country migration, feminist politics, class identity, and working-class political struggles as transnational experiences. Additionally, in a class of US-educated students, studying domestic workers' histories brought them into a more critical engagement with US history. For example, while all students in the class were well-aware of the history of the Montgomery Bus Boycott (1955–56), none knew of the key role that domestic workers played in ensuring its success. In the process of studying and translating this history, from the perspective of domestic workers, students in *Doméstica* were also developing critical social justice questions, chief among them being who decides how history is narrated and whose voices and actions become authorized (or not) as representatives of that history. Like the Matahari member-organizers, students were reevaluating their knowledge of the past, as well as drawing inspiration and learning strategies for building a different, and more just, future that uplifts the historical contributions of women of color, domestic workers, and immigrants, in the US as well as Latin America.

Doméstica students were paired and assigned three slides to jointly translate. They were also required to write a set of reflections on the process of collaborative translation, to document and reflect critically on their methods, challenges, successes, and unanticipated insights and outcomes of the paired translation work. The pedagogical intention was to reproduce the conditions for achieving language justice goals: equalizing space so that all voices are heard, prioritizing a process of dialogue and discussion to reach a common agreement, and commitment to an alternative vision of academic work that values collective, community advancement over individualistic and competitive models of language development. As in the movement-building that Matahari was doing to envision and create a more just society, student pairs were challenged to consider the collective good, rather than individual gain, as they produced an instrument that would be used outside the academic setting. In *Doméstica*, the guiding CBR ethos of collaboration and democratization of knowledge functioned as a kind of prefigurative politics of the classroom and nurtured a community of practice that rehearsed the social and language justice that Matahari was committed to performing. I invoke prefigurative politics to underscore the kind of behaviors the term describes, that is "modes of organization and social relations between participants . . . that anticipate the future . . . society" they seek to create (Lightsey). Reflection and critical awareness – of language, of each other, of collective work, of listening and being heard – became core values of our classroom meetings and practice, focused mainly (though not solely) on the translation project. To support Matahari's language justice goals, the time line project required that we practice translation as a political project integral to an on-going historical struggle for domestic workers' rights. Additionally, because language justice is an expressed commitment to creating the conditions for all voices to be heard, syallabi and classroom practices had to be structured in service of those conditions. For me, as the professor, this meant structuring classroom meetings so that there would be time for students to dialogue, debate, and discuss the translations they were creating. By extension, individual language "performance" was de-centered, and a higher academic and community value was placed on collaborative, responsive and dialogic "processes." Asking questions, offering suggestions, and sharing knowledge accrued greater value for both the individual and the group and of course for the translations themselves. Students cultivated greater awareness that their listening and response behaviors were key not just to their individual grades but to their classmates' progress and to our partner's goals.

Along a similar grain, but with an outward focus, critical reflection on whose voices were at the center of our translations strengthened language acquisition by nurturing a metacritical perspective on the heterogeneity of Spanish. Students became sensitized to the social contexts of language production by exposure to US southern and African American vernacular expressions in English, for example, and grappled with the complexities of Spanish as a heterogeneous language that contained and expressed similarly diverse national, regional, class, racial, and ethnic identities. Because the time line would be used by domestic workers from various parts of Latin America – including Honduras, El Salvador, and Colombia – students had to dig deeper and wider for help with the subtleties and nuances of language, including turning to non-academic expertise. For example, in one instance, seeking accurate rural Colombian (or Honduran or Salvadoran) translations for rural, southern African American women's terms of endearment, students turned to organizers at Matahari, online newspapers, and *telenovelas* and other popular cultural materials. As they built collaborative, non-academic knowledge networks for the translation project, students likewise reflected critically on the question of knowledge making, including the at-best minimal (if not wholly absent) representation of diverse registers of Spanish in the language classroom. The material conditions of producing the time line nurtured a critical coming-to-awareness of the ways in which class, racial, ethnic, and gender hierarchies have an unspoken hold on second language acquisition. In this, and other ways, language justice in the classroom and the curriculum became a goal to strive for as well as an intellectual object of analysis.

Doméstica's curation-translation collaboration with Matahari is one example of how technology and community partner-driven goals can combine to shape innovations in pedagogy and practice. This hybrid, scholar-student-activist research and learning community radically shifted second language acquisition away from an individualistic language development model to a collective, dialogic, and intercultural practice that centered our community partner's needs and commitment to language justice. It cultivated writing and communication skills that are simultaneously responsive to digital platforms, facilitate a democratization of knowledge, and nurture students' language development. A key pedagogical innovation of implementing a language justice–focused community of practice was the expectation that students critically consider, at every juncture, *whose* voices and *whose* stories were at the center of their work. To this end, our practice of language study required critical considerations of regional forms of speech, vernacular and popular expressions, racial and ethnic communities and their idioms, and the vocabularies of working-class-identified communities. By consistently prioritizing their academic responsibility to uplift and make the histories and voices of domestic workers accessible to other domestic workers, students necessarily questioned hierarchies of "appropriate" Spanish. This led to critical intellectual engagement with Spanish as a heterogenous language, dynamically created in distinct social and economic classes, genders, regions, and generations. A significant outcome for students was the cultivation of an alternative social vision of language learning, the development of relational and intercultural language skills, and a critical engagement with the social contexts of their language study. Collective and collaborative work models required students to build a community of co-learners that was committed to the co-creation of narratives rooted in communities, histories, and cultures historically excluded from the academy's higher education language classrooms. Finally, rather than experiencing second language acquisition as one more competitive quest within an academic model that rewards individual achievement, students had to de-center their individualized relationship to reimagine second language acquisition practices. Aligning with the language justice goals of our partner motivated a more creative and expansive pedagogical engagement with the study of Spanish. Equally important, it led to a transformation of social space and social relations in our second language acquisition classroom that reflected domestic workers' vision for social and multilingual justice.

Notes

1. More information on the Matahari Women Workers' Center is available at www.matahariјustice.org.
2. *SPN 230: Doméstica, Precarious Subjects and the Politics of Intimacy* is taught in the Department of Spanish and Portuguese as a high-intermediate-level language and cultural studies course that focuses on the representation of domestic workers in Latin America and the Latinx US in fiction, film, and visual arts. I have taught it once a year since the fall semester of 2015.
3. For full text, see https://labor.ny.gov/legal/domestic-workers-bill-of-rights.shtm.
4. See, for example, Mary Louise Pratt's "Lessons for Losing: Language in Vulnerable Times."

References

Arguelles, Pancho, et al. "Language Justice Toolkit: Multilingual Strategies for Community Organizing." 2012. https://nesfp.org/sites/default/files/resources/language_justice_toolkit.pdf. Accessed 12 October 2018.

Boris, Eileen, et al. "Enforcement Strategies for Empowerment: Models for the California Domestic Worker Bill of Rights." *UCLA Institute for Research on Labor and Employment Research and Policy Brief*, no. 30, 2015, pp. 1–22.

Burnham, Linda, and Nik Theodore. "Home Economics: The Invisible and Unregulated World of Domestic Work." *National Domestic Workers Alliance*, 2012. www.idwfed.org/en/resources/home-economics-the-invisible-and-unregulated-world-of-domestic-work/@@display-file/attachment_1. Accessed 10 October 2018.

Cass, Melnea. "Letter to William Sargent." 11 August 1970. Personal Collection of Monique Nguyen.

Global Language Justice. "Institute for Comparative Literature and Society." Columbia University. icls.columbia.edu/initiatives/global-language-justice/. Accessed 20 November 2018.

Klein, Hilary. "One Movement, Many Languages: Building Muli-lingual Capacity at the US Social Forum." *The United States Social Forum: Perspectives of a Movement*, edited by Karides, et al. Changemaker, 2010, pp. 77–88.

Kuznesof, Elizabeth. "A History of Domestic Service in Spanish America, 1492–1980." *Muchachas No More: Household Workers in Latin America and the Caribbean*, edited by Elsa M. Chaney and Mary García Castro. Temple University Press, 1989, pp. 17–35.

Lightsey, Louisiana. "Prefigurative Politics." *Global South Studies: Collective Publication with The Global South*, 2017.

Nguyen, Monique. "Multilingual Justice." Received by Michelle Joffroy 27 January 2019.

Pratt, Mary Louise. "Lessons for Losing: Language in Vulnerable Times." *Modern Languages Association Blog*, 2014. https://profession.mla.org/lessons-for-losing/. Accessed 4 December 2018.

Strand, Kerry, et al. "Principles of Best Practice for Community-Based Research." *Michigan Journal of Community Service Learning*, vol. 9, no. 3, 2003, pp. 5–15.

"Universal Declaration of Linguistic Rights." *Wikipedia*. en.wikipedia.org/wiki/Universal_Declaration_of_Linguistic_Rights. Accessed 10 October 2018.

11 Language Acquisition Through Service Learning and Community Engagement

Critical Reflection, Intercultural Competence, and Action Agency

Alison Maginn

Service Learning and Community Engagement (SLCE)[1] is a potentially transformational mode of project-based teaching and learning which traces its roots to the theories of experiential education offered by John Dewey (1938). SLCE and Project-based Learning (PBL) intersect in many strategies and goals such as their emphasis on student-driven, collaborative, interdisciplinary and authentic learning, connected to real-world issues relevant to students' cultures and lives. Both pedagogies aspire to push students toward "comprehension of concepts and principles rather than knowledge of facts; development of complex problem-solving skills rather than learning building block skills in isolation" (Newell 5). Furthermore, best practices in both approaches underline the importance of critical thinking, self-reflection, and the production of a public document or performance that can be assessed and critiqued.[2] That said, a fundamental difference between the two pedagogical approaches is that SLCE always emphasizes civic and social responsibility, an emphasis not necessarily present in PBL experiences.

Educational theorists, such as Paolo Freire (*Education*, *Pedagogy*), David Kolb, and Ernest Boyer expanded Dewey's fundamental concepts of learning through experience to develop theories of democratic engagement, community involvement, and civic responsibility through learning. Over the last two decades, we have seen emerge an increasing body of quantitative and qualitative research from practitioner-scholars who straddle the fields of SLCE and second-language acquisition (SLA). There is credible evidence to suggest that the pedagogies and practices of SLCE align well with the goals and desired learning outcomes of world language programs, language acquisition classes, and their PBL approaches. This study will consider the far-reaching implications of second-language acquisition and project-based learning within SLCE and the intentional and unintentional consequences of this practice for our students and community partners.

SLCE can be an exhilarating, inspiring, and transformative experience for all involved; however, for stakeholders entering the terrain for the first time (instructors, students, and community partners), indeed for experienced practitioners too, this "counter normative" (Howard) pedagogical enterprise can be difficult, even intimidating. Furthermore, as its purposes and academic integrity can be misunderstood or undervalued, the field warrants ongoing and different kinds of research in order to give account of its diverse modes, successes, and challenges. My contribution to the discussion of SLA through SLCE emerges from an autoethnographical process of self-reflection as a practitioner-scholar over the past four years. I offer my own professional narrative from the field as a story of engaged, reciprocal collaboration in a bilingual dynamic of Spanish and English, between undergraduate students, community partners (leaders and program participants), faculty members, and administrators. Acknowledging and dialoguing with the findings of research in the field of SLCE and its intersection with SLA theories, my story situates itself as a qualitative analysis of the shared journeys I embarked upon with my students and our various community partners.

Literature Review

In their overview of the field of practice, Palpacuer Lee, Curtis, and Curran emphasize the importance for the researcher in SLA/SLCE to recognize that we are not pioneers in the field of teaching and learning through community engagement. It is incumbent upon us, therefore, to place our work within the trajectory of scholarship that has come before us. This review of research in the field does not intend to be exhaustive; rather, it will highlight some of the key inquiries that foreground the particular interests of this study within the discipline of language acquisition. These are: the benefits experienced by all stakeholders in the SLCE enterprise; entering into and nurturing relationships with diverse, multicultural, and multilingual community partners; and reflection and assessment that can best address some of the sensitive issues and unexpected situations that we face in this "realm of human interaction" (Felton and Clayton 77).

A considerable body of evidence demonstrates that service-learning is a "high-impact" educational practice. The affective dimension and the role of emotions on learning and community engagement are discussed by Astin and Sax and Felten, Gilchrist, and Darby, while Eyler, Giles, Stenson, and Gray discuss the personal, social, academic, and career benefits for all participating stakeholders within the academy. For their part, Astin, Volgelgesang, Ikeda, and Yee published a study that is both broad and deep and provides data analysis on some 200 universities in the US. Their conclusions indicate multiple positive learning outcomes ranging from academic performance and civic responsibility to personal values and critical thinking skills. In 2009, Bringle, Clayton, and Price developed the SOFAR model of partnership (Students, Organizations in the community, Faculty, Administrators on the campus, and Residents in the community) expanding and deepening their analysis of this dynamic in their 2010 piece that addresses differentiating and assessing relationships in SLCE. Based on their conviction that "the field needs clearer nomenclature and tools to conceptualize, investigate, evaluate, monitor, and nurture partnerships" (Clayton et al. 5), they also present three different kinds of relationships in which SLCE practitioners can become involved: exploitative, transactional, or transformational. They describe each kind of relationship and using the Transformational Relationship Evaluation Scale (TRES), they advocate for careful and intentional design in order to avoid exploitative or merely transactional relationships, aiming instead to establish transformational relationships with our partners (Clayton et al. 8–19).

Along these lines, researchers such as García and Guerra, Yosso, and Tilley-Lubbs call for a deconstruction of the traditional asset/deficit binary models of viewing the academic versus the local community and, through the lens of critical race theory, raise some crucial questions and present some groundbreaking concepts. Tilley-Lubbs, for example, interrogates the role of whiteness, power, and privilege in preparing educators to teach in immigrant and refugee communities, while Yosso re-evaluates the idea of cultural capital and presents the concept of "community cultural wealth" (Yosso 70). Taking into consideration the complexities involved in SLCE, which may not exist in other forms of PBL, it is not enough to ask only "What are our students learning through this experience?" Instead, we must re-frame the question as "How do our students learn and grow with our community partners, and how do our community partners learn and grow with our students?" It is worth repeating that this approach is not easy. To engage in this kind of practice requires bravery, honesty, and acknowledgment of the failures as well as the successes. It is imperative that we monitor, question, and calibrate our practice through ongoing self-reflection as well as assessment involving all of the constituent participants as laid out in the SOFAR model. Thanks to my university's Center of Excellence for Teaching and Learning (CETL), which launched a Service-Learning Faculty Fellows Program in the summer of 2016, alongside my fellow faculty colleagues, I entered into ongoing training and professional development with our invited senior scholar-practitioner, Patti Clayton. I found Ash and Clayton's model for generating, deepening, and documenting learning through the DEAL model of critical reflection to be essential to my practice. I used this framework for intentional SLCE program design, reflection, and assessment, the processes and outcomes of which I will elaborate upon in the following sections.

SLCE and Second-Language Acquisition

Research at the intersection of SLCE and SLA began 20 years ago with the sponsored series on service-learning across the disciplines. Under the auspices of the AAHE (The American Association for Higher Education) Josef Hellebrandt and Lucía T. Varona co-edited in 1999 the groundbreaking volume *Construyendo Puentes [Building Bridges]: Concepts and Models for Service-Learning in Spanish*. Among the many important contributions of *Construyendo Puentes*, two key concepts resonate with this present volume on project-based learning and remain at the very core of second-language acquisition theories: 1) "[B]ecoming proficient in a second language cannot be separated from learning the culture of the people who speak that language" (1), and 2) "Meaningful language study and training then requires that learners participate in these processes by interacting with community members, participating in their pursuits, and learning *with* them as opposed to learning *about* them" (Hellebrandt and Varona 1; emphasis in the original). Within *Construyendo Puentes*, various studies describe an array of learning outcomes ranging from affective factors, such as motivation and confidence, to academic factors, such as enhanced critical thinking skills, intercultural competence, and changed attitudes. This early research paved the way for subsequent researchers in the intersecting fields of SLA/SLCE to explore further and carry out more detailed quantitative and qualitative analyses. Arries, for example, examines the roles of critical pedagogy and critical thinking as a means to destabilize myths and question stereotypes (33–47). In later years, these objectives are explored and expanded by theorists such as Nieto or Glynn, Wesely, and Wassell. Nieto argues for the important role of language educators who can, as Papalcuer Lee and colleagues explain, "challenge, confront, and disrupt misconceptions, untruths, and stereotypes that lead to structural inequality and discrimination based on social and human differences" and "promote critical thinking and agency for social change" (Nieto 46; quoted in Papalcuer Lee et al. 178).

Hale considers the affective facets of SLCE like motivation and self-confidence, which can then lead to the application of meta-cognitive skills such as connecting language use with culture and changing attitudes (Hale 9–25). Mullaney's article in this same volume maps out the important connections between SLCE and the theories of second-language acquisition (differentiated from second-language learning) proposed by Krashen in 1982 (Mullaney 51–52). Following Krashen, Mullaney argues that carefully planned experiences for language students within the community can create a context for the desired affective variables to exist, thereby minimizing the negative affective filter of anxiety. Krashen's theories of language acquisition are still central to the proficiency-oriented second-language teaching of the present; nevertheless, the traditional measures of language acquisition are adapting to the global dynamics and demographic shifts of today's world. The most recent update and expansion of ACTFL's national standards, incorporating the five C's of language proficiency (Communication, Cultures, Connections, Comparisons, and Communities) emphasizes World-Readiness Standards (National Standards Collaborative Board) within the context of our current multilingual and multicultural world. The standards value 21st-century skills, such as translingualism, intercultural competence, problem-solving, and community connections, as Baker, Barreneche, and Ramos-Flores; DuBord and Kimball; and Palpacuer Lee and colleagues have discussed. In her study on community-based service-learning in a dual-language classroom, Baker highlights the importance of a "community of practice in which . . . [k]nowledge is co-constructed, and learners build their language capacity in their communication with others as they become part of the community" (797).

Palpacuer Lee and colleagues, in their survey of the current state and future directions of the SLA/SLCE field, propose the following:

> As we move into the future, we believe that we need critical community-based models for language classes, degree programs in languages, and teacher preparation programs that aim to produce a specific outcome: speakers who can use their pluricultural and plurilingual experiences and expertise in and out of academic settings. Advanced language preparation often seeks to replicate the competence of an educated native speaker, an unrealistic and unnecessary goal that postadolescent learners rarely reach or need. In contrast . . . the idea of translingual and transcultural competence places value on the ability to operate between languages as informed and capable interlocutors who are prepared to reflect on the world and themselves through the lens of another language and culture. Through meaningful relationships with diverse members of linguistically and interculturally competent communities, possibilities emerge for engaging in democratic and ethical action.
>
> (181)

Increased learning experiences in and with the community by no means minimize the importance of in-class learning of grammar, vocabulary, and the four skills of reading, writing, listening, and speaking. Nonetheless, students need to apply and practice this knowledge and these skills in authentic situations that excite and engage them so that they will want to become life-long users of the second language. Pellettieri has drawn attention to the importance and challenge of sustained, authentic practice since even high-achieving learners tend to be reticent to use their language skills outside the classroom. She correctly points out that

> particularly after their formal studies cease, learners' active use of the L2 is crucial for the continued development and maintenance of their communicative competence. Language educators must therefore strive to understand what is necessary to take students from being L2 learners to independent L2 users.
>
> (285)

By facilitating students' engagement and relationship building with target-language community members and in keeping with the tenets of project-based learning, which nudges students toward taking more responsibility for their own learning, SLCE starts to build a path for students' life-long involvement with the language, which in turn can lead to a commitment to social justice and equity. The ethos of intercultural competence and its potential for social change agency is at the heart of ACTFL's world readiness standards. Research shows that learning goals in all areas of the five C's are supported through SLCE, as Bettencourt has summarized:

> by providing students with opportunities for communicative language use in authentic situations (Standards 1.1, 1.2, and 1.3), understanding of cultures different from their own (Standards 2.1 and 2.2), making connections to other disciplines (Standards 3.1 and 3.2), comparing differences and similarities in their own language and culture with that of others' (Standards 4.1 and 4.2), and engaging in meaningful and personally satisfying interaction with members of communities in which the language is used (Standards 5.1 and 5.2).
>
> (474)

Measuring Language Acquisition

This analysis focuses on traditional and nontraditional measures of student learning in two editions of an Advanced Spanish Conversation and Oral Discourse class. Language acquisition outcomes are measured in achievements in oral and written analyses of class content (see Appendix 1) and in the formative and summative oral and written reflections that students provided on their SLCE experiences (see Appendix 2 for DEAL model of reflection). As a counter-normative pedagogy, SLCE is unpredictable and involves so much more than teaching and learning, as if that in itself is not already challenging. Acknowledging this complexity, Felton and Clayton remind us that "community organizations are not merely learning laboratories but rather realms of significant problem-solving and human interaction, which means that much more than student learning is at stake" (77).

Given that there is so much at stake in service-learning, it seemed appropriate while assessing what and how my students learned in their language acquisition journey through the SLCE experience that I should also assess my own thinking process and engagement in what was a new and complex pedagogical approach. Blending introspection with objective analysis, an ethnographic "layered account" emphasizes the experiential nature of research itself, taking the researcher through a self-reflective process in meaning-making, mirroring the students' pedagogical journey as they learn how to learn and generate meaning through their critical self-reflections.

With these acknowledgments and admissions brought to the fore, my inquiry examines the following questions:

- How does SCLE facilitate and enhance L2 acquisition and development?
- What is the role of critical reflection?
- How does an increasingly diverse and multicultural student body benefit from SLCE in an increasingly diverse and multicultural community?

Academic Context

In the first offering of the course, 18 students attended class twice per week and collaborated with a local church in a town close to our campus. The service occurred outside of class time with most students giving between 10 and 15 hours of service during the course of the semester. The second time the class was taught, there were sixteen students, and in addition to the church partnership, we began a relationship with a local public library in a different nearby town. Intentional, reciprocal design is essential to the successful implementation of an SLCE experience so before launching the partnerships with the church and library, I met frequently with the organizations' leaders in order to discuss our mutual interests and potential for co-creative, reciprocal collaboration. I knew that the church in question had a progressive, inclusive, and deeply committed social justice program, including a food justice program with one of the largest food pantries and soup kitchens in the area. Furthermore, they offered an after-school chorister and music program for children aged seven through 18, most, if not all of whom attended the local schools. This school district faces many challenges such as underfunding and the problems exacerbated by the socio-economic disadvantages of poverty. The Hispanic immigrant population of the town has grown significantly over the past decade, and the church saw a need to offer not only religious services in Spanish but also attractive, educationally focused programming especially for children. This is where we saw a potential area of mutual enrichment, learning, and growth, and I continued to meet with the lay and religious staff of the church over the course of six months before beginning the program that fall.

In a different adjacent town, I was familiar with the public library and knew that they offered high-impact programming, including ESL and citizenship classes, tutoring, and English conversation practice, as well as a range of after-school programming for children. I had a series of meetings with the head librarian, the children's librarians, and other cultural and educational programming staff. It was fascinating and exciting to discover that 80% of the library's patronage was Hispanic, and it was clear on all visits that they were frequent and engaged patrons. The librarians proposed that we pilot a bilingual storytelling program, which would also include crafts, art, and tutoring as needed.

Following Ash, Clayton, and Moses's *Learning Through Critical Reflection Tutorial*, the syllabus was redesigned to ensure that the academic learning outcomes of the class aligned with the three main goal areas for service-learning: academic enrichment, civic learning, and personal growth. The syllabus shared this information with students (see Appendix 1).

During the first two weeks of class, aside from discussing the general syllabus, the introductory pages of the *Learning Through Critical Reflection Tutorial* manual were assigned. We discussed key concepts of SLCE were discussed, such as democratic versus hierarchical teaching and learning; the re-evaluation of asset/deficit models of teaching and learning; reciprocal co-creation; the importance of interrogating condescending language and attitudes, such as "helping" and "saving"; and the differences between service-learning, "volunteering," and "community service." During the second to third weeks of the semester, guest speakers from our partner organizations visited class and presented essential background information about the community members we were about to work with. One of our guest speakers, a Hispanic pastor who worked closely with the Hispanic immigrant community remained for the full 80 minutes of class and answered many questions from the students. The information and insight he provided went far beyond any research to be found on the immigrant population and experience of the town in question. One of the concepts that he explained was how undocumented immigrants "viven en las sombras" [live in the shadows], which has many implications. Census data, for example, can only be approximate, as undocumented immigrants often fear answering the door or responding to requests from the census takers. The pastor addressed how most undocumented immigrants do indeed pay taxes, as they purchase Social Security numbers in order to be able to work; however, they do not have access to the services and health-care benefits that other citizens receive. Students were surprised to learn that immigrant families frequently share one apartment and one car between many, taking turns and shifts to sleep, cook, shower, and live in the space. Around the third or fourth week, I shared a handout on the DEAL model of reflection that I had translated into Spanish and summarized from the *Tutorial* (Ash et al.) and the article on generating, deepening, and documenting learning (Ash and Clayton; see Appendix 2).

During those early weeks, we worked together to come up with some of the personal learning goals the students were interested in examining. We did these exercises on the white board so that all students could brainstorm and listen to one another's ideas. Relinquishing control is often one of the greatest challenges that instructors face, but in the context of SLCE, it can be even more difficult. While traditional classes can and do present unplanned occurrences, questions, and problems, we know with reasonable certainty where we will hold class, for how long, with whom, and more or less what material we will cover. This is not the case with SLCE. All of these variables can change at any time. All partners in this enterprise must be flexible and patient, but if things do not go to plan, it is helpful to remember that everything is worthy of reflection and that meaning can be generated from even the "messiest" of situations. Although I had thought a great deal about the objectives and desired learning outcomes of the class and had expressed them formally on the syllabus, I still wanted to give the students some ownership of these goals and their own reflections. It also gave me the opportunity to assess students' understanding of some of the counter-normative aspects of SLCE.

Samples of Student Reflections

No corrections have been made to the grammar or vocabulary of these reflections, which students wrote in Spanish. The only alteration made was to de-identify people and places. I have provided translations into English.

Raw Language Gains

While raw language gains through SLCE were difficult to measure since students were learning in many different contexts in a three-credit, 14-week class, the community engagement experience led to the use and understanding of some new concepts and terminologies, which were important to the development of sensitivity, empathy, and an appreciation of the complexity of people's lives. Students began to use terms such as "inseguridad alimentaria" (*food insecurity*) rather than *poor*, "personas que viven sin techo" (*people experiencing homelessness*) rather than *homeless*, and "inmigrantes indocumentados" or "sin papeles" (*undocumented immigrants*) rather than *illegal immigrants*. At the beginning of the semester, some students mentioned or wrote about "la cocina de sopa" as a direct translation from the English *soup kitchen* but soon changed to the correct terminology "comedor público." Another student used and understood the term "interseccionalidad" (*intersectionality*) and went on to discuss "las ideas preconcebidas que tengo y mi ignorancia a mi privilegio" (*the preconceived notions I hold and my ignorance to my privilege*). We can attribute the acquisition of this new vocabulary and these concepts specifically to the service experience, and it marks an important shift toward democratic as opposed to hierarchical thinking.

Connectedness and Willingness to Continue

There was much evidence of connectedness and emotional bonds forming through conversations with the children about their lives. We cannot underestimate the power of the affective dimension as it leads to deeper engagement, an appreciation of the assets that everyone in the community has, regardless of their circumstances, and a desire to continue the collaboration when the semester is over. Students' words attest to this:

> Al principio yo pensé que esto solo era un requisito para una clase y quería terminar con esto. Pero cada vez que regresaba, una amistad y una relación desarrollaron con los niños, especialmente con xxx. (*In the beginning, I thought of this as a class requirement and I wanted to get it over with. But every time I returned friendships and relationships developed further with the children, especially with xxx.*)
>
> Me sentí invitada a su segunda casa . . . típicamente soy tímida en cantar en público pero ellos me ayudaban con leyendo la música y me hacían sentir cómoda. Alguien ha dicho que es importante estar vulnerabilidad transparente para hacer conexiones profundas. (*I felt like I was being invited into their second home. . . . I'm usually shy about singing in pubic, but they would help me with reading the music and they made me feel comfortable. Someone has said that it's important to show vulnerability in order to make deep connections.*)
>
> Estos niños me inspiraban porque muchos vienen de areas o familias dificiles pero participan en el coro y usan sus talentos para el beneficio de la comunidad aunque es posible que sus vidas sean dificiles afuera del coro. (*These children inspired me because many of them come from difficult neighborhoods or family situations, but they participate in the choir and use their talents for the benefit of their community although it's possible that their lives outside of the choir are difficult.*)
>
> A través de esta actividad yo aumento mi confianza en mi competencia en el idioma del español y yo voy a seguir una actividad voluntaria como un traductor médico. (*Through this experience, my confidence in my competence in the Spanish language has grown, and I'm going to do another voluntary activity as a medical translator.*)

Intercultural Competence

In speaking Spanish with the children in the library, students started to develop an understanding of the importance of bilingualism and the inextricable connection between language, culture, and identity. Again, the affective dimension lowered the anxiety filter so that students could enjoy the encounters and really start to understand what speaking with these children in their native language meant within the context of their bilingual, bicultural lives:

> Los niños estaban tan emocionados de vernos cuando íbamos. Creo que fue una oportunidad para ellos para hablar en español con nosotros porque nunca hablan en español en la escuela. . . . Creo que

> es importante hacer aprendizaje-servicio y otras actividades con la comunidad local. Aprendí mucho de los niños porque son de un origen diferente al mío. Personalmente también me sentía bien cuando estaba allí porque los niños disfrutaban cuando les leíamos. Nunca he hecho algo como esto antes sin embargo me gustaría hacer más servicios en el futuro. Estoy agradecido por la oportunidad y la experiencia. (*The children were so excited to see us when we would go. I think it was an opportunity for them to speak in Spanish with us because they never get to speak in Spanish in school. . . . I think it's important to do service-learning and other kinds of activities with the local community. I learned a lot from the children because they're from a different background than me. Personally, I also felt good when I was there because the children enjoyed when we read with them. I've never done anything like this, but I'd like to do more service in the future. I'm grateful for the opportunity and experience.*)

Another student remarks,

> Creo que es muy importante tener personas presentes que hablan su idioma, principalmente a los niños que se están integrando en una cultura nueva. (*I think it's important to have people present who speak their language, especially for children who are integrating into a new culture.*)

Heritage-Speaker Learners and Community Members

Barreneche and Ramos-Flores discuss the changing demographics of the United States, where, by 2020, minority students will comprise the majority of school-age students and consequently will participate increasingly in higher-level education (221). The authors raise concerns about how our increasingly multicultural and multilingual students will respond in service-learning experiences with community partners who come from the same backgrounds as them. They state that minority students tend to keep away from SLCE classes and pose the question "Can service-learning still be used to help students achieve multicultural awareness when multicultural students are the very pupils that institutions are teaching?" (221). I would argue, based on my experience over the past four years and on research on heritage learners, that we must do more, rather than less, to include and encourage heritage learners to participate in such community engagement since they have so much to offer the community, their peers, their professors, and the pedagogies of language acquisition and SLCE. Contrary to Barreneche and Ramos-Flores's fears, in my experience, many heritage learners signed up for these classes and expressed enormous interest in and solidarity with the community members. Integrating heritage learners into the community learning experience provided the important opportunity to honor their voices, recognize their unique insights, and acknowledge their personal, cultural, and linguistic histories, which traditionally have been marginalized and undervalued at all levels of education in the US. In their discussion of critical pedagogy beyond the classroom walls, Leeman, Rabin, and Román-Mendoza underline the necessity to revise the hierarchical orientation of language teaching and learning. These authors outline how their departmental reform

> sought to bring students' home and community knowledges and experiences in from the margins and to integrate the language, language practices and cultural production of US Spanish speakers in an effort to . . . resist the language subordination of Spanish in relation to English.
>
> (Leeman, Rabin, and Román-Mendoza 3)

In my classes, the heritage learners' reflections on the connections between language and identity were poignantly introspective and stressed the importance among the immigrant community to maintain the language and culture of their heritage through the generations:

> Yo conseguí verme en estos niños porque ya pasé lo que están pasando ahora. (*I could see myself in these children because I already went through what they are experiencing now.*)
>
> En un punto de mi vida yo era como xxx, mis padres no hablaban el inglés y me tocaba hacer la tarea yo sola. Aunque yo aprendí rápido, no todos los niños aprenden igual. Cuando xxx terminaba de leer un libro solita, celebrábamos pintado hojas. (*At one point in my life, I was like xxx, my parents couldn't speak English, and I had to do my homework all by myself. Although I learned quickly, not all children learn the same way. When xxx would finish reading a book by herself, we would celebrate by painting leaves.*)
>
> Esta conexión me hizo sentir mucha felicidad. A pesar de que esta es una nueva generación, todavía hay conexiones y comparaciones que yo vi en ellas por la cultura y en su creatividad. (*This connection made me feel so happy. In spite of the fact that this is a new generation, there are still connections and comparisons that I saw in them through the culture and in their creativity.*)
>
> Son momentos como estos que son inolvidables y te motivan a ser un ejemplo para la nueva generación. (*It's moments like these that are unforgettable, and they motivate you to be a model for the new generation.*)

Civic Responsibility and Action Agency

My students were between 18 and 22 years old, with quite a few in their first year of study. The children they collaborated with in the library were between six and 10 years old. This is not a huge age difference, but the college students saw the younger children as the next generation, and they developed a civic responsibility to support the non-English-speaking parents and encourage the children to be successfully bilingual and bicultural. Many students also commented that they had not realized the crucial role played by public libraries:

> Aprendí cuán importante es tener una biblioteca pública. También es una manera para que la comunidad se unir y trabajar juntos para un futuro mejor para los niños. (*I learned how important it is to have a public library. Also, it's a way for the community to unite and work together for a better future for their children.*)
>
> Esta experiencia me enseñó que cada vez hay más inmigrantes. Enseguida es importante dar apoyo a los padres y a los niños. (*This experience taught me that there are more and more immigrants. It is urgent to give support to the parents and the children.*)
>
> No todos los padres que hablan español pueden o tienen el tiempo o el dinero para ayudar a sus hijos con el inglés. Esto no es justo porque todos los niños deben de tener las mismas oportunidades. (*Not all Spanish-speaking parents can or have to time or the money to help their children with English. This is not fair because all children should have the same opportunities.*)

Co-Creativity and Asset-Based Thinking

The students, community partners, and I all collaborated to create a symbolic "artefact," and for the choristers, this was an invitation to the university to give a concert and join us for a special Christmas dinner in our university's most famous and elegant building. My administrative colleagues from our CETL also helped me with this event, as the logistics were complex. This was a beautiful and emotional culminating event and an excellent example of co-creativity. Some of my students (who were not musicians) had learned a piece of music alongside the children during their service, and the choir director invited them to sing a song with the choristers in the concert. In this case, the young children had taught the college students, illustrating so well Tara Yosso's point about community cultural wealth and the importance of embracing an asset rather than deficit-based approach to all people, no matter their circumstances. This event resonated with everyone in very special ways, as the following remarks show:

> A mi el parte más gratificante fue cuando el coro vino a xxx para cantar. Fue increíble ver todos sus trabajos duros valen la pena.

Después en la cena hablé con xxx y le di consejo y le aviso continuar sus estudios. (*For me, the most gratifying part was when the choir came to xxx. It was incredible to see that all their hard work had paid off. After the dinner, I spoke with xxx and I gave her advice about continuing her studies.*)

Yo dibujé un dibujo para xxx y pensé que lo tiraría. Pero cuando vino a la universidad a cantar yo he realizado que lo puso en el enfrente de su cuaderno para el coro. Fue una gran sensación. (*I drew a picture for xxx, and I thought that she would throw it away. But when she came to the university to sing, I realized that she had put it on the cover of her choir folder. It was a great feeling*).

Me encantó verlos hacer su presentación de canto en la universidad y estaba sorprendido de qué tan bien podían cantar porque son tan jóvenes. (*I loved seeing their choral performance at the university, and I was surprised at how well they sang because they were so young*).

Conclusion

In data analysis of the average final grades from two previous semesters teaching this course without the service component compared with those of the two editions of the course taught with the service component, no significant statistical difference emerged. That is to say that the average final grades were the same in all versions of the class. The final grade was based on all the required components of the class, plus the final exam (see Grading Criteria, Appendix 1). This is in keeping with data analyses carried out in comparative studies, such as that of Moreno-López, Ramos-Sellman, Miranda Aldaco, and Gomis Quinto. However, based on my qualitative analysis of the two service-learning courses, I did find evidence of additional learning in the three areas of academic enhancement, civic learning, and personal growth. Students' reflections through the DEAL model showed enhancement in language acquisition in some of the specific vocabulary and nuanced terminology acquired within community contexts. Students demonstrated important gains in personal growth and intercultural learning, such as confidence, interest in the community members, and positive feelings of empathy, solidarity, and identification with and appreciation of the challenges that immigrant families face. Furthermore, the kinds of issues learners discussed in class and in their formative and summative reflections showed significant development in the understanding of socio-political and social justice issues, such as educational equity, food insecurity, economic hardship, homelessness, and the discrimination suffered by immigrants. Across the board, students expressed their enthusiasm for practicing their Spanish outside the classroom regardless of whether they were native English speakers or Spanish heritage speakers. Heritage learners in particular were able to help their monolingual peers to understand some of the behaviors that bilingual Hispanic students display because of the desire to fit in and speak the same language as everyone else. At first, some of the Hispanic immigrant children who had become bilingual did not want to speak in Spanish with the college students, but after a few weeks when trust had been established, they were happy to switch back and forth between the languages. Since the university heritage learners had gone through similar socio-cultural and linguistic journeys themselves, they had an immediate understanding of this socio-linguistic phenomenon. My findings, then, contradict those discussed by Barreneche and Ramos-Flores but are in keeping with other research which finds that measurable learning gains are evidenced through the specific context of engaging with the community. As Bettencourt argued, "Overwhelmingly, the literature has pointed to SL as a means of providing students with meaningful learning opportunities that would otherwise be unattainable while simultaneously supporting our common goals as foreign language educators" (Bettencourt 475).

Finally, students' ongoing critical reflection was instrumental to their ability to generate meaning from the service experience and to understand the value of bilingualism, multiculturalism, and the potential for civic agency through intercultural competence. A good number of my students went on to engage in post-semester reflection in the form of research, which is an important indication of the value they placed on the SLCE experience from the vantage point of temporal distance. I will give the last word to one of my students:

> Lo más importante es que seguí aprendiendo que no se puede asumir cosas sobre las vidas de otras personas sin conocerlas y sus situaciones. Algunos de los niños están "en riesgo" pero son muy talentosos y tienen sus propios intereses. Y esto es especialmente importante en la atmósfera política actual." (*The most important thing is that I continued to learn that we can't assume things about other people's lives without knowing them and their situations. Some of the children were "at risk," but they are very talented and they have their own interests. And this is especially important in the current political climate.*)

Notes

1. In this inquiry, the terminology I use to describe my practice is *service-learning and community engagement*, abbreviated as SLCE. In the field of second language acquisition (SLA), the commonly used term is *community-based learning* (CBL). I prefer the term *SLCE* since it clearly names concepts that I consider essential to this pedagogy. Everything that is implicated within the hyphenated noun service-learning (which can also be an adjective) is part of my ongoing reflection as an educator and participant in this nontraditional, outside-of-the-box approach to teaching and learning. Within this particular

approach, there can be no service without the learning, nor learning without the service. I also prefer the term *community engagement* to *community-based* since one could be based in the community without being engaged.

2. See Boss and Larmer for a discussion of the Gold Standard of PBL developed by the Buck Institute of Education.

References

Arries, Jonathan. "Critical Pedagogy and Service-Learning in Spanish: Crossing Borders in the Freshman Seminar." *Construyendo puentes (Building Bridges): Concepts and Models for Service-Learning in Spanish*, edited by Josef Hellebrandt, and Lucía T. Varona. American Association for Higher Education, 1999, pp. 33–47

Ash, Sarah L., and Patti H. Clayton. "Generating, Deepening, and Documenting Learning: The Power of Critical Reflection for Applied Learning." *Journal of Applied Learning in Higher Education*, vol. 1, no. 1, 2009, pp. 25–48.

———, and Myra G. Moses. *Learning Through Critical Reflection: A Tutorial for Students in Service-Learning*. Instructor version, PHC Ventures, 2009.

Baker, Lottie. "From Learner to Teacher Assistant: Community-Based Service-Learning in a Dual-Language Classroom." *Foreign Language Annals*, vol. 51, no. 4, 2018, pp. 796–815.

Barreneche, Gabriel I., and Héctor Ramos-Flores. "Integrated or Isolated Experiences? Considering the Role of Service-Learning in the Spanish Language Curriculum." *Hispania*, vol. 96, no. 2, 2013, pp. 215–228.

Bettencourt, Michelle. "Supporting Student Learning Outcomes Through Service Learning." *Foreign Language Annals*, vol. 48, no. 3, 2015, pp. 473–490.

Boss, Suzie, and Larmer, John. *Project Based Teaching: How to Create Rigorous and Engaging Learning Experiences*. ASCD, Buck Institute for Education, 2018.

Boyer, Ernest L. "The Scholarship of Engagement." *Bulletin of the American Academy of the Arts and Sciences*, vol. 49, no. 7, 1996, pp. 18–33.

Bringle, Robert G., Patti H. Clayton, and Mary F. Price. "Partnerships in Service Learning and Civic Engagement." *Partnerships: A Journal of Service-Learning and Civic Engagement*, vol. 1, no. 1, 2009, pp. 1–20.

Clayton, Patti H., et al. "Differentiating and Assessing Relationships in Service-Learning and Civic Engagement: Exploitative, Transactional, or Transformational." *Michigan Journal of Community Service Learning*, vol. 16, Spring 2010, pp. 5–22.

Dewey, John. *Experience and Education*. Macmillan, 1938.

DuBord, Elise, and Elizabeth Kimball. "Cross-Language Community Engagement: Assessing the Strengths of Heritage Learners." *Heritage Language Journal*, vol. 13, 2016, pp. 298–330.

Freire, Paolo. *Education for Critical Consciousness*. Continuum Publishing, 1970.

———. *Pedagogy of the Oppressed*. The Seabury Press, 1973.

García, Shernaz B., and Patricia L. Guerra. "Deconstructing Deficit Thinking: Working With Educators to Create More Equitable Learning Environments." *Education and Urban Society*, vol. 36, no. 2, 2004, pp. 150–168.

Glynn, Cassandra, Pamela M. Wesely, and Beth A. Wassell. *Words and Actions: Teaching Languages Through the Lens of Social Justice*. ACTFL, 2014.

Hale, Aileen. "Service Learning and Spanish: A Missing Link." *Construyendo puentes (Building Bridges): Concepts and Models for Service-Learning in Spanish*, edited by Josef Hellebrandt, and Lucía T. Varona. American Association for Higher Education, 1999, pp. 9–31.

Harrison, Barbara, Patti H. Clayton, and Gresilda A. Tilley-Lubbs. "Troublesome Knowledge, Troubling Experience: An Inquiry Into Faculty Learning in Service-Learning." *Michigan Journal of Community Service Learning*, vol. 20, no. 2, 2014, pp. 5–18.

Hellebrandt, Josef, and Lucía T. Varona, *Construyendo puentes (Building Bridges): Concepts and Models for Service-Learning in Spanish*. American Association for Higher Education, 1999.

Howard, Jeffery P. F. "Academic Service Learning: A Counter Normative Pedagogy". *Academic Service Learning: A Pedagogy of Action and Reflection*, edited by Robert A. Rhoades and Jeffery P. F. Howard. Jossey-Bass, 1998, pp. 21–29.

Kolb, David A. *Experiential Learning: Experience as the Source of Learning and Development*. Prentice Hall, 1984.

Leeman, Jennifer, Lisa Rabin, and Esperanza Román-Mendoza. "Critical Pedagogy Beyond the Classroom Walls: Community Service-Learning and Spanish Heritage Language Education." *Heritage Language Journal*, vol. 8, no. 3, 2011, pp. 1–22.

Moreno-López, Isabel, et al. "Transforming Ways of Enhancing Foreign Language Acquisition in the Spanish Classroom: Experiential Learning Approaches." *Foreign Language Annals*, vol. 50, 2017, pp. 398–409.

Newell, Ronald J. *Passion for Learning: How Project-Based Learning Meets the Needs of 21st Century Students*. Scarecrow Press, 2003.

Pellettieri, Jill. "Measuring Language-Related Outcomes of Community-Based Learning in Intermediate Spanish Courses." *Hispania*, vol. 94, no. 2, 2011, pp. 285–302.

Sigmon, Robert L. "Service-Learning: Three Principles." *Synergist*, Spring, 1979, pp. 9–11.

Tilley-Lubbs, Gresilda A. "Troubling the Tide: The Perils and Paradoxes of Service-Learning in Immigrant Communities." *International Journal of Critical Pedagogy*, vol. 2, no. 1, 2009, pp. 67–87.

Yosso, Tara J. "Whose Culture Has Capital? A Critical Race Theory Discussion of Community Cultural Wealth." *Race Ethnicity and Education*, vol. 8, no. 1, 2005, pp. 69–91.

Appendix 1

Course Description

This is a content-based, student-centered language class designed to bridge the gap between the 200- and 300-level courses in Spanish. This course includes a service-learning component providing students with optimal opportunities to connect the issues discussed in class with our local community, to enter into a collaborative relationship of co-creativity with our partners, and to practice language skills at the mid- to high-intermediate level. Students will practice Spanish in authentic contexts through the community engagement experiences, in-class discussions, partner chats, and intentional and ongoing reflection using the DEAL model. While the course provides practice in all four language skills, special emphasis is placed on oral communication.

Objectives

Through analysis of and reflection upon an array of different texts and experiences, including Hispanic film, short literary and non-literary selections, and the service experience in xxxx, students will

- become familiarized with and converse in Spanish on a number of high-interest topics relevant both to their own lives and Hispanic cultures, especially the immigrant experience
- engage in debates, "tertulias," oral presentations, mock interviews, role-plays, and recorded partner chats in order to reflect upon the course content, at the same time practicing and improving upon all aspects of spoken Spanish, including vocabulary expansion and improved grammatical accuracy
- analyze the service-learning as an experience that connects with the other texts of the class, thereby permitting the cross-fertilization and illumination of in-class and community learning
- generate, deepen, and document in Spanish the learning taking place through ongoing critical reflection structured around the three learning

goal areas of academic enrichment, civic learning, and personal growth. Reflection will be based on the service experience with the xxxx after-school chorister program and/or the xxxx food justice program or xxxx Public Library's bilingual storytelling program

Using the DEAL method of critical reflection (see accompanying handout), the following learning outcomes will be assessed over the course of the semester in each learning goal area:

LO#1 Examine an area of weakness in your oral communication – how does this impinge upon your interaction and learning within the classroom and in the service experience?
LO#2 Analyze a personal strength that you think can be applied successfully to in-class learning and community engagement.
LO#3 Analyze a belief/perception you hold to be true and subject it to scrutiny within the context of class readings, films, and the service experience.
LO#4 Examine your understanding of empathy within the context of class content and the service experience.

Evaluation

The emphasis of this class is oral proficiency; therefore, a large part of the assessment is based on participation, presentation, and improvement in oral communication skills. Written evaluation will be based on the homework exercises, the written reflections on the service-learning community engagement, two tests, and the final exam. Please note that you will not earn credit for the service itself; rather assessment and credit are based on the reflection upon and documentation of the learning that takes place through the service.

Grading Criteria

Attendance	10%
Homework & critical reflections	25%
2 Tests (including SL reflection)	20%
Partner chats	5%
Oral Presentation	5%
Conversation lab	10%
Final exam (written & oral including final SL reflection paper)	25%

Appendix 2

El Aprendizaje-Servicio (ApS) – Service Learning (SL)

El Aprendizaje-Servicio es la integración de material académico, actividades relevantes en la comunidad y la reflexión crítica en una colaboración recíproca (co-creada). Esta colaboración involucra a estudiantes, profesores y miembros de la comunidad para que los estudiantes cumplan con las metas de

enriquecimiento académico
aprendizaje cívico
crecimiento personal

Asimismo se avanzan los propósitos públicos.

- Este método de aprendizaje **no es normativo.** No se limita al aprendizaje dentro de la sala de clase, ni a un libro de texto. Más bien, se combina el aprendizaje en clase y el estudio de varios textos CON una experiencia **intencional y bien planificada en la comunidad.**
- **Es recíproco:** el proceso y la experiencia se planifican en colaboración con un profesor, unos estudiantes y una organización cívica. El aprendizaje y los beneficios de la experiencia **son recíprocos.**
- Hay que pensar en el aprendizaje-servicio en la comunidad como **una experiencia pedagógica** que hay que analizar.
- **La reflexión crítica** es fundamental para **conectar** el aprendizaje con el servicio.
- La reflexión crítica **genera, profundiza y documenta** el aprendizaje.
- **Todo merece reflexión.**

El ApS es una manera no normativa de aprender por lo cual el estudiante tiene que aprender cómo aprender, cómo crear significado (make meaning) y finalmente cómo entender el proceso mismo de este tipo de aprendizaje.

La experiencia por sí sola no significa aprendizaje. Se puede tener la experiencia y perder el significado (you can have the experience and miss the meaning). Para hacer la reflexión final, ustedes van a seguir un método de reflexión propuesto por dos estudiosas y practicantes del ApS: Las Dras. Sarah L. Ash y Patti H. Clayton.

Estas investigadoras proponen el método **D.E.A.L** para reflexionar sobre el ApS:

D – Describir la experiencia objetivamente (¿quién, qué, dónde, cuándo y por qué?)
E – Examinar la experiencia con preguntas en cada categoría de las metas de aprendizaje (crecimiento personal, aprendizaje cívico y enriquecimiento académico)
A – Articulate **L** – Learning. Articular el aprendizaje con otros contextos a través de un proceso de razonamiento con argumentos sólidos, considerando estas 4 preguntas:

- ¿Qué aprendí?
- ¿Cómo lo aprendí?
- ¿Por qué importa?
- ¿Qué puedo hacer para mejorar mi aprendizaje?

Service Learning and Community Engagement (SCLE)

Service Learning is the integration of academic material, relevant service activities in the community, and critical reflection in a reciprocal (co-created) collaboration. This collaboration involves students, teachers, and community members to help students meet the learning goals of academic enrichment, civic learning, and personal growth. Likewise, public purposes are advanced.

* *This method of learning is not normative. It is not limited to learning within the classroom, nor to a textbook. Rather, it combines in-class learning and the study of several texts* **WITH** *an intentional and well-planned experience in the community.*
* *It is reciprocal: the process and experience are planned in collaboration with a teacher, students, and a civic organization. The learning and benefits of the experience are reciprocal.*
* *Critical reflection is fundamental to connecting the service with the learning. Critical reflection* ***generates, deepens, and documents*** *learning.*
* *Everything is worthy of reflection.*

Since SCLE is a non-normative way of learning, the student has to learn how to learn, how to make meaning, and finally, how to understand the process itself of this type of learning. Experience alone does not necessarily lead to learning. You can have the experience and miss the meaning. To carry out their critical reflections, students will follow a method proposed by two scholars and practitioners of SCLE: Drs. Sarah L. Ash and Patti H. Clayton.

These researchers propose the **DEAL** *method to reflect on the SLCE:*

D-*Describe the experience objectively (who, what, where, when, and why?)*
E-*Examine the experience with questions in each category of the three learning goals (personal growth, civic learning, and academic enrichment)*
A-*Articulate* **L**-*Learning. Articulate the learning through a reasoning process with solid arguments, considering these four questions:*

* *What did I learn?*
* *How did I learn it?*
* *Why does it matter?*
* *What can I do to improve my learning?*

Part VI

Case Studies in Creative Communications

12 *¿Y tú quién eres?* Interviews as Project-Based Learning at a Multicultural College Community

Adrián Gras-Velázquez, Julia Chindemi-Vila, and Ah-Young Song

Project-based learning (PBL) is a student-driven approach to learning organized around complex tasks, in which the teacher acts as a facilitator, and students are given "ownership of the project" (Mikulec and Chamness Miller 81).[1] In this approach, there are explicit educational goals and learning outcomes, and the projects engage students in cooperative learning, problem-solving, decision making, and investigative activities. Additional defining features of project-based learning are how these learning activities offer students the "opportunity to work relatively autonomously over extended periods of time" (Thomas 1) over the course of days, weeks, or months. Activities typically culminate in the creation of a project that is shared with an authentic audience. Importantly, project-based learning within the realm of second language acquisition also promotes "communication and the functionality of language, both of which are key elements in contemporary language instruction" (Mikulec and Chamness Miller 81). Therefore, project-based learning helps integrate language learning within particular contexts and fosters the "gathering, processing, and reporting of information from target language resources" (81).

This descriptive case study traces a project-based learning assignment in a Beginning Spanish language classroom. Data collection involved examinations of student work, such as transcripts of interviews with community partners as well as student surveys completed following the class. This methodological approach allowed researchers to examine the significance of a "phenomenon . . . as it is socially enacted within a particular case" (Dyson and Genishi 10). Through an exploration of interactions between individuals situated in a foreign-language learning context, this study explores how one classroom case serves as a useful example of how project-based learning can engender and extend communities of practice for novice language learners. The *¿Y tú quién eres?* project[2] was based on a communicative approach to second language acquisition and highlighted the use of language in contextual situations, positioning the learner in a meaningful task for live purposes after three months of Spanish-language instruction. This project integrated major language learning skills (e.g., listening, speaking, reading, and writing) that students developed interdependently as they developed "communicative competence" (Mikulec and Chamness Miller 82). In this PBL unit, communicative competence was defined by the following:

1) the ability to use basic grammar structures in present and past tenses
2) the ability to comprehend general ideas in a basic interaction
3) the ability to have a simple conversation with a native speaker without reliance on English

The project also encouraged students to expand their linguistic repertoire beyond foundational literacy skills and consider how "culture plays a central role in establishing communicative competence" (82). This project encouraged language learners to engage with Spanish speakers on campus and illustrated the importance of intercultural dialogue in facilitating language acquisition.

¿Y tú quién eres? was designed for Beginner Spanish students. In this course, students completed two consecutive semesters of language instruction and met five days a week with two instructors. By the end of the second semester, learners were expected to communicate at a level of low-intermediate proficiency. The objective of this learning project was to start building a community of practice[3] in the classroom and then engage with members of the wider college community. By week nine, when the project started, the students had reached a low level of proficiency in Spanish, and engaging with a wider community of practice helped the students build their understanding of sociocultural dimensions of literacy. The aim was to encourage them to converse with diverse speakers of Hispanic[4] descent in the target language through an interview directed by the students' own questions. Centered on the goal of building cultural and global competencies, this project allowed students to appreciate the campus's cultural diversity. For students of Hispanic descent, the project also encouraged deeper engagement with fluency in their heritage language through in-person exchanges.[5]

College communities in the United States are often considered to be a microcosm of a globalized network because of the high rates of racial, cultural, and socioeconomic diversity. The term *globalization*, however, can also be considered reductive. As Waters and Brooks assert, "by capturing 'everything', globalization actually succeeds in explaining very little" (26).[6] Although the term itself is a fashionable concept that captures "the vast, complex and seemingly unstoppable changes occurring in economies and societies around the world" (26), it also potentially reduces the understanding of international environments into that of an "undifferentiated sameness" (Ley 4). This type of project-based learning therefore helps students understand their local college community from a transnational perspective and develop an appreciation of multidimensional racial, ethic, and cultural identities. As Pauwels argues, many universities have significant international student populations, and the college campus has therefore become "a multilingual and multicultural hub" (46). In addition, international faculty and staff have multicultural backgrounds that contribute to campus diversity. By interviewing Spanish-speaking students, faculty, and staff in the college community, language learners in this PBL unit could interact with a range of speakers and gain some insight into transnational experiences, while also making progress in their target language.

This project also shares some of the tenets of a *multiliteracies framework*, which positions learners to leverage a wide range of semiotic tools to connect with diverse communities, societies, and cultures (The New London Group). A pedagogy of multiliteracies assumes that "learning is not simply a series of rules to be obeyed, facts to be learned, and knowledge authorities to be followed" (Fenice and Tochelli 91). This approach strives to prepare learners for "multilingual, multicultural and, in a Bakhtinian sense, multivocal communication, digital communication, global and local participation and a complex knowledge society" (Breidbach and Küster 136). In this sense, second-language acquisition should enable students to foster social awareness and critical literacy instead of "mere instrumental skills" (136). This framework helps position both learners' identities and their social participation at the center of the learning process, inspiring them to "negotiate and generate (new) meaning in linguistically and culturally heterogeneous life worlds," while at the same time "adopting responsibility for themselves as well as for the community" (136).

A multiliteracies pedagogy involves more than just integrating "digital tools and technology, multiple modalities, or popular culture into an existing curriculum" (Boyd and Brock 2); it encourages students to engage with multiple media, such as visual, gestural, spatial, and linguistic affordances, to learn and communicate across cultures. Drawing from a pedagogy of multiliteracies requires instructors to reshape curricula that expand beyond traditional literacy skills (e.g., reading, writing, speaking, and listening) and instead include interdependent social practices "that honor the vast array of linguistic, racial, cultural, sexual, and gendered identities" (2). A multiliteracies approach attends to social diversity and the "variability of conventions of meaning in different cultural, social, or domain-specific situations" (Kalantzis and Cope, as cited in Boyd and Brock 6).

In the following sections, we present the motivations for this project, desired learning outcomes, students' engagement with components of the project, and reflective comments about pedagogy. The chapter then concludes with results from the case study, followed by a discussion about project modifications recommended for future iterations.

The Project

The idea of the project was to build a classroom community that acknowledged sociocultural dimensions of literacy and the diversity of Hispanic cultures on campus. The concept of "communities of practice" in education, as introduced by Lave and Wenger, is built around the principle that "learning is to be understood within the context of interpersonal experiences" (Breidbach and Küster 132). Second language learning is therefore a "process of individual experience, in which the learner is gradually involved and integrated in the speech community" (132). By increasing their active participation in language exchanges, students can expand their linguistic competencies. This communicative approach to language learning follows Kramsch's definition of learning activities that expose "learners as much as possible to spoken or written texts that have not been fabricated for pedagogic purposes" (185). Instead, language learners can engage in more authentic communication experiences that help them "better *understand* the speaking customs and ways of life of the target country" (185).[7] Therefore, the project was a means to develop not only language skills but also intercultural understanding, which is "valued as an equal complement to language learning and as an activity valid in its own right" (Byram et al. 10).[8] While this learning project may not be reflective of a completely impromptu or natural interaction embedded in what Collentine and Freed would term "authentic target culture situations" (156), it involved sociocultural learning through interactions with native speakers in communicative situations outside of the course.

In small groups, students researched the interviewees' national or regional backgrounds, created a list of possible interview questions, contacted the interviewee to arrange a meeting time, recorded the interview, and edited the recording for a two-to-three-minute final product to present to the class. Each student also separately composed a personal 500-word essay about what they learned from the interview, the process of working with others, and their experience with the target language. All of these activities, of course, had to be in Spanish.

The students started working on the project around week nine of the Beginning Spanish class. By then, they were familiar with the present tense form and could understand and use everyday expressions, such as basic phrases to introduce themselves and others. In speaking to their interviewees, students could use any of the Spanish-language forms of address (tú/usted/vosotros/ustedes) as long as they were consistent. They could also ask and answer questions about personal details, such as likes, dislikes, locations of residence, and basic information about a person. Students were proficient enough to complete project tasks without major difficulties, including the creation of meaningful questions to communicate in the target language at a basic level during the interview.

Part of the reasoning for the timing of this project was to test the probabilistic model of language processing and acquisition at a novice level. Language is often represented in Chomskian terms as a natural and inherent system of grammar, or a "system of rules that specifies all and only allowable sentences" (Chater and Manning 336). However, language rules are also somewhat ambiguous,[9] as grammar is often shaped by particular contexts and situations. As Chater and Manning express, language use, "with probabilities of use, [is] capturing what is linguistically likely, not just what is linguistically possible" (335). Students can generalize concepts from sparse linguistic data, an ability that is crucial for learning not only the meaning of words but also "the properties of objects, cause-effect relations, social rules, and many other domains of knowledge" (Tenenbaum et al. 309). Similarly, Seidenberg notes that language learning varies because it consists of both standardized and nonstandardized grammar patterns that are at times indiscernible to the learner. By engaging with the community outside of the classroom, students are able to use grammar at a dialogical or sociocultural level. Working with linguistically and culturally diverse people allows them to develop linguistic strategies to sustain interpersonal communication, exposes them to grammatical exceptions to conventional rules, and enhances understandings of regional and cultural differences.

The Process

Before the project-based learning unit, the course professors undertook several tasks to set the project in motion, including finding interviewees, arranging for media equipment, and structuring the project into a feasible timeframe with specific deadlines and guidance points for students. For students, important project tasks involved conducting background research, preparing questions for the interview, recording the exchange with a device, editing the interview, and presenting the product to their classmates. The following sections elaborate further on the professors' and students' roles for this PBL unit.

Professor-Led Tasks

Finding Community Members to Participate as Interviewees

The class of 20 students was divided into five groups of four to five students, with each group interviewing one community member from the college campus. Therefore, professors strove to find a minimum of five people to interview, with the aim of having as much national diversity within the interviewees as possible. They chose not to include interviewees who shared the instructors' countries of origin so that students could engage with community members with different cultural backgrounds and regionalisms. The professors wanted students to have access to a variety of people across the college community, so they looked for not only faculty members but also students and staff who would be willing to participate in the project. The professors of the course endeavored to connect student groups with a Spanish-speaking member of the college community at large, rather than just a professor in the modern languages department.

The professors reached out to potential interviewees through personal connections, such as volunteers across Hispanic social organizations at the college. Five candidates were selected (See Table 12.1), with demographic information outlined in the following table:

Table 12.1 Interviewees general demographic information

Candidate	*Job*	*Gender*	*Nationality*[10]	*Age Group*
1	Faculty	Female	Cuban	31–40
2	Staff	Male	Puerto Rican	31–40
3	Staff	Female	Mexican	31–40
4	Student	Male	Mexican	21–30
5	Staff	Female	Mexican	21–30

Once the interviewees were confirmed, the professors paired each group of students with one interviewee. They introduced the students to the candidate over email, offered some basic information about the interviewee (name and position within the college community), and provided students deadlines for the interviews and final project.

The Media/Technology Component

The professors worked with the college's IT and media department to simplify the technological component of the project for students. Students needed unobtrusive recording equipment that would not detract from the interview exchange since, as Blake summarizes, "a second language is best learned and taught through interaction" (3). They used the Zoom H1 Handy Recorder, a portable audio recorder whose auto-level function prevented sound distortion and supported WAV and MP3 files for easy editing. The primary audio editing program was Audacity, which professors recommended to students because it was a free, open-source, cross-platform software that was easily accessible online.

Setting the Time Frame and Facilitating the Opening Conversation

The professors set the following time frame (See Table 12.2), with particular professor- and student-directed tasks:

Table 12.2 Professor- and student-directed tasks

Week	*Activity*	*Student (S)/ Professor (P) led*
9	—Create groups	P
	—Recruit volunteer interviewees	P
	—Pair groups with interviewees	P
	—Facilitate an initial class discussion	P
10	—Conduct cultural and background	S
	research	S
	—Prepare questions	P
	—Give feedback on questions	
11	—Begin recording interviews	S
12	—Continue recording interviews	S
	—Edit interviews	S
13	—Complete final edits and prepare	S
	for presentation	S
	—Optional: Submit first draft of essay	P
	—Provide feedback on first draft	
14	—Present projects	S
	—Grade projects	P

At the beginning of the unit, the professors organized an initial discussion to elicit students' thoughts on the project and to frame tasks. The discussion had two goals: to make the students more aware of campus diversity and to discuss the linguistic and social differences across cultures. The class started with an open discussion of general topics about the college community, such as meals in the cafeterias, schedules, academics, sports, family, and jobs.

Afterward, the professors focused the conversation around the following topics:

- how international students talk about their personal experiences and cultural differences
- how Hispanic members of the community talk about their background and family traditions in the US
- how different community members talk about regionalisms and cultural differences
- how students connect immigration to the cultural diversity of the United States
- who speaks Spanish in the United States and why
- what kind of jobs students associate with Hispanic immigrants and why
- what stereotypes students associate with Hispanic communities in the US
- who speaks Spanish in the college community and from which countries they originate.

Student-Led Tasks

Research and Preparation

After the initial discussion in class, students had two main tasks before the interviews. First, once they learned about their interviewee's country of origin, they conducted research using various online resources on relevant customs and cultural practices. This background research supplemented intercultural exchanges and the development of linguistic competence while engaging "with complexity and multiple identities" rather than stereotyping during the interview (Byram et al. 9).

However, acquiring intercultural competence is an ongoing and unfinished process (7). Thus, the aim of conducting research was not the "transmission of information about a foreign country" (14) in a decontextualized manner. Gaining an understanding of the interviewee's general cultural, social, and national background allows students to prepare themselves to understand

- how intercultural interaction takes place,
- how social identities are part of all interaction[s],
- how their perceptions of other people and other people's perceptions of them influence the success of communication,
- how they can find out for themselves more about the people with whom they are communicating.

(Byram et al. 14)

This pre-interview research also built on previous in-class discussions about diverse Hispanic communities on campus. As Byram and colleagues state, "[U]nderstanding the target culture" is sometimes seen as "a support to linguistic proficiency" (7), but this project encouraged that cultural learning was "valued as an equal complement to language learning and as an activity valid in its own right" (10). This kind of exercise could also help dispel the danger of culture "being limited to the all-too-familiar stereotypical icons of the target culture" and the belief "that there is one authoritative account of another country and its cultures, that there is a 'real' account which only the native speaker can know" (11).

The second activity was for groups to create a series of questions to ask their interviewees. To promote creativity and spontaneity, the professors did not place restrictions on the types of questions, and students were free to explore any subjects that seemed interesting or pertinent during the interview. Professors also encouraged the students to depart from the script and delve into unplanned topics if they wished, but not many ended up asking questions that had not been previously written down, except for some clarifying questions. Once they formed their list of questions, professors checked them for grammar and spelling. The groups had different approaches but similar levels of proficiency. The following are examples[11] of questions that students decided to use or discard for the final interviews, based on time constraints or relevance of the topics:

Questions Used During the Interviews

1) ¿Como se llama usted?
   What is your name?
2) ¿De dónde es tu familia?
   Where is your family from?
3) ¿Tienes hermanos o eres un hijo único?
   Do you have siblings, or are you an only child?
4) ¿Que lugares viviste antes llegando a Swarthmore?
   What places did you live before coming to Swarthmore?
5) ¿Como sabes español?
   How do you know Spanish?
6) Cual es tu trabajo en Swarthmore? ¿Cuáles son sus principales responsabilidades?
   What is your job at Swarthmore? What are your primary responsibilities?
7) ¿Qué haces en tu tiempo libre?
   What do you do in your free time?
8) ¿Cuál es el mejor parte de estar trabajando en Swarthmore? ¿Cual es el peor parte?
   What is the best part about working at Swarthmore? And, what is the worst part?
9) ¿Cual es tu comida favorita?
   What is your favorite food?
10) Cual es uno consejo que usted tiene por los estudiantes en el clase de espanol?
    What is one piece of advice you have for the students in Spanish class?

Students were reminded to be mindful of certain syntactical, grammatical, and linguistic norms, but professors did not make explicit corrections on their papers. As agents of their own learning, students drew from their class notes and books to make their own corrections. After receiving feedback on spelling and grammar, students had two weeks to finalize questions, get in touch with their interviewees, schedule a time and place to meet, and send questions ahead of the interview. All communication had to be in Spanish, and at the end of the project, all emails and recordings had to be submitted to the professors for the purpose of grading either as a Zip file or shared through Google Drive.

Interview Recording and Editing

In project-based learning, students gain knowledge and skills through problem-solving, critical thinking, collaboration, and self-management. Finding resources and applying information are key elements of this approach. Students can also make their own decisions and take charge of their project after considering certain constraints, such as time and resources. Although professors were available if there were any questions, students had total freedom on how to conduct and edit the interviews. Students edited their recordings on Audacity and downloaded five- to ten-minute recordings into a cohesive, two-minute piece that they then emailed to the professors, in addition to the raw recordings.

Final Product, Presentations, and Product Display

Due to unforeseen technical and timing circumstances,[12] students were unable to share the audio interviews in a manner that did justice to the time and effort that they had taken to complete the project. Therefore, the class did not have the opportunity to experience one of the most essential parts of project-based learning: exhibiting the final product to a larger community.[13] As Larmer and Mergendoller assert, "[S]chool-work is more meaningful when it's not done only for the teacher or the test" (37). As the following section will demonstrate, displaying the final product for a wider audience is an integral part of project-based learning and must be considered in order for students to benefit fully from the PBL activity.

Results

An effective way to assess skills at low proficiency levels is to apply a holistic criteria[14] and make a general assessment of a student's level of performance as a speaker, writer, and learner. However, it is also possible to take into account analytical criteria that, although often used at higher levels, can serve as guidance for the instructor in any evaluation task.

Group Interviews

The evaluation of students groups' written and oral work were considered using a very simplified rubric (see Table 12.3). Overall, students engaged in different kinds of negotiation strategies and responded to implicit feedback from fellow group members or from interviewees to keep the conversation moving forward and resolve minor misunderstandings. Students engaged in simple but effective interactional modifications like comprehension checks and error reformations. For example, during their conversation with one of the members of staff (an Environmental Building Services employee), students had the following exchange:

STUDENT: *¿Nosotros tenemos . . . tienes las cucarachas . . . nosotros tenemos en los dormitorios?*/Do we have . . . you have cockroaches . . . we have in the bedrooms?

Table 12.3 Evaluation rubric

	5	*4–3*	*2–1*	*0*
Interview Preparation Score______	The group prepared many questions to ask.	The group prepared between four and five questions to ask.	The group prepared less than three questions to ask.	The group did not prepare any questions.
Communication Skills Score_____	The students listened carefully to the person being interviewed and asked several relevant follow-up questions and/or made clarifications.	The students listened carefully to the person being interviewed and asked at least a relevant follow-up question and/or made clarifications.	The students listened to the interviewee but did not ask any relevant questions or make clarifications. Students did not engage with interviewee.	Incomprehensible (due to language misuse or technical issues) communication or lack of audio sample.
Mechanics (Writing) Score: _____	No grammatical, spelling, or punctuation errors.	A few grammatical, spelling, or punctuation errors.	Many grammatical, spelling, or punctuation errors.	Too many mistakes OR no writing sample.
Final Product Score: _____	The students edited and organized the audio interview in a way that made the information clear and interesting.	The students edited and organized the audio interview in a way that made the information clear or interesting.	The students edited and organized the audio interview, but the information was not as clear or as interesting as it could have been.	The students did a poor job editing and organizing the audio interview, or the students did not edit it.
Final Score				

INTERVIEWEE: *Una vez más . . . Repíteme la pregunta . . .* /Again . . . Ask me the question again . . .

STUDENT: *Oh, si . . . ¿Tenemos las cucarachas? Porque nosotros tenemos en nuestros dormitorios . . .* /Oh, yeah . . . Do we have cockroaches? Because we have [cockroaches] in our bedrooms.

INTERVIEWEE: *¿Ustedes tienen cucarachas en sus dormitorios? Lo único que te puedo decir es no comas en tu cuarto . . .* /Do you have cockroaches in your bedroom? All I can say is do not eat in your room.

This excerpted conversation illustrates how students were able to engage actively in the conversation using beginning Spanish language skills and respond instantly to the interviewee with incremental adjustments based on perceived misunderstandings, especially as interviewees asked for repeated questions and modeled more conventional structures and phrasings.

The interviewees also responded to students' clarification requests, as exemplified by this interaction[15] between a group of interviewers and another college employee:

STUDENT 2: *¿A ti te gusta la comida de Swarthmore?*/Do you like the food at Swarthmore?

INTERVIEWEE: *¿La comida de Swarthmore? Pues bueno, esta tarde, en la tarde comí en Sharples,*[16] *no está tan mal, está bastante bien . . .* /Food at Swarthmore? Well, this afternoon, this afternoon I ate at Sharples, it is not that bad, it is quite good . . .

STUDENT 2: *¿Cual es tu comida favorita?*/What is your favorite food?

INTERVIEWEE: *¿En el mundo?*/In the world?

STUDENT 2: *Si.*/Yes.

INTERVIEWEE: *Pues, como comida individual* jitomate, *en México, o tomate en general, misma cosa, tiene diferente nombre y cheesecake.*/Well, as a single food *jitomate*, in Mexico, or tomato in general, same thing, it has a different name in México and cheesecake.

Interviewees' follow-up questions often helped lead students to advance conversations, as this example evolved from a discussion about local to worldwide contexts.

Most students demonstrated mastery of basic grammatical structures that enabled them to complete the interview. They were able to ask and answer questions about personal details, even while using only the present tense, as exemplified by this conversation between one of the groups and a faculty member:

STUDENT 3: *¿Cuándo empiezas enseñar en Swarthmore?*/When do you start teaching at Swarthmore?

INTERVIEWEE: *Empecé en septiembre de este año, así que sólo hace 3 o 4 meses*/I started in September this year, so only 3 or 4 months ago.

Although students were at a more novice level of Spanish, these fluid exchanges with interviewees helped them understand the distinctions between past and present tenses. Some students even asked for explicit explanations about interviewees' biographical details, such as where they had been born. These options for differentiation gave students the freedom to direct and demonstrate their own learning within a community of practice in ways that traditional multiple choice exams might not have allowed.

Students' Survey Responses[17]

At the beginning, some students seemed indifferent to the project, as exemplified by Student 2's feelings about the assignment at the start of the PBL unit: "*I was pretty neutral about the idea, but it was fine doing it.*" At the conclusion, however, many of the students expressed enjoying the project, as they noted in their post-project questionnaire responses. Student 1 stated,

> *At first I was really reluctant to do this project but it turned out I actually really liked it. I liked getting to hear the perspective of the person I interviewed on his culture and how he felt that fit into going to a liberal arts college in America.*

This sense of enjoyment and learning from the interactions with members of the college community was echoed in many of the responses.

The students' most significant concern about the project had been their relatively low level of Spanish proficiency. At the beginning, they were concerned that their Spanish was not "*good enough*" to communicate with someone outside of the classroom setting. Student 3 stated, "*I didn't feel really comfortable having a conversation with a native speaker that early in my Spanish-learning experience.*" Student 4 feared not only the language barrier but also a cultural one, explaining, "*I just needed to be reassured that I wasn't going to embarrass myself or offend the person I was talking to.*" Students felt unsure whether the wording in the questions could be misinterpreted or lost in translation, resulting in intercultural miscommunication.

After completing the project, however, students stated that they felt "*more comfortable with the language*" (Student 5), especially across multiple dialects (Student 3). Students had the benefit of being able to talk to a native speaker who understood the nature of the project. The interviewees were aware of the students' limited exposure to the language and were "*not judgmental*" (Student 6). Therefore, they "*at no point made us feel stupid or attempted to use language he knew we wouldn't understand*" (Student 2). Student 2 also enjoyed being able to create questions that "*you could ask anyone in any language from any place, but then hearing how his cultural experience led him to have a very different response than I would have had*" (Student 2). Students learned about cultural differences, noting that native Spanish speakers "*had to adjust to other Spanish-speaking folks who didn't have the same heritage as her. At the college they were kind of all lumped into the same group*" (Student 4). In addition, as Student 5 noted, listening to the whole audio conversation multiple times in order to create the two- to three-minute piece helped them "*really understand*" the language "*in order to edit it*."

At the same time, Student 2 added that the project highlighted how much they still needed to learn in order to master a second language: "*I think it put in perspective how much we needed a native speaker to slow down in order for us to understand, which is kind of a bummer to realize*." While the PBL unit facilitated students' understanding and use of more complex Spanish dialogue, they also recognized the relative levels of experience that distinguished them from native speakers.

Conclusions

The project helped expose lower-proficiency students to authentic conversations that placed them in interactive settings that exceeded basic linguistic skills. Through the use of a communicative approach to language learning, the project offered a balance between comprehension and production skills at the beginner's level. As Han and D'Angelo assert, learners may rely on non-linguistic information, such as "contextual clues and world knowledge" to infer meaning (178–179). Furthermore, the project drew from the language socialization framework that emphasizes the "development of linguistic, cultural, and communicative competence through interaction with others who are more knowledgeable or proficient" (Duff and Talmy 95). By understanding language through contextual semantics, students could then practice the target language at the beginning level, while also practicing grammar, syntax, and vocabulary that might not have been covered in a traditional classroom unit. The students became familiar with more advanced grammar structures through conversations with native speakers that would be solidified later on in the course curriculum and beyond.

Students developed linguistic and sociocultural understandings, and they felt more "comfortable" with the language, in part due to the native speaker's linguistic accommodations for the learners. More fluent speakers were clearly attentive to the varying needs of a novice speaker's vocabulary, language structure, and pace, which helped learners of Spanish not only improve their language skills but feel equipped to communicate without fear of judgment. In this way, students developed their language skills in part because of the native speakers' social allowances, which helped them feel a sense of acceptance and a capacity to take risks as less-experienced speakers.

Lecture-based classes with strict formal instruction driven by the instructors could offer similar learning outcomes in regards to grammar and vocabulary, but this project supported students' capacity to engage in a wider community of practice with native speakers. As Duff and Talmy contend, language socialization exercises promote a sense of "agency, contingency, unpredictability, and multidirectionality" in learners (97). Interview-based projects promote active learning, as students navigate and transform conventional language practices.

This PBL assignment also encouraged lifelong skills such as critical thinking, decision making, cross-cultural understanding, problem-solving, collaboration, communication, and technological fluency. Projects like this provide opportunities for greater engagement with the broader community outside of a single classroom. Learning is then situated across social contexts through the exchange of emails, the formation of interview questions, relevant research of cultural backgrounds, and interviewing and editing processes.

To further improve and expand the activity, instructors might consider having more in-class practice, which students suggested as a modification for future classes. Professors could assign a class activity in which students could interview and record each other to develop greater confidence and fluency. In addition, per the students' recommendation, instructors might invite students to create a shared set of questions to ask their interviewees and make cross-cultural comparisons during a later class. This activity could serve an in-class exercise in which questions are modeled, brainstormed independently, and then discussed in small groups. However, students should not be limited to only these questions, since part of the exercise is to encourage learners to develop their own creative ideas and respond with extemporaneous follow-up questions.

A second-semester activity could also involve more intensive work with native speakers on a series of mini-projects that could provide more comprehensive insights into the diversity of the campus community. These smaller exercises could be linked to different grammatical points. For instance, a series of photographs of interviewees' daily lives could be used to practice the present or present perfect tense. Or a short narrative of interviewee's childhoods could help students learn the two basic past tenses in Spanish, the preterit and the imperfect. Interviewees could also share a list of their short- and long-term plans to help students practice the future and the conditional tenses. In addition, students could collaborate with community members to co-construct a rubric that could be used in their final assessment. This process could help engage students in building their own accountability standards rather than having an instructor independently define the scoring criteria.

As previously mentioned, the audio interviews could not be displayed because of technical issues, but with sufficient planning and coordination, this project could be part of an exhibition. During the last weeks of the semester, students could share their work, answering questions and offering reflections on the project to friends, interviewees, and interested community members. They could also contribute to a larger campus-wide activity, such as Hispanic Appreciation Week.

While most literature on project-based learning underscores frameworks that facilitate the process of language acquisition at higher levels, this case study serves as an example of what is possible when novice Spanish speakers participate in an interview project. Overall, the *¿Y tú quién eres?* project demonstrates that many of the benefits of project-based learning can be successfully implemented and adapted for beginning learners.

Acknowledgments

The authors wish to thank all of the fall 2015 SPAN001: Intensive First Year Spanish students for their participation and the Department of Modern Languages and Literatures at Swarthmore College for their support at the time.

Notes

1. See Stoller "Project Work" or "Establishing a Theoretical Foundation" or Haines for further definitions and discussions of the main features in PBL.
2. This project took place during the fall 2015 academic year while the two Spanish professors were teaching at Swarthmore College.
3. A community of practice provides a learning context in which students can simultaneously build knowledge of language and communicate in a foreign language across a range of contexts and activities (Hall).
4. The term "Hispanic," rather tan "Latinx," was preferred by the interviewees.
5. As Kern states, "It is important not to lose sight of the fact that what one sees on one's computer screen is a highly mediated, filtered, and designed version of the world" (341). Online venues for second language acquisition can be beneficial and enhance the class environment (see, for example, Clark and Feldon, Butcher, or Erneling), but this particular project stressed the interactivity of face-to-face encounters.
6. See also Block and Cameron, Blommaert, or Gorter for a discussion about the homogenizing effect of the term *globalization* and its contradictions.
7. Emphasis in original.
8. See Byram et al. for a discussion on language and culture learning theory (4–40). See also Kramsch ("The Cultural Component") for an interesting discussion on the cultural component of language pedagogy.
9. Instructors can, for example, make students aware that standardized grammar rules presented in class are not infallible and that at times there are exceptions to the rule.
10. The nationalities of the interviewees varied in official citizenship and heritage. The only requirement for volunteers was that Spanish had to be a primary language in the home, either as the dominant language or in conjunction with English.
11. Questions are transcribed without corrections as to best exemplify the students' levels of Spanish at the time of the project.

12. Several groups needed extra time because of their interviewees' schedules, while one group had to re-do their interview several days later, after realizing that they had not in fact recorded it properly.
13. See Larmer and Mergendoller, Boss and Krauss, or Cooper and Murphy for more on culminating activities and the need to showcase students' work.
14. For a discussion on the benefits and pitfalls of a holistic approach to grading, see Charney or Sadler ("Indeterminacy," "Transforming Holistic Assessment").
15. The transcriptions are directly taken from students' own work, so any non-standard spelling and punctuation choices are inherent to the original texts.
16. Sharples is Swarthmore College's dining hall.
17. Of the 20-plus students in the class, only eight agreed to answer a questionnaire regarding the project. The low number of responses was due in part to the fact that questionnaires were sent during the summer, when students do not always check their emails with great frequency, rather than during the semester in which this course was offered.

References

Allen, Heather Willis. "Embracing Literacy-Based Teaching: A Longitudinal Study of the Conceptual Development of Novice Foreign Language Teachers." *Research on Second Language Teacher Education: A Sociocultural Perspective on Professional Development*, edited by Karen E. Johnson K and Paula R. Golombek. Routledge, 2011, pp. 86–101.

Blake, Robert J. *Brave New Digital Classroom: Technology and Foreign Language Learning*. Georgetown University Press, 2008.

Block, David, and Deborah Cameron. *Globalization and Language Teaching*. Routledge, 2002.

Blommaert, Jan. *The Sociolinguistics of Globalization*. Cambridge University Press, 2010.

Boss, Suzie, and Jane Krauss. *Reinventing Project-Based Learning: Your Field Guide to Real-World Projects in the Digital Age*. 2nd ed. International Society for Technology in Education, 2014.

Boyd, Fenice B., and Cynthia H. Brock. "Reflections on the Past, Working Within the "Future": Advancing a Multiliteracies Theory and Pedagogy." *Social Diversity Within Multiliteracies: Complexity in Teaching and Learning*, edited by Fenice B. Boyd and Cynthia H. Brock. Routledge, 2015, pp. 1–10.

Breidbach, Stephan, and Lutz Küster. "'Bildung', 'Multiliteracies' and 'Identity' – Key Concepts in Language Education in the Light of Sociocultural Theory and Dynamic Systems Theory." *Plurilingualism and Multiliteracies: International Research on Identity Construction in Language Education*, edited by Dagmar Abendroth-Timmer and Eva-Maria Hennig. Peter Lang, 2014, pp. 129–144.

Butcher, Kirsten R. "The Multimedia Principle." *The Cambridge Handbook of Multimedia Learning*, 2nd ed., edited by Richard E. Mayer. Cambridge University Press, 2014, pp. 174–205.

Byram, Michael, et al. *Teaching-and-Learning Language-and-Culture*. Multilingual Matters Ltd, 1994.

———, et al. *Developing the Intercultural Dimension in Language Teaching: A Practical Introduction for Teachers*. Council of Europe, 2002.

Charney, Davida. "The Validity of Using Holistic Scoring to Evaluate Writing: A Critical Overview." *Research in the Teaching of English*, vol. 18, no. 1, 1984, pp. 65–81.

Chater, Nick, and Christopher D. Manning. "Probabilistic Models of Language Processing and Acquisition." *Trends in Cognitive Sciences*, vol. 10, no. 7, 2006, pp. 335–344.

Clark, Richard E., and David F. Feldon. "Ten Common But Questionable Principles of Multimedia Learning." *The Cambridge Handbook of Multimedia Learning*, 2nd ed., edited by Richard E. Mayer. Cambridge University Press, 2014, pp. 151–173.

Collentine, Joseph, and Barbara F. Freed. "Learning Context and Its Effect on Second Language Acquisition." *Studies in Second Language Acquisition*, vol. 26, 2204, pp. 153–171.

Cooper, Ross, and Erin M. Murphy. *Hacking Project Based Learning: 10 Easy Steps to PBL and Inquiry in the Classroom*. Times 10 Publications, 2016.

Duff, Paula A., and Steven Talmy. "Language Socialization Approaches to Second Language Acquisition: Social, Cultural, and Linguistic Development in Additional Languages." *Alternative Approaches to Second Language Acquisition*, edited by Dwight Atkinson. Routledge, 2011, pp. 95–116.

Dyson, Anne Haas, and Celia Genishi. *On the Case: Approaches to Language and Literacy Research*. Teachers College Press, 2005.

Erneling Christina E. *Towards Discursive Education: Philosophy, Technology, and Modern Education*. Cambridge University Press, 2010.

Gorter, Durk. *Linguistic Landscape: A New Approach to Multilingualism*. Multilingual Matters, 2006.

Haines, Simon. *Projects for the EFL Classroom: Resource Material for Teachers*. Thomas Nelson, 1989.

Hall, Mark R. "Theory in/to Practice: Using Dialogic Reflection to Develop a Writing Center Community of Practice." *The Writing Center Journal*, vol. 31, no. 1, 2011, pp. 82–105.

Han, ZhaoHong, and Amy D'Angelo. "Balancing Between Comprehension and Acquisition: Proposing a Dual Approach." *Second Language Reading, Research and Instruction: Crossing the Boundaries*, edited by ZhaoHong Han and Neil J. Anderson. The University of Michigan Press, 2009, pp. 173–191.

Kalantzis, Mary, and Bill Cope. *Literacies*. Cambridge University Press, 2012.

Kern, Richard. "Technology as Pharmakon: The Promise and Perils of the Internet for Foreign Language Education." *The Modern Language Journal*, vol. 98, no. 1, 2014, pp. 340–357.

Kramsch, Claire. *Context and Culture in Language Teaching*. Oxford University Press, 1993.

———. "The Cultural Component of Language Teaching." *Language, Culture and Curriculum*, vol. 8, no. 2, 1995, pp. 83–92.

Larmer, John, and John R. Mergendoller. "Seven Essentials for Project-Based Learning." *Educational Leadership*, vol. 68, no. 1, 2010, pp. 34–37.

Lave, Jean, and Etienne Wenger. *Situated Learning. Legitimate Peripheral Participation*. Cambridge University Press, 1991.

Ley, David. *Millionaire Migrants: Trans-Pacific Life Lines*. Wiley-Blackwell, 2010.

Mikulec, Erin, and Paul Chamness Miller. "Using Project-Based Instruction to Meet Foreign Language Standards." *The Clearing House: A Journal of Educational Strategies, Issues and Ideas*, vol. 84, no. 3, 2011, pp. 81–86.

The New London Group. "A Pedagogy of Multiliteracies: Designing Social Futures." *Harvard Educational Review*, vol. 66, no. 1, 1996, pp. 60–93.

Pauwels, Anne "Rethinking the Learning of Languages in the Context of Globalisation and Hyperlingualism." *Plurilingualism and Multiliteracies: International Research on Identity Construction in Language Education*, edited by In Dagmar Abendroth-Timmer and Eva-Maria Hennig. Peter Lang, 2014, pp. 41–56.

"Reaching Global Competence." *American Council on the Teaching of Foreign Languages (ACTFL)*, 2004. www.actfl.org/sites/default/files/GlobalCompetence PositionStatement0814.pdf. Accessed 12 March 2017.

Sadler, Royce D. "Indeterminacy in the Use of the Present Criteria for Assessment and Grading." *Assessment & Evaluation in Higher Education*, vol. 34, no. 2, 2009a, pp. 159–179.

———. "Transforming Holistic Assessment and Grading Into a Vehicle for Complex Learning." *Assessment, Learning and Judgement in Higher Education*, edited by Gordon Joughin. Springer, 2009b, pp. 45–63.

Seidenberg, Mark S. "Language Acquisition and Use: Learning and Applying Probabilistic Constrains." *Science*, vol. 275, no. 5306, 1997, pp. 1599–1603.

Stoller, Fredricka L. "Project Work: A Means to Promote Language and Content." *Methodology in Language Teaching: An Anthology of Current Practice*, edited by Jack C. Richards and Willy A. Renandya. Cambridge University Press, 2002, pp. 107–118.

———. "Establishing a Theoretical Foundation for Project-Based Learning in Second and Foreign Language Contexts." *Project-Based Second and Foreign Language Education: Past, Present, and Future*, edited by Gulbahar H. Beckett and Paul Chamness Miller. Information Age Publishing, 2006, pp. 19–40.

Tenenbaum, Joshua B., et al. "Theory-based Bayesian Models of Inductive Learning and Reasoning." *Trends in Cognitive Sciences*, vol. 10, no. 7, 2006, pp. 309–318.

Thomas, John W. "A Review of Research on Project-Based Learning." 2000. www.bie.org/object/document/a_review_of_research_on_project_based_learning. Accessed 9 May 2017.

Waters, Johanna, and Rachel Brooks. "Transnational Spaces, International Students: Emergent Perspectives on Educational Mobilities." *Changing Spaces of Education: New Perspectives on the Nature of Learning*, edited by Rachel Brooks, et al. Routledge, 2012, pp. 21–38.

13 Every Poem Matters

World Language Acquisition and Community Building Through Spoken-Word Poetry

Inés Arribas

Spoken-word poetry, a form of poetry specifically written to be performed, is live poetry. Slam poetry, the version of spoken-word performed for a live audience as part of a contest, is a collective art of poetic delivery, which brings into play an array of voices, words, and emotions. The poetry slam – the competition itself – is an increasingly popular artistic, cultural, and social movement in most urban centers on an international scale, which makes of poetry a living spectacle that fully engages those involved in it. It sets in motion a large communication system between the poets and their audience, as it seeks to establish a first-hand relationship between the public and the poets through a flexible, participatory, and dynamic format. Poetry slam is about performance, community, and audience (Eleveld). It is a link between writing and performance that encourages the poets to focus on what they say and how they say it.

When used as a teaching tool in the world language classroom, spoken-word poetry presents an array of pedagogical possibilities for students and instructors. By the workshops that I have led in my Spanish language classes, I have observed that the creation of original poetic texts and their performance enable students to embark on a personal journey through the language they learn and to become the active agents of their language acquisition. Because they become the holders of their learning process, they usually acquire a greater sense of accomplishment, while they create bonds with their peers. Poetry workshops and slams are also spaces where a sense of community develops and builds itself. All students become poets and discover their classmates in that function. Writing and performing poetry is a way to open up one's soul and to trust others to acknowledge it. And for a poet, being able to move an audience with one's own creative words is the best reward that proves the power of spoken-word poetry.

After discussing the advantages and challenges of integrating this form of project-based learning (PBL) in the language classroom, I provide instructional samples implemented in Spanish classes at the intermediate level and above in a college context that demonstrate the process of the L2 acquisition through this motivating method.

History of Poetry Slam/Slam Poetry in the US and Spanish-Speaking Countries

The Poetry Slam was born some forty years ago in the United States, originating in the Black Arts Movement (Thomas). In the 1980s, construction worker Marc Kelly Smith gave a new breath to oral poetry by organizing poetic competitions at the Green Mill Tavern in Chicago. He called them "slams," as in boxing slams, positioning oral poetry against the rigid conventions of its written form. Smith wanted the public to constitute the jury and gave them the chance to have a voice in their evaluations and preferences. The stage was open to all; it became a free forum for expression and exchange. Every week, slammers from diverse backgrounds would gather in bars or clubs to engage in real poetic battles (Hewitt 21). This is how "slam poetry resurrected the spoken-word literary tradition" (Smith xxxiii). This collective art advocating free expression and creativity without limit had everything to conquer many audiences.

Marc Kelly Smith did initiate poetry slam in Chicago; however, throughout social history, oral literature and poetry have always been fundamental in communicating all aspects of the human condition. Already in Greek antiquity, accompanied by a lyre, the poets recited poems on a vast array of topics. The minstrels and troubadours in the European Middle Ages were in charge of transmitting and composing oral poetry, touring villages and castles where they performed dances, songs, and poetry of all sorts. Today, the *griots* in West African culture, the Basque *bertsolaris* (*bertzolaritza*), and the Italian *canto a braccio* are examples of how traditions of oral poetry existing in the world since ancient times have remained vibrant and healthy. Several of these traditions included poetry competitions, like the literary *Justas* popular in the time of Cervantes's Spain or the demanding Puerto Rican *décimas* dating back to the 19th century or even the *payadas* of the Southern Cone. Furthermore, the types of performance in which two or more adversaries measure their poetic capacity in front of an audience that is often also in charge of judging them is actually common to many cultures and times. We could name very different competitive poetic acts typical of different times and places, from the flyting in the Anglo-Saxon sphere to the *cantastori* and *stornellatori* in Italy, the already mentioned Basque *bertsolaris*, the Galician *enchoiadas*, the *Trovos* of the Alpujarra (Spain), or the Cuban *repentismo*. Many of these forms here are still preserved today in a very vital state. In this sense, modern poetry slam is not a new concept but can be seen as homage to those times when oral communication was the most widespread way to connect with the world. They consolidate the literary tradition of orality.

There are national and international poetry slams, slams of women, slams of young people, and bilingual slams in schools, to name just a few. These cultural practices continue to grow and to build communities of slammers and poetry fans. It is becoming a notable platform for people to "take the floor" in a literary sense in many cities and towns around the world, hosted by multiple cultural institutions, universities and schools, museums, libraries, and bars. In the Spanish-speaking world, numerous cities in countries such as Mexico (2007), Spain (2008),[1] Guatemala (2011), Colombia (2013), Argentina (2013), Chile (2013), Costa Rica (2014), and Peru (2014) have embraced the genre with art and passion.

Nowadays, the Poetry Slam is a vibrant artistic and social movement on every continent. The topics addressed in the poems are extremely varied, from love, the pursuit of happiness, and mere plays with words to social issues and current events, such as racism, women's rights, oppression, politics, violence, sexuality, or identity. The poetry slam serves then as a platform to address these issues and to give a voice to oppressed groups of people. As Laura Wagner points out, "It is an empowering and influential form of activism that plays an important role in the progression of social change." It is, most of all, a space that opens the path for community building and shared emotions.

Poetry slams carry specific rules that the slammers must respect: each poem must be an original text, no props are allowed, and the performance is limited to three minutes. The goal of the poets is to "seduce" the audience and jury with the poetic quality of their text, their voice, and their staging abilities. Five members from the audience are picked randomly as jury and give marks based on their emotional and intellectual reaction to the performance (Glazner 13). In an academic setting, as Jamie Banks remarks, it is "a powerful statement about who gets to decide what good art is, and potentially powerful for students in a classroom just as much as for adults at a performance venue." The rest of the audience can question or approve the grading of the jury by interjecting or applauding their decision. The season's finalists of contests held in major cities get to compete in national slams, which eventually culminate in the Poetry Slam World Cup, held once a year in Paris.

Slam Poetry as a Pedagogical Tool in the World Language Classroom – Why?

Over the last decade, the idea of implementing performance poetry in the English class curriculum in the United States has seduced more than one teacher of English, from elementary schools all the way to college. It constitutes a new approach to teaching poetry and a new manner to develop writing and oral skills, as it encourages students to write about their own lives in their own words, to perform these stories before their peers, and to share with them a common experience. Martina Pfeiler explains,

> The crucial difference between a silent discourse in the world of reading and a live performance is that it lacks something of a communal atmosphere that surrounds poetry events. One's own attendance takes the perception of poetry to a different level. In a simple way, this means that we engage with poetry individually as well as with other people's receptions to the poem by joining in their laughter or applause; we also experience the poet as a living artist.
>
> (76)

The "communal atmosphere" created by this group event here is certainly one of the most important elements of this activity, as we will discuss later.

In spoken-word poetry, words and sounds are protagonists. Poetry in general touches our senses, our inner being, our intellect, and our imagination, as it directly stimulates our emotions and transforms us. But the performative part of slam poetry is even more empowering, both for the poets who deliver their poems and the members of the audience who are impacted by them. As a matter of fact, several practices of slam poetry in the classroom have proven that, as Grace Rubenstein vehemently states,

> Through slam poetry, students reach new heights in literacy and in life. . . . In fact, surveys, classroom observations, and interviews with students and teachers show a relationship between the poetry program and improvements in student attendance, language arts test scores, motivation, attitudes toward literacy, social skills, self-confidence, and (for English-language learners) language acquisition.
>
> (Online)

This pedagogical approach works within the lines of the emotional pedagogy principles, which emphasize creativity and emotional experiences as the base for students' motivation for learning and their retention of material and skills. Research in psychology and neuroscience has shown that positive emotions "play an important role to improve creativity and flexibility in problem-solving and could enhance performance on the task at hand" as they "are widely related to diverse cognitive processes, such as attention, long-term memorizing, problem solving, decision making, etc." (1). Daniel and Michel Chabot, who have largely studied the role of one's emotional awareness in the learning process, point out that this process happens not only in the cognitive brain, but also – and most of all – the emotional brain. The fact that "[t]he true learning process takes place when we feel more than when we understand" (80) is one of the central lines of thought to their emotional pedagogy. And what spoken-word poetry does is just that: it engages the emotions of the poet who composes the poem and delivers it; it calls for an emotional reaction from the audience that listens; and it creates a sense of community by sharing a mutual experience.

Since the outcomes of spoken-word poetry practices in the curriculum of English classes are very positive on many levels, as they enhance the students' learning experience, there is no doubt that they have a vital role to play in an academic curriculum in general. And if slam poetry is a privileged space for language appropriation, why not exploit it in our world language classes, as a pedagogical tool for developing the language and communicative skills of our students?

Research has shown that learning through educational projects that require the students' active participation helps them to acquire deeper knowledge. Project-based learning (PBL) develops in learners the "soft skills" necessary for success in the 21st century, such as problem-solving, teamwork, critical thinking, communicative competence, cooperation, decision-making aptitude, and creativity (Bell, Vaca Torres and Gómez Rodríguez, Stanley, Kavlu, O'Brien) – in part because it involves the emotional phenomena described earlier.

PBL is an instructional method in which "students gain knowledge and skills by working for an extended period of time to investigate and respond to an authentic, engaging, and complex question, problem, or challenge" (*PBLWorks* n.d.). This definition encapsulates the very essence of the spoken word activities as a tool for language acquisition. Indeed, throughout the diverse steps of this practice, scattered over a period of time, students acquire both linguistic knowledge and social skills, as they work in part collaboratively in the creative process. By putting their linguistic tools and creative minds into play, they are engaged in using the language in a new way, where sounds, rhythm, word choice, and grammatical accuracy accompany the message they want to convey. In this sense, it represents the "engaging, and complex question (and) challenge" stated earlier. Having to deliver their poems in a slam format requires students to challenge themselves and to look at the target language through a different lens.

Spoken word poetry activities meet the three main characteristics of PBL identified by Maggie O'Brien, as being "inter-disciplinary," "rigorous," and "student-centered." Indeed, spoken word poetry involves not only language but also literature and performance. The topics that students choose to write on are quite varied, ranging from social issues to personal matters. Students need to reflect on these issues, invoking both research and introspection. Furthermore, the linguistic rigor required in the poetic creation is a process that is mainly determined by their needs for specific vocabulary words, accuracy in their grammar, and exactitude in their pronunciation. Students are exposed to playing with the language, by researching it on a lexical level, paying attention to its prosody, understanding grammar as a whole (i.e., as a complete toolbox needed to convey meaning). This is what makes action-based learning a venue for "meaningful learning opportunities" (O'Brien). Finally, as a student-centered methodology, it focuses on students' collaborative and individual efforts and presentational skills and engages them in increasing their agency over their own language acquisition (Bell, Kavlu).

Main Goals

Integrating and practicing spoken-word poetry in the foreign language classroom is not an activity like any other. It entails many steps, from brainstorming to writing, from writing to revising, from revising to memorizing and finally to "staging." It is a process, and as such, it requires time and planning. Each step has its own objectives and goals. In the writing portion of the activity, students may be exposed to different poetic texts, be asked to observe linguistic traits, to identify and apply grammatical structures, or to pinpoint and learn how to use stylistic devices. In the oral/performative section of the process, students work in groups, engage in different types of dialogs with each other, and go through exercises aimed at developing their diction and fluency in the spoken language.

Challenges

Asking students to write and perform poetry in the language classroom represents sizable challenges whose process and outcomes, however, undeniably outweigh them.

Challenge 1: "Me? Writing Poetry?"

While some students are already writers and will dive into the activity with no fear, with joy and eagerness, others will carry with them the common preconception that poetry is not for them but for a chosen people who belong to higher realms. Indeed, the perception that poetry is difficult to read and to understand is quite shared. Poetry is usually considered to be an obscure genre, widely felt as socially coded within selected, elitist spheres. In many introductory classes of Spanish literature, poetry is more often than not perceived as that part of the curriculum that could be skipped, because it is too unintelligible or too obscure. In most Spanish language textbooks, the poem finds its place at the end of the chapter, frequently left alone and ignored in its peripheral place because of lack of time in the syllabus – or the teacher's lack of confidence and students' apprehension.

The first step is to demystify the scriptural act. Most students who fear poetry in reality apprehend the constraints imposed by the literary canon to which they were exposed in their English literature classes. They fear to have to use a registry of language they have not mastered, to have to imitate the poems from a literary tradition they do not necessarily feel connected with. Amber Regis exposes that for many students,

> It can be difficult to foster a sense of reading as identification, participation and shared exchange when a student is separated from a poem not only by obstacles of technical form and language, but also by a gulf of years and a strange cultural context.

This "sense of disenfranchisement" dissipates, however, when students are immersed in the writing of their own poetry. Slam poetry can desacralize the act of writing and restore confidence with regard to it. If writing allows students to become aware of their singularity as individuals, it is our duty to make accessible the object of writing and to change the negative representations of it. It coincides somehow with the notion of "liberation" that educator Paulo Freire defended as a necessary step to enhance learning as he exposed in *Pedagogy of the Oppressed*, outlining a new type of education that creates a partnership and dialog between teacher and student and gives the students agency over their learning process.

Moreover, writing in a language whose literary standards are unknown makes the endeavor all the more easy. Students writing in Spanish are not faced with the same literary constraints as when writing in their own language. They are freer, less confined with the restrictions they believe are imposed upon them. As such, they establish a different relationship with the language and with themselves, which facilitates identification with their writing.

By exploring slam poetry in the language classroom, the erroneously negative perception of poetry can be debunked, paving the way for new pedagogical and learning practices and opening up channels for a new relationship with the language and oneself.

Challenge 2: Writing Poetry in a Foreign Language When Proficiency Is Not Acquired May Seem a Difficult Endeavor to Undertake and Can Be Intimidating

World language students do face the limitations of grammar and vocabulary, but not in any different way than when they write a composition in prose. The exercise of writing a poem can be focused on a specific grammatical structure (for example, the hypothetical clauses involving past subjunctive and conditional in Spanish), and as such, students practice it in a more stimulating way. As far as vocabulary is concerned, students are free to search the exact words they desire or choose to use in order to make their poems more vibrant. As one of my students stated, "I believe that I learn more vocabulary when I write poetry in Spanish because I have to find the words I need." And it is this sense of empowerment that is key to the whole process, as we will see reappearing in many instances.

Challenge 3: Performance

To some students, performance appears an overwhelming aspect of the task. Standing in front of the class to perform one's own poem takes courage. It represents opening one's heart to the group, and reciting in a foreign language adds to the effort. As one of my students expressed,

> In terms of performing, it was certainly a very interesting experience. I worried a bit over it, because . . . this was my first time memorizing Spanish and it proved much harder than even memorizing long Shakespearean monologues. All of the minor intonation changes also made it difficult to work with memorization and recitation. In the end, however, I think it was quite fun and I will definitely consider writing a poem in Spanish again.

Furthermore, the shy students surprised me and moved me greatly. I was not expecting that the most timid, insecure, or inhibited students would experience such release through the active practice of poetry. Spoken word actually gives them a place, their place, and their voice. Naturally, fostering a welcoming and embracing environment is key to making everyone feel confident, and it should be encouraged in all sequences of a poetry workshop. In my workshops, some students who were reticent at first ended up recognizing the benefits of the activity and expressed their positions in the following terms:

> I like to write poems and the creativity of this activity, but I do not like to perform, although it is important to practice. But it also helps me to improve my confidence because the atmosphere is relaxed and comfortable.

Once students feel they belong to this community of poets in the making, they gain confidence (Weiss). "I do not like speaking in front of the group but it is a nice way to practice Spanish," another student wrote. Most students acknowledge that the journey from writing to performing poetry constitutes a whole process worth the effort, because this effort is crowned with a beautiful sense of accomplishment and pride – pride for oneself and for the other members of the group. Students do admit that the practice of slam poetry in the Spanish classroom is a novel and enjoyable way to acquire the language.

Uniqueness of Spoken-Word Poetry as a World Language Teaching Tool

"Sense of Community"

Whether they are formed by people of other cultures or people who share a common interest regardless of their geographical location, communities are important to their members, for they create a feeling of belonging and identification. Social psychologists McMillan and Chavis, in their study of how communities work and come together, have formed and developed the concept of "sense of community," defined as "a feeling that members have of belonging, a feeling that members matter to one another and to the group, and a shared faith that members' needs will be met through their commitment to be together" (9). They go on to say that the "definitive element for true community" (14) is when a shared emotional connection takes place. This connection is based on a shared history or identification with that history.

Be it in a classroom setting during a poetry workshop or at a poetry slam event, spoken-word poetry intrinsically builds and develops a sense of community. The performative aspect of spoken-word invites an audience who, because of its participative nature, becomes a community. Poets and audience, who often play both roles simultaneously, are drawn together as they share not only a common language (the poetic language) but also the same desire to be immersed in it and to participate in each other's stories. In a society where social media tend to physically isolate individuals rather than to bring them together, a face-to-face interaction with peers is a valuable human experience.

Establishing this sense of community in the language classroom is challenging but necessary for guaranteeing the success of the experience. In writing and performance workshops, group-centered activities must be privileged over individual ones to guarantee that students will bond, listen, and give feedback to each other, as a team.

Addressing the Language Skills

The goal of integrating slam poetry in the wold languages curriculum is to enhance the students' language acquisition and increase their confidence in using it as a tool of communication. The advantages of doing so are multiple. In the practice of poetry slam, all four language skills are put to work:

- Reading – It is crucial to open a spoken-word workshop with a piece of poetry, either relevant for its theme or for its use of the language (vocabulary/grammar). Students take this opportunity to observe also the different types of verses, rhymes, sounds, and rhythms of the verses.
- Writing – Through a series of exercises and activities, learners are geared toward the practice of their own writing process, in class and outside of class.
- Speaking – Every workshop embraces brainstorming activities in groups and other venues for interpersonal communication. In addition, every single text produced by the students is read to the class,

in the format of a slam scene. Pronunciation and intonation through performance are a significant component of the activity, and students are given several occasions to work on them.

- Listening – Besides reading poetry, students watch and listen to slam poets on video. These are samples of the art of poetry performance, through which students are exposed to the language's prosodic elements: its rhythm, its intonation, and its melody. Seeing slammers in action also brings students models of performance and can inspire them to add body movement and nuances to their renditions. In addition, if students are given the time to listen to each other's poems before the "official slam" and to offer each other feedback, they are compelled to focus on the listening activity and to put into action their critical thinking skills.

Poetry Slams and Community

Spoken-word Poetry events are times to share stories, words, images, and emotions. They constitute spaces to listen to each other, spaces where tolerance, compassion, and involvement are protagonists. These events can take an array of formats: as a competition within the classroom itself or between language classes in the same school or language classes in schools of the same district or institutions in the same state. It can also be organized as an open mic event in the community, in a local venue such as a coffee shop or a library, which would also involve members of the larger community. As follow-up projects suggested by Danielle Berg, the students' poems may be gathered in an anthology and sold as a fundraiser in support of a local organization that the students themselves would identify in their community. She adds, "Regardless of the amount of money students raise, the important goal is that students are taking action and working together to benefit their community – preparing them to be responsible citizens."

Addressing the 5 C's

In addition to addressing the four language skills, slam poetry as a teaching tool in the world language classroom speaks to several of the goals as outlined in ACTFL's World-Readiness Standards for Learning Languages. These standards are connected with five broad goal areas, referred to as the five C's (Communication, Cultures, Connections, Comparisons, and Communities), which reflect the knowledge and skills students need in order to communicate with competence and cultural sensitivity in a world language.

Communication: While working with spoken-word poetry, students engage in "interpersonal communication" at different stages of the project, where they "interact and negotiate meaning in spoken . . . conversations to share information, reactions, feelings, and opinions." They also work with the "presentational" aspect of communication, in particular using the specific tools of poetic performance in order to "convince" their audience. Their "interpretive communication" skills are put to work as well, as they "understand, interpret, and analyze what is heard, read, or viewed" (Standards 1.1, 1.2, and 1.3).

Comparisons (between languages): This goal focuses on the learners' abilities to understand use of the language to "reflect on the nature of language through comparisons of the language studied and their own." It addresses the students' abilities to examine and understand their first language when in contact with the target language (Standard 4.1).

Connections: Learning a language allows students to acquire information and increase their content knowledge using sources produced in that language. It enables them to connect with other disciplines, in our particular case, poetry and other literary expressions, without mentioning all the themes that students may want to explore in their writings. Additionally, through slam poetry, they can read or listen to pieces of literature that will make them aware of the cultural and personal sensibility that the native speakers of the language possess (Standards 3.1 and 3.2).

Communities: This goal speaks to the fact that learning a language gives students access to communities within and beyond the classroom by enabling them to participate within these communities.

Teaching Slam Poetry in the Spanish Classroom: A Sample Process of a Poetry Writing Workshop

There is no single formula to organize and lead activities around spoken-word poetry. They will vary according to the instructor's available time and specific goals. Activities can be gathered in two or three hour-periods or broken down into series of twenty minutes. The instructor is free to decide the length of the activities done in class or at home. Additionally, the level of language acquisition will determine the complexity or sophistication of the poem students will write. But in general terms, with very little, a lot can be achieved.

The following workshop took place in an Intermediate Spanish 2 class in a college setting. It entailed composing a poem as a recipe "For a better world" that used culinary vocabulary and commands as they are often used in recipes in Spanish. I started with an example of poetry to give them a base, related to the theme of the prompt. Samples of poetry can be chosen from the literary canon or from slam poetry, designed as a point of departure for the students. The poem chosen for this activity was "La luna" by Mexican poet Jaime Sabines, from which the students were to observe the poetic handling of the moon as a concrete object, and to identify its diverse usages: as a medicinal plant, an amulet, a delicacy, a dividable item, a liquid, a nutrient, or a breathable entity. I played a recording of it read by the author himself, before we read it together for pronunciation, rhythm, and clarification of vocabulary. We discussed students' reactions to it and the verses they found interesting. We analyzed briefly its content with some questions prepared in advance. We observed it for its shape and examined the rhetorical figures used and the choice of vocabulary to understand what distinguishes poetry from prose.

From this example, students worked in groups to identify major world problems and were sent to the board to write them down to make them visible to everyone. A brief discussion followed on the justification of their choices. We proceeded to list solutions to these issues, as they would become the ingredients for their recipe. In pairs, students selected the ones that called their attention the most. They were then instructed to treat their solutions in a similar manner Sabines did with the moon in his poem "La luna": that is, as concrete objects to measure, cut, add, boil, fry, and sprinkle. Students received a handout with specific vocabulary on the culinary arts with measures and verbs. The activity was closely timed, for them to write fast and not overthink their lines. They shared their "raw" lines with the class when time was up. And from there, students individually wrote their poem. I imposed some constraints, such as the use of commands (tú, Ud., nosotros) and a minimum of 12 lines. They had 20 minutes to "quick write" the rough draft of their poem.

The poems were finalized and reviewed at home, with special instructions: since these poems were to be recited and performed, students needed to pay close attention to the rhythm, the sounds, and the images that they conveyed. Reading their personal text aloud was a necessary component of their proofreading endeavor. Beyond the revision of grammar, students were to ask themselves the following questions: How does my poem sound? Do I like the words I have chosen? Do I combine concrete elements with abstract ones, as Sabines did in "La luna"? Have I created surprising images? How strong is the message?

Once they handed it in to me, my reading was two-fold: polishing language issues and proposing "more poetic" resources, as I would with a composition regarding the organization and the content of the text. After they went through second revisions, the corrected version was ready to be memorized and performed.

This workshop is one example of the multiple possibilities of playing with the poetry writing process in the language classroom, according to the instructor's specific pedagogical goals. However, this is only the first part of the whole process. Performing it is next.

Process of a Performance Workshop

This is the oral and auditory part of the activity. The goal of the performance is to help the audience members to understand and perceive the poem better than if they had read it silently. The interpretation of the poem through movement and nuances of the voice accompany its message. It deepens it and enlivens it. However, mastering verbal delivery is not sufficient. On stage, nonverbal communication is crucial, as body language conveys messages as well. Thanks to a number of techniques and exercises on verbal and nonverbal language, students are able to acquire a strong physical presence on stage and achieve a good performance.

Verbal Language Exercises

- Diction and enunciation: Since pronouncing the Spanish vowels is often a challenge for English speakers, work on enunciation is essential to ensure a good delivery of words. A series of exercises is designed to observe the quality of the vowels and the articulation of the syllables. Enunciating words clearly, even if said quickly, is key to clarity.
- Tones: Tones carry emotions. Varying tones while reading or reciting a poem adds dimension to it. It enhances its message, meanings, allusions and other nuances. To this aim, we practice reading the same verses in different tones: happiness, anger, sadness, impatience, and so on. This exercise can be expanded to an array of emotions, such as nervousness, surprise, fear, amusement, pride, or confidence, to name just a few.
- Tempo: Varying the pace and speed of recitation also intensifies the dramatic effect of the performance. To attract the students' attention on this aspect, several readings are done slowly, at normal pace, and fast – while paying attention to diction. Pauses can be added if the poet desires to let the words soak in.
- Volume of the voice: Volume is yet another important component to performance. Whispering verses or shouting them will not have the same impact on the audience. Knowing how to increase or decrease volume (*crescendo/decrescendo*) when needed in the poem is a great tool to master in order to build emotion and accomplish a convincing performance.

Body Language Exercises

- Posture and gestures: A large part of performance is to be aware of the signals that body language emits. For this reason, some movements are prescribed and others dissuaded. Showing confidence by staying firm on both feet will prevail over the swaying from side to side, crossing and uncrossing feet, or gestures that betray nervousness. The goal is to deliver the poem with fewer possible distractions for the public.
- Eye contact: Maintaining eye contact with members of the public, without looking at anyone in particular more than one or two seconds, will capture their attention.

The Poetry Slam

Once the poem is ready in its written form, it is time to observe it with its performance in mind. Students review their piece thinking about the intent of each verse and therefore all the elements stated earlier: tone(s), speed of enunciation, and volume of the voice. Students practice their own poem in class with peers who give them their perceptions, comments, and observations on their interpretation.

Right before students are ready to "slam" their poems – that is, to participate in the competition, their names are entered into a container (hat, basket, jar, and so on). The audience (i.e., the students not performing) receives a "performance assessment" sheet and is in charge of evaluating the poet on stage. The first student goes on stage and performs his or her poem. As the audience marks their points, the poet pulls out another name from the container and calls on the next poet, until the last one is called out.

At the end of the slam, all the assessment sheets are collected. I draw the average of the points for each poet and announce the three "official winners" at the following class session – although everyone clearly understands that in this activity, there are no losers. Everybody wins.

Conclusion: Relevance of the Method

The implementation of PBL in the world language classes has a lot to offer. Integrating activities related to reading, writing, and staging of poetry in world language classes allows instructors to work with the language in an innovative way. And through this project, students not only learn its lexical wealth, its grammar, its codes, its standards, and its prosody, but they approach it as an instrument for personal expression and communication that is relevant to them. This project offers them an original tool through which they can express their emotions, think critically, engage in an introspective journey of the self, and build bonds with their peers, while putting into practice all four language skills. It improves their proficiency and their confidence in using it as a tool for communication. By creating and performing their own texts, they embark on a personal journey through the language and become their own negotiators in their language acquisition. They get personally involved and develop active agency over their learning. Last but not least, spoken-word poetry in the language classroom unites the students and instills a great sense of community. By the end of the slam, they will have shared a piece of themselves with their peers and been the witnesses of many other slices of life. They will have been drawn together as a community that will have supported and applauded them all along.

Note

1. Today, Spain alone counts 21 cities that organize regular poetry slams (Phillips).

References

ACTFL. "World-Readiness Standards For Learning Languages." www.actfl.org/sites/default/files/publications/standards/World-ReadinessStandardsforLearningLanguages.pdf. Accessed 9 March 2019.

Banks, Jamie. "Slam Poetry: Social Justice, Identities and the Culture of Power." *Poetry at the Core*, 2013. poetryatthecore.wordpress.com/2013/05/08/slam-poetry-social-justice-identities-and-the-culture-of-power/ Accessed 9 March 2019.

Bell, Stephanie. "Project-Based Learning for the 21st Century: Skills for the Future." *The Clearing House: A Journal of Educational Strategies, Issues and Ideas*, vol. 83, no. 2, January 2010, pp. 39–43.

Berg, Danielle. "Crossing Boundaries Through Bilingual, Spoken Word Poetry." *Readwritethink.Org*. www.readwritethink.org/about/bio/danielle-berg-602.html. Accessed 9 March 2019.

Chabot, Daniel, and Michel Chabot. *Emotional Pedagogy: To Feel in Order to Learn*. Trafford, 2004.

Eleveld, Mark, and Marc Kelly Smith. *The Spoken Word Revolution (Slam, Hip Hop and the Poetry of a New Generation)*. Sourcebooks MediaFusion, 2003.

Freire, Paulo. *Pedagogy of the Oppressed*. 30th anniversary ed. Continuum, 2000.

Glazner, Gary Mex. *Poetry Slam: The Competitive Art of Performance Poetry*. Manic D Press, 2000.

Hewitt, Geof. *Hewitt's Guide to Slam Poetry and Poetry Slam*. Discover Writing Press, 2005.

Kavlu, Aziza. "Implementation of Project Based Learning (PBL) in EFL (English as a Foreign Language) Classrooms in Fezalar Educational Institutions (Iraq)." *International Journal of Social Sciences and Educational Studies*, vol. 4, no. 2 (Special Issue), October 2017, pp. 67–79.

McMillan, David W., and David M. Chavis. "'Sense of Community: A Definition and Theory.'" *Journal of Community Psychology*, vol. 14, January 1986, pp. 6–23.

O'Brien, Maggie. "What Is Project-Based Learning?" *Defined STEM*, 2017. www.definedstem.com/blog/what-is-project-based-learning/. Accessed 9 March 2019.

Pfeiler, Martina. *Sounds of Poetry: Contemporary American Performing Poets*. Gunter Narr Verlag, 2003.

Phillips, Abril. "Lo último en poesía se llama poetry slam y cada día suma más seguidores." *La Vanguardia*, 2018. www.lavanguardia.com/cultura/20181111/452762010197/lo-ultimo-en-poesia-se-llama-poetry-slam-y-cada-dia-suma-mas-seguidores.html. Accessed 9 March 2019.

Regis, Amber. "Why Do Students Fear Poetry and How Can They Access It Better?" *The Guardian*, 2013. www.theguardian.com/higher-education-network/blog/2013/mar/21/world-poetry-day-student-occupy. Accessed 9 March 2019.

Rubenstein, Grace. "Kids Feel the Power of Poetry in Performance." *Edutopia*, 5 May 2009. www.edutopia.org/poetry-slam-global-writes. Accessed 9 March 2019.

Smith, Marc Kelly, and Joe Kraynk. *The Complete Idiot's Guide to Slam Poetry*. Alpha, 2004.

Stanley, Todd. *Creating Life-Long Learners: Using Project-Based Management to Teach 21st Century Skills*. Corwin, 2016.

Thomas, Lorenzo. "Neon Griot: The Functional Role of Poetry Readings in the Black Arts Movement." *Close Listening: Poetry and the Performed Word*, edited by Charles Bernstein. Oxford University Press, 1998, pp. 300–23.

Vaca Torres, Ady Marcela, and Luis Fernando Gómez Rodríguez. "Increasing EFL Learners' Oral Production at a Public School Through Project-Based Learning." *PROFILE: Issues in Teachers' Professional Development*, vol. 19, no. 2, 2017, pp. 57–71.

Wagner, Laura. "Top 15 Slam Poems Addressing Social and Political Gender Issues." *Her Campus*. www.hercampus.com/school/gettysburg/top-15-slam-poems-addressing-social-and-political-gender-issues. Accessed 10 March 2019.

Weiss, Jen, and Scott Herndon. *Brave New Voices. The Youth Speaks Guide to Teaching Spoken-Word Poetry*. Heinemann, 2001.

"What Is PBL?" *PBLWorks*. Buck Institute for Education. www.pblworks.org/what-is-pbl. Accessed 5 March 2019.

14 Films for Inclusion

LGBT+ Perspectives in the French Language Classroom

Aurélie Chevant-Aksoy and Ericka Knudson

Over the past few years, we have been hearing more and more about inclusion. On a broad level, we think about the need for inclusion of underrepresented communities in political and corporate leadership, in certain professions, and in the arts. In France and other Francophone countries, there has also been debate over inclusive writing (*écriture inclusive*) to try to repair inequalities inherent in the language and to challenge heteronormative practices in society. As educators, it is our responsibility to open the doors of our classroom and the minds of our students to include perspectives that may not have been considered. Indeed, in education today, embracing diversity is imperative, yet, the language classroom traditionally has not been so inclusive, still drawing most of its material from heteronormative narratives. To foster better understanding and build empathy, we must start by hearing other voices, other stories. We can do this in a number of ways, notably by integrating different perspectives told through text and image in our curriculum.

This chapter presents a way to integrate LGBT+ perspectives in the French language classroom, using a cinema class to illustrate methods to challenge the heteronormative framing of identity. Through films such as *Ma vie en rose* and *Laurence Anyways*, students discuss representations of gender and sexuality in the French-speaking world. Students, engaged in four-skills activities and project-based activities, analyze gendered social constructions, make cross-cultural comparisons of the LGBT+ community in the French-speaking world and in the US, and investigate the challenges posed by French as a gendered language. It is our hope that through screening these films, guided class discussions, and project-based activities, students will gain insight, helping them become more informed, responsible and concerned global citizens.

LGBT+ Perspectives in Francophone and French Contexts

It is not hard to notice that, when opening American textbooks to teach French, most of the chapters or the lessons only briefly mention LGBT+

issues, if at all. A few will offer some cultural information on gay marriage in France and on the change of family structure in some countries of the Francophone world, but this is usually as far as it goes. On the one hand, this can be explained by the fact that the language being taught is extremely gendered and that it represents societies that are strongly based on the masculine vs. feminine dichotomy and also that governmental discussions on gender equality, fluidity, and preferences in these societies are currently very controversial.

As Annabelle Timsit clearly summarizes in her article *The Push to Make French Gender-Neutral*,

> in French, pronouns, nouns, and adjectives reflect the gender of the object to which they refer. So, *le policier* is a policeman; *la policière* is a policewoman. The language has no neutral grammatical gender. And there are many nouns (including those referring to professions) that don't have feminine versions. So, a male minister is *le ministre* and a female minister is *la ministre*. What's more, French students are taught that "the masculine dominates over the feminine," meaning that if you have a room full of ten women and just one man, you have to describe the whole group in the masculine.

So how can instructors approach French language and Francophone cultures in order to be more inclusive? How can we still be culturally authentic when making the classroom more inclusive in French? In the same article, Timsit points out that the French publishing house Hatier released in France in September 2017 an "inclusive" textbook for children in the third grade, based on the 2015 recommendations of the High Council for Gender Equality. This "innovation" faced a wave of strong opposition from politicians, scholars, and philosophers who claimed that inclusive writing would lead to "a disunited language, disparate in its expression, creating a confusion that borders on illegibility" (Timsit). However, as Timsit explains, the supporters of inclusive writing say that "the strong institutional pushback in France is rooted in a misunderstanding of what language is meant to do; it should be a vector for social progress." This example shines a light not only on the rigidity of the French Academy practices and of French language rules but also on the limited social definitions of gender in France.

What is the current discourse on gender in France, then? France's political turmoil can be a great indicator of the general social perception of LGBT+ issues. In 2017, several candidates for the presidential election expressed their intention to "rewrite the Taubira law" on same-sex marriage and adoption. François Fillon even received the support of *Sens commun*, an organization openly opposed to the rights of LGBT+ individuals. More recently, in October 2018, some three thousand people attended a rally in Paris to denounce assaults on lesbian, gay, bisexual, and transgender people and demand urgent action from the government. In his article "French LGBT Groups Denounce 'Culture of Hate' After Spate of Attacks," Benjamin Dodman notes that the campaigning group *SOS Homophobie*, which runs a hotline where victims can anonymously report assaults, has registered a 15% increase nationwide in the number of homophobic assaults from last year. The website *Rainbow Europe* ranks 49 European countries on a scale between 0% (gross violations of human rights, discrimination) and 100% (respect of human rights, full equality). France still manages to come in sixth place.

And what about other Francophone countries or provinces like Belgium or Quebec? It seems that France's French-speaking neighbor, Belgium, is a much better advocate for LGBT+ rights. According to the "Rainbow Index," Belgium ranks second in terms of respect of human rights and equality for the LGBT+ community. In 2015, Belgium approved, acknowledging that in the case of a lesbian couple undergoing IVF, both mothers are immediately considered legal mothers. Additionally, since 2017, the Parliament approved a reform bill to the Belgian gender recognition law, which means that sterilization and a mental health diagnosis are no longer requirements for legal gender recognition. By looking at the online presence of LGBT+ blogs or forums, such as *Blogs Genres Pluriels*, it also seems that there is more support online and more helpful tools available to navigate a more fluid gender identity and identification. In November 2017, the Prime Minister of Canada, Justin Trudeau, publicly apologized for years of oppression of the LGBT+ community in Canada. Additionally, by the end of August 2017, the minister of immigration said that people who do not identify as male or female could now use an X on their Canadian passports and other official documents. However, there are still noticeable differences in practices and values between Canadian provinces. For instance, in the west of Canada, in Alberta, for example, or even in Ontario, people are much more conservative when talking about religion, homosexuality, or abortion.

It is clear, then, that in order to bring about changes that ensure the rights of everyone, perspectives need to be broadened and different points of view considered. When others' stories are told, it is easier to understand and identify with them, to see the world through different eyes, and therefore, to recognize their humanity. The use of stories is always a good way to build empathy. By showing on screen the stories of those from underrepresented communities, such as those from the LGBT+ community, and by discussing them in the classroom, it is possible to make the necessary first step toward that understanding.

The Need for Inclusion: Focus on Transgender Youth

According to research, as many as 150,000 gender nonconforming adolescent students live in all parts of the country and a growing number live in alignment with their gender identity (Campos). However, the psychological effects from the discord stemming from the desire to be treated according to their gender identity while being classified as the other gender can be devastating. Some studies of the transgender population have shown rates of suicide ideation as high as 64% and suicide attempts as high as 38% as compared to non-transgender populations. Changes in perception are necessary to change attitudes and to create acceptance. Since 2010, the *DSM-5* (*Diagnostic and Statistical Manual of Mental Disorders*) now uses "gender dysphoria" instead of "gender disorder" to identify those whose gender identity differs from their biological sex. The challenges transgender youth face include maltreatment and lives filled with adversity. Statistically, transgender youth are at greater risk of harassment. In fact, they are two to four times more likely to be harassed than their counterparts. As many as 80 percent of the transgender student population in one study was verbally harassed, which was largely attributed to their gender-nonconforming behavior and expressions, and 12% of transgender students have been sexually assaulted (Campos).

Because transgender students are often targets of maltreatment by their peers and because of changes in the law, which no longer protects them (Campos), it is imperative that we, as educators, work from the inside, creating an environment of understanding and inclusion through our curriculum and classroom environment. It is important to mention gender identity explicitly: inclusiveness is critical in the classroom so that it translates to change outside of it.

Working With Films in the Language Class

Over the past few decades, films have been taking a more central place in the foreign language curriculum. This trend in French was visible, in the early 2000s, with the increasing number of first editions of language or cultural textbooks with a focus on films, such as *Cinema for French Conversation* by Anne-Christine Rice (1999), *Séquences* by Michele Bissiere (2008) or *La France contemporaine à travers ses films* by Anne-Christine Rice (2011). In 2007, the MLA report emphasized the importance of translingual and transcultural competence. Using films and other media was encouraged to "challenge students'" imaginations and to help them consider alternative ways of seeing, feeling, and understanding things." The report continues by stating that through these media, students "are taught critical language awareness, interpretation and translation, historical and political consciousness, social sensibility, and aesthetic perception." Therefore, films are an easy tool to give students access to a quite authentic rendition of cultural habits and practices. Students can thus develop socio-cultural sensitivity to different cultures, learn more about key historical changes, and practice analyzing cinematography as well. Sébastien Dubreil explains in his article "Rebels With a Cause: (Re)defining

Identities and Culture in Contemporary French Cinema," that "through the narratives that it presents, cinema offers examples of language as culturally situated semiotic practice as it reflects cultural values and beliefs, worldviews and daily behaviors" (179). He adds that this

> can lead students to develop more refined Intercultural Communicative Competence (ICC – as elaborated by Byram, 1997), which describes the ability to navigate multiple cultural identities and multiple cultural contexts or multicultural contexts, and to see how different cultures relate to each other.
>
> (178–179)

Students reflect upon their own cultures through the prism of other cultural narratives. Films create a bridge tying language patterns and specificities to cultural perceptions and behaviors. This is especially useful when talking about social struggles, racial tensions, and gender considerations. In the same volume, in his article "New Approaches to Exploiting Film in the Foreign Language Classroom," Mark Kaiser also emphasizes the fact that films "often incorporate a wide variety of sociolects of the target language" and that "making students aware of the varieties of L2 sociolects should be an important part of their language learning" (233). Films allow us to cast a wider net to grasp more dialects, idioms, and speech patterns and thus to understand more cultural differences and specificities. In summary, films are a great tool in the language classroom to access authentic material that allows learners to study broader categories of vocabulary, to discuss a various range of cultural topics and sociopolitical issues, and to reflect upon the parallels and differences between their native cultures and the cultures studied.

Films in this way can provide a pedagogical tool to increase awareness and can serve as a basis for project-based activities. Through guided instruction, movies can help students think critically, increase their interest, and incite enthusiasm for topics that expand beyond the classroom (Russell). Through real life, context-rich dilemmas in which characters must exercise higher-order thinking skills to make decisions (Blickenstaff; Russell), students can participate in new "experiences" by identifying with the on-screen characters. By learning to analyze film narratives and the representation of characters, for example, students can become more aware of how a film's construction can influence their point of view. Project-based pedagogy can also stimulate higher levels of critical thinking in applying concepts explored in class discussion: imagining role reversals and alternate endings or creating parodies, for example. More important, an engaging film that incites bonding and identification with characters (Marcus), followed by project-based activities can, in a word, build empathy (Campos and Knudson).

Our Course: "The Contemporary Francophone World Through Cinema"

Course Description

The course "French 40: The Contemporary Francophone World Through Cinema" is an advanced French language class at Harvard University. Students usually take French 40 in the first semester of their third year in the French program. In this course, students view contemporary Francophone movies to study various cultural issues relevant to Francophone identity, such as immigration, education, the workplace, regional differences, sexuality and gender, relationships, and so on. They participate in a range of written and oral activities and advanced grammar exercises and practice.

This course allows students to deepen their knowledge of French language and culture while considering broader issues through class discussion as well as creative projects that correspond to the ASCD guidelines for project-based learning.

Framework and Lesson Planning

In designing our lessons for this course, we consider the following basic framework that can be adapted to any film. This framework can also be applied to the study of other foreign languages or as a base from which to incorporate films in a multicultural classroom.

Aiming to develop students' cultural awareness and language skills, we scaffold our lessons using these basic steps:

1) Instructional Goals for the Film

This encompasses background knowledge and what collaborative activities can be planned to engage students to reflect on what they will see, focusing on cinematographic devices, narrative elements, or literary, historical, social, and cultural content and concepts embedded in the film (Sommer 2001). This stage is critical for instructors to plan the overall goals for studying a particular film from both a linguistic and cultural point of view.

2) Background on the Director and the Film's Context

To situate the film in its socio-historical context, we ask students to conduct an informal search on cultural background information concerning a particular issue or aspects the film might address, and to look for the film that make it significant, such as its critical impact in film history (aesthetic aspects, important actors, directors, or storyline, for example), the period and social context at the time the film was made, how the point of view is presented, if the topic being depicted is fair, and whose viewpoint might be lacking (Marcus and Stoddard). At this point, to anticipate the film screening, vocabulary can be introduced and preview questions can be structured that will incite critical thinking, allowing students to consider different perspectives that will prepare class discussion. To go deeper, we also suggest instructional strategies, such as comparing movie posters and/or trailers from different countries to sensitize students to image analysis and make them aware of multicultural viewpoints and foci according to the respective Francophone countries and cultures. Assigning students to do an informal research assignment on the historical or socio-cultural context also helps prepare their viewing of the film and class discussion following.

3) Screening the Film and Scene Analysis

Ideally, students should be able to watch the film together without interruption on a big screen, providing a holistic experience, but because of outside constraints, our students usually view the film on their own time through the Media Gallery on the course website. Then, in the following class, certain scenes that are significant or interesting to explore for narrative subtleties or representation of characters (Nielsen) are shown and analyzed in class. For a more constructivist approach, the scene can be shown before the instruction, asking students to identify what is important about a scene (Saltau). We prefer, however, the use of guided questions, where students are encouraged to analyze the scene aesthetically (color, composition, angle, point of view, and so on), and talk about the storyline or characters in more depth.

4) Post-Viewing Activities

For class discussion, questions should inspire students to reflect on complex issues, sharing their ideas that can also inspire debate. According to Buchanan, good questions engender divergent-thinking responses, get students emotionally invested in the film, and can apply to their lives (Buchanan). Before class, students are asked to consider certain complex questions and to write their reactions and thoughts on the class website, also responding to another classmate's text to prepare class discussion. In the next class, students gather in small groups to continue the dialogue face to face. Topics could include basic questions, such as describing certain characters and the relationships among them, to more complex aspects of the *mise en scène*, bringing in cinema-specific vocabulary to analyze certain dynamics, emotions, and perspectives. Students can consider a dilemma faced by one of the characters in the film and discuss motivations or explore how they might react or solve it if they were the character. Through the openness provided by the discussion in these small groups, students can also identify other issues or other aspects they find interesting, encouraging their creativity and valuing different perspectives from their peers. These small group activities encourage participation and develop speaking skills in an environment that is less intimidating and in turn help prepare discussion with the whole class about more difficult or complex issues that can be covered in more detail or through closer readings.

5) Project-Based Activities

Project-based activities are usually enjoyable for students, providing them a chance to exercise higher-level thinking through processing, synthesizing, and applying the knowledge and skills developed in the previous steps. Developing new ideas and imagining new perspectives inspires broader thinking, and these activities that encourage students to be flexible and creative also strengthen their language abilities while opening their minds. For each film, we draw from activities, such as rewriting a scene from another character's perspective or imagining an alternate ending, as a writing assignment or, collectively, writing a parody of a scene, using a different genre or register of language (slang, formal speech, subtitles of thoughts, and so on), together as a group and acting it out in a skit in front of the class, creating a different trailer, and so on. On a smaller scale, students could also redesign the movie poster to emphasize a different aspect of the story or keep a diary of their experiences as a secondary character in a certain scene, for example. At the end of the semester, students use these types of ideas to create their own short film, applying both the content and language skills they have acquired throughout the course. These activities aim to strengthen students' communication skills in French, to encourage more critical thinking and analysis, and to broaden their point of view. By examining socio-cultural codes and norms conveyed in films from different Francophone countries, teachers may better guide students to embrace a multitude of perspectives in today's complex intersection of cultures worldwide and, in effect, promote the development of deeper understanding (Campos and Knudson). To do this, it is important to choose carefully films that are inclusive and representative of a multitude of Francophone cultures, communities, and perspectives.

Our Selected Movies

As a model, we will share, here, examples from the films we have used in the course over the past five years. This template can be applied to many other interesting Francophone films that explore LGBT+ issues and can be used for classes in other languages and cultures as well. Over the past few years (under the supervision of Dr. Ericka Knudson), we have used the Xavier Dolan film, *Laurence Anyways* (Quebec, 2012) that addresses the challenges of coming out as a transgender teacher, under the theme of "Le Soi et la mise en scène" – that includes Marjane Satrapi's *Persepolis* and Agnès Varda's *Les Glaneurs et la glaneuse*. This unit comes at the end of the semester after students have studied more mainstream films. From 2013 to 2016, Dr. Aurélie Chevant-Aksoy used Alain Berliner's *Ma vie en rose* (Belgium, 1997), reflecting a similar perspective of a transgender child.

Ma vie en rose *by Alain Berliner (Belgium, 1997)*

Synopsis: Seven-year old Ludovic and zir (we use the gender-neutral pronouns here as will be discussed later in this chapter) family move to an upper-middle-class Belgian suburban neighborhood. Ludovic is obsessed with a program about a Barbie-like doll called Pam, who lives in a flowery, girly, pink cartoon fantasy world. Ze wants to be like her: ze loves makeup, wants to wear dresses, and is quite convinced that ze will be marrying a neighborhood boy, the son of zir father's boss. However, zir family and neighbors do not see it that way.

a) **Pre-viewing activities:** In this phase, we push students to research how gender can be constructed at an early age, especially how society encourages children to fulfill specific gender roles. The aim is to motivate students to answer the question: How do people address gender fluidity and gender identification in France and Belgium, especially regarding children? For this purpose, students are asked to explore the Internet and the city to find out how toy catalogues and stores, clothing lines, and other types of advertising or products identify specific gender roles for children. They can then analyze how some activities, colors, shapes, and characters are clearly associated with being male or female, which corresponds to a cisgender representation of the world. Through the Internet, we can guide students to websites that are not only Belgian or French but also from other Francophone countries and their countries of origin. One example we suggest for France is an advertising campaign for the bank *Société Générale*, portraying girls as smiling ballerinas in pink tutus and boys as frowning dirty rugby players. In class, students then share and compare their multicultural discoveries and analyses. Following this, students analyze the poster of the movie and elements like the rose and the quite androgynous shadow. To that, we provide a famous French proverb: "*Les garçons naissent dans les choux et les filles dans les roses*" (Boys are born among the cabbages and girls among the roses).[1] Students can then start formulating questions or hypotheses about the movie, its characters, its topic, and its possible social commentaries.

b) Scene analysis, follow-up activities, and discussion: In general, we try to analyze four or five brief scenes in class. In *Ma vie en rose*, the story is about oppositions: a heteronormative society vs. a genderfluid main character, reality vs. magical realism, children vs. adults, science vs. religion. In the accompanying dossier, which they work on at home, students compare images describing scenes where Ludo tries to assert hir transitioning process and scenes where society resists and rejects hir wishes and expression of identity. Students are thus asked to analyze how the school fails in protecting Ludo against other discriminating families, how the community isolates Ludo and hir family, and how and why the parents impose gender-normative practices onto Ludo. Before the session in which we analyze scenes about school practices, students are asked to look at websites designed to help LGBT+ children and young adults. For instance, we suggest the Canadian website *Enfants Transgenres* and the site of a Belgian federation *Les Cheff* to find out how Canadian and Belgian governments support LGBT+ youth and what other resources are available in terms of rights and physical and mental health. Students are encouraged to find resources on their own from other Francophone countries in Africa, Canada, or the Caribbean.

Additionally, following the aforementioned session, students study a case that occurred in the French educational system in 2010. The short film *Le baiser de la lune*, directed by Sébastien Wastel, is a love story between two male fish. Intended to be used as an educational tool for elementary schools to educate children on different forms of love and the dangers of homophobia, it received the approval of the minister of national education. As soon as this approval was announced, however, many associations and politicians opposed its use. In our class, in a blog entry, students write on what happened and what they think of the short film and the arguments from supporters and opponents. This will then be used as a brainstorming tool for the following session focusing on how the community isolates Ludo and hir family and why the parents impose gender-normative practices on their child. In 2015–2016, when we did this activity in class, a lot of students were surprised by the amount of documentation that could be found on Canadian websites and that there seemed to be many efforts of support at the governmental level. In contrast, some of them were surprised to discover that France was not as progressive.

c) Final project: For other films studied in the class, students can opt for a creative project, which usually consists of imagining and filming a new ending to the movie or a scene that might come after the end, for example. For this movie, however, we found it best not to risk any inappropriate depiction of Ludo or of being transgender that might come from an otherwise well-intentioned project. Therefore, we chose to take the documentary route. After the students start research on LGBT+ issues in education and, by extension, in child development, they are given the task of exploring these topics in their community. On the one hand, students can go visit the "Office of BGLTQ Student Life" on campus and ask about LGBT+ students' rights and school policies. They can focus on interviewing the student population about what they know of said rights at school, what they think is lacking, and other LGBT+ initiatives they support in the community. They are also encouraged to venture off campus and explore other organizations in Boston and on other local campuses. On the other hand, students are asked to look through the website for *Welcoming Schools*, the professional development training for educators to support transgender and non-binary students, offered by the Human Rights Campaign. Going further, students can visit, for example, the Harvard Medical School on campus and interview faculty about children's mental health and transgender youth. They can also contact local elementary schools and teachers to interview them on what they and their schools do to support their LGBT+ students. Students can also share with the teachers they interview elements of the film they are studying and discuss what happens to Ludo at school and how they would approach the situation. Because many interviews are conducted in English, students should create subtitles in French for the video and make sure that, in between interviews, they provide comments and explanations in French as well.

Laurence Anyways *by Xavier Dolan (Quebec, 2012)*

Synopsis: *Laurence Anyways* "tells the story of an impossible love between Frédérique and her long-term boyfriend Laurence, a man who reveals his inner desire to become his true self: a woman." This introduction is the first line of the synopsis on the film's website. We can see here that the focus is set on the "doomed love of Fred and Laurence" and the "trials and tribulations they face" instead of the main character's revelation to her girlfriend that she feels she was born in the wrong body and that she wants to start her life again as a woman. We also note the ambiguity of the use of pronouns here that we will address in a subsequent section. The film, set in the late '80s in Quebec, follows the transformation of Laurence in the search of her identity and that of the couple whose love is put to the ultimate test.

a) **Pre-viewing activities:** To provide a framework for discussion in the scope of a multicultural classroom, we start by situating the film in terms of LGBT+ social and political rights in students' culture and language of origin as a base to compare with those of different Francophone countries. First, as part of a background, investigative assignment, students are asked to photograph and make a list of posters, brochures, and other resources that advocate for LGBT+ rights on campus and in the city. At the same time, the class is broken into smaller groups that are asked to go online to research the situation of rights and awareness in different Francophone countries (through forums, governmental websites, and so on) and share their findings with the class the following session. To continue the discussion, and to provide students with deeper context about perceptions and levels of awareness regarding transgender issues in Quebec, the setting of the film, we prepare the students by assigning a reading before they view the film. The article, "Xavier Dolan 'dégoûté' par les prix récompensant les films gays," published in *Le Monde* in September 2014 (Marques 2014), centers on the director's own dislike ("disgust") of his movie being categorized as an LBGT+ film, refusing a "ghettoization" and the Queer Palm awarded him in Cannes. This polemical stance lays the groundwork for animated class discussion in the aim of exploring what might be the benefits and detriments of such an award or label. Students are sometimes challenged in their own beliefs by hearing the views of the film's director.

After this initial discussion, we move to a more specific analysis of the film, in a preview activity comparing posters that promote the film in Canada, France, and the US. During this exercise, students are encouraged to infer which type of genre or storyline is focused upon in each poster, how they differ by country, and what that might say about the preferences or values of different cultures. Students also describe the ambiance they expect in the film according to the colors and graphics used on each poster, and they discuss which one makes them want to see the film (or not) and why. This activity is followed by viewing the film's trailer together, where students describe how the main characters are represented and discuss different aspects of the film's aesthetics. As homework, we ask students to watch another trailer from a list of films from different countries that treat transgender issues (*Tomboy*, *The Danish Girl*, *Todo sobre mi madre*, *Ma vie en rose*) and to present and describe it as a point of comparison regarding stereotypes and representation in different countries in the following session. Along with these activities, students are asked to choose from three more complex questions about the film and post their response on the class website after having seen the film and respond to the text of a classmate before coming to class in order to prepare for class discussion.

b) Post-viewing activities: During the class session following the film, students discuss their responses (posted on the website) and continue the conversation in small groups before coming together as a class to share their insights and continuing with the more detailed analysis of scenes. In order to prepare one of these scenes further, we ask students to deepen their knowledge about gendered pronouns.

As we have seen, the film's director makes a choice to present the main character using pronouns in the feminine, corresponding to gender choice. Because this is an important, conscious choice, it is important to address the debate around gender-neutral and gender-inclusive pronouns (a pronoun that does not associate a gender with the individual who is being discussed) in the context of the film in the multicultural classroom. Looking at the BGLTQ Student Life website at Harvard, we can see the aim of raising awareness about the issue while avoiding giving a definitive answer. As they explain, "language does not exist in a vacuum, but rather is subject to the specific historical, cultural, and political context in which it develops." Moreover, as groups of people with different backgrounds come together and communicate, especially through the Internet, they point out that "new terms are coined, and existing terms are expanded to account for these newfound similarities and differences." Because language is constantly in flux, as they state, the Harvard BGLTQ site does not "purport to serve as a definitive, up-to-date resource regarding the many ways in which words – especially identity terms – change in meaning over time," but instead, they provide a list of glossaries curated by organizations they deem reputable. For example, the first resource, MyPronouns.Org explains the importance of pronouns and again aims at increasing sensitivity instead of prescribing pronoun use:

> Often, people make assumptions about the gender of another person based on the person's appearance or name . . . and the act of making an assumption (even if correct) sends a potentially harmful message.

They go on to explain that "using someone's correct personal pronouns is a way to respect them and create an inclusive environment," adding "it can be offensive or harassing to guess at someone's pronouns and refer to them using those pronouns if that is not how that person wants to be known." Besides building awareness, in the language classroom, we must also address specifics and explain to students that, in search of greater equality, gender-neutral pronouns have been created by some communities in languages that do not already include them. In English, for example, some people prefer to use the singular "they," "their," and "them," while others prefer new gender-neutral pronouns ze, sie, hir, co, and ey (as seen in the lesson on *Ma vie en rose* earlier). In French, new pronominal forms such as "iels," "ille s," "iel," "ul," "ol," or "ele" are suggested, or the indefinite pronoun "on" can be used. The pronoun debate in both French and English raises many questions.

In order to deepen the awareness of students around this debate, we open discussion about genderfluid pronouns, using the heritage and background of the students, by asking them to inform themselves about the situation on different levels, starting by conducting an informal investigation in their community (on campus at the LGBT+ center, for example, or asking friends and teachers around campus) about their familiarity, opinion, and use of genderfluid pronouns. As in the first assignment, we then ask them (divided into smaller groups of students) to widen their search to different Francophone countries, looking online for blogs, forums,

YouTube videos, and so on, that inform each country's situation regarding the use of genderfluid pronouns. Students will share and discuss their findings in the following session to gain perspective on pronoun use and its implications according to different countries and cultures. As a result, students will be better able to discuss meaning behind the choice of pronouns and gender identity in the film.

In effect, as applied to the film, before analyzing scenes, we start as a class by identifying and describing the characters, mainly Laurence and Fred, and discussing the ambiguity inherent in their names. In order to make students more attentive to the way gender in language constructs meaning, students complete a grammar activity on object pronouns. Here, they are made explicitly aware of how French works as a gendered language through the subtleties required in the task of choosing pronouns for Laurence in various stages of his/her transition from man to woman.

c) Scene analysis, follow-up activities, and discussion: In class, we analyze four short scenes from the film that provide different points for discussion. Students are shown the scene and asked to consider certain questions and share their opinions in small groups before discussing them with the whole class. We begin with the opening scene, before Laurence appears on screen. From the point of view of Laurence, shots of different people in the street looking straight into the camera (at Laurence) establish the importance of the gaze, of the vision of others in constructing identity. We ask students to describe here how these people are looking at Laurence and what emotions they convey. This exercise is meant to incite students to think about judgment and the role of different perspectives. The second scene examines Laurence's coming out in front of her class. Students describe Laurence's visible signs of femininity, the reaction of her students, and her attitude upon leaving the classroom (here again, we use the feminine pronoun in accordance with Dolan). Following these two analyses, we show a short video with Judith Butler about the concept of gender performativity, central in *Gender Studies*, to inform and provoke deeper discussion.

In the following session, for scene three, we bring in the pronoun debate and have students share and discuss their findings after examining the scene in the film that involves an argument in a café between a waitress, Fred, and Laurence. We use a transcript of this scene to focus on the language, to go more in depth in the analysis of pronouns, showing the scene two times. The first time, students are asked to pay attention to the characters' physical appearance, attitudes, and body language illustrating their dynamic and how Fred and Laurence provoke the waitress and then decide if her reaction is justified. The second time, using the transcript, students are asked to pay closer attention to the language and the use of pronouns in the scene.

After sharing what they noticed in small groups, students are given an exercise involving direct and indirect pronouns, inviting them to hypothesize as to ways the waitress could have reacted, aimed at further sensitizing students to the importance of the use of pronouns in constructing identity. This exercise is followed by a more general discussion where students share their findings regarding the differences in genderfluid pronoun use and the surrounding debate in their assigned Francophone country.

In the final scene that we analyze together, students are first asked to contemplate and discuss the different types of love and how they are portrayed on screen. We end by showing the very strong cinematic scene where Fred receives a book of poems from Laurence and breaks down. Students discuss the role of emotions and the topic of the love story, favored by Dolan, and how they are conveyed through the *mise en scène*. With discussion focused on the love story between Laurence and Fred, we follow Dolan's stance against ghettoization, choosing to explore instead a truly inclusive narrative that considers the characters above all as two people who share a story of love and hardship together in their search for identity as individuals and as a couple.

d) **Composition topic:** To explore the concept and construct of identity further, students are asked to write a three-page essay where they analyze how Laurence's identity evolves with the narrative and how certain aspects of the *mise en scène* communicate Laurence's identity and transformations, supporting their arguments through scene analyses and outside research.

e) **Final project:** At the end of the semester, students create short films in groups of three or four (as described earlier) that are inspired by one or more of the films or characters we have studied in the course. The following suggestions are examples of how choosing Laurence could lead to creative thinking that would also deepen students' capacity to identify with the character. For instance, students can imagine a short biopic or interview where Laurence or another protagonist tells the story of her childhood, adolescence, transition into adulthood, and so on; they could also choose to do a spinoff where that character shows what happens next in her life. Another option is having the directors of some of the films we study over the semester appear on a talk show about film where students imagine their exchange with the host. Projects focusing more specifically on *Laurence Anyways* and LGBT+ rights could include a documentary in French on the situation and resources on campus and in the city, including interviews, or interviews with French speakers on campus or in the city from different Francophone countries on specific issues such as rights ("mariage pour tous," for example), pronouns, and so on. All of these topics are geared toward real inclusivity, steering away from marginalization, in that students are encouraged to consider many different viewpoints as conveyed through the various films we cover throughout the semester, all of which explore different aspects of identity. The goal is visibility and representation that fosters an environment where all people feel free to affirm their own identity and to be open to the perspective of others.

Results so far have been very positive. In fact, according to the comments in the evaluations of the course and in other feedback, *Laurence Anyways* has been students' favorite film overall, and they have enjoyed the corresponding activities as well. Instructors notice a positive effect in students after viewing and studying this film in that they are able to discuss openly subjects that could be controversial and challenge preconceived ideas and stereotypes through this touching character and story. Their eyes are also opened to the limitations of the French language and how language in general can work to construct identity and perceptions. We consider this film an important addition in the development of the curriculum in French 40 and hope to continue advancements in other areas that will foster inclusiveness.

Expansion of Our Course Material

International Movies

As discussed previously, the lessons we share here, on these two films, are also meant to serve as a model. The suggested template can provide a framework that can be adapted to other films and expanded to other language courses, cross-cultural courses, or those that wish to incorporate film as a means to work toward a more inclusive and multicultural classroom. Instructors might consider integrating other international films that include LGBT+ perspectives, for example. Besides our suggestions for other Francophone films with characters from the LGBT+ community, we also propose the critically acclaimed and very popular films *Moonlight* (2016) by Barry Jenkins or Luca Guadagnino's *Call Me By Your Name* (2017) that, because of their popularity, can provide characters who are already accessible. For another perspective from the transgender community, that also discusses other issues, we can suggest Almodovar's *La mala educación* (2004) from Spain, which includes a situation with a priest; Céline Sciamma's award-winning film, *Tomboy* (2011), providing the perspective of a transgender girl who wants to be a boy; or Kimberly Peirce's *Boys Don't Cry* (1999), based on the real-life story of an American transgender man. Finally, the films *Viva* from Cuban directors Juan Carlos Cremata and Iraida Malberti Cabrera (2015) and the Franco-Brazilian *Madame Satã* (2002) by Karim Aïnouz, both portray drag performers. We imagine these films could help open dialogue on LGBT+ issues as students hear the voices of their characters and are exposed to a variety of stories that shed light on different experiences and challenges that inspire empathy.

Comic Books and Graphic Novels

Another medium that has increasingly ignited interest among language teachers, researchers, and students consists of comic books and graphic novels. Comics, like films, provide access to a variety of sociolects; represent an authentic report of socio-historical trends, events, and ideologies; and allow students to identify visual codes linked to cultural beliefs and habits. Gretchen Schwarz in her article "Expanding Literacies Through Graphic Novels," mentions that graphic novels give access to a form of

> literacy that affirms diversity, gives voice to all, and helps students examine ideas and practices that promulgate inequity. Many graphic novels offer more diverse voices than traditional textbooks and can open up discussion about issues such as social justice.
>
> (62)

For the last decade, we have seen an increasing number of graphic novel publications about LGBT+ issues, stories for young adults and adults alike. Instructors can draw parallels among graphic novels from different countries on specific topics of interest. In the course "Graphic-Literary Representations of Francophone Identities," taught in Fall 2015 by Dr. Chevant-Aksoy at Harvard, students examined how the representation of gender identity and sexual orientation in Francophone graphic novels could inform socio-cultural and historical norms. The first book students analyzed, *Mauvais Genre* by Chloé Cruchaudet (2011), is a story about a World War I deserter who starts cross-dressing to avoid going back to the war and discovers polysexual practices in the Bois de Boulogne. Students discussed symbols and values associated with masculinity and male duties in France in the World War I era and what it meant to challenge those norms. In the case of a cross-cultural course, instructors could also use the Italian *In Italia Sono Tutti Maschi* by Luca de Santis and Sara Colaone (2008), which depicts the confinement and exile of gay people under the fascist rule in World War II. To continue to explore LGBT+ issues, students then studied *Bleu est une couleur chaude* by Julie Maroh (2010), a coming-of-age story about a lesbian teenager, where they discussed LGBT+ rights in Europe in the 1990s and the psychological issues of being in and coming out. In the case of a cross-cultural course, instructors could also study excerpts of the Japanese yuri manga series *Sasameki Koto* (ささめきこと) by Takashi Ikeda (2007–2011), also a coming-of-age story about lesbian teenagers. In Fall 2015, one student decided to compare *Bleu est une couleur chaude* to the American graphic memoir *Fun Home* by Alison Bechdel (2006). The student drew parallels between the two heroines' coming-out stories, focusing on their relationship with their families, gender roles and stereotypes, and emotional and psychological distress. Most of the students in the class felt a strong connection to *Bleu est une couleur chaude* as they commiserate with the main character's first heartache and her feelings of loss, confusion, and social inhibition. They also mentioned that the format of the graphic novel (drawings, colors, concise sentences, and onomatopoeias) helped them feel more comfortable commenting on themes they were not necessarily comfortable with or that were less familiar to them.

Conclusions

As teachers of French, we have seen changes in the curriculum over the past few decades that move it away from Francocentric or even Paris-centered points of view, opening it to the Francophone world through literature and film. Intuitively, we also know as instructors that we are teaching much more in the language classroom than just how to speak French. We are introducing our students to different cultures, certainly, but through the focus of our curriculum, class discussion, and projects, we are also implicitly teaching them cultural norms, whether they challenge or actually reinforce stereotypes. In today's global climate, it is even more imperative, then, that we provide an environment that is inclusive and open to all points of view, and that we cultivate understanding in our students so that they become open-minded, responsible, and culturally rich individuals. One way of doing this is by *including* perspectives of some of the most vulnerable through the stories we propose and explore together in the classroom. Transgender students represent one of these populations that is the most vulnerable and faces many challenges. As the transgender and larger LGBT+ population in general becomes more visible nationwide, schools need to become more responsive in working toward promoting an inclusive school environment that deters hate-motivated attitudes and behaviors. Indeed, concerted efforts should be made to support LGBT+ students and affirm their gender identity (Campos 2018). A first step in this direction is easily within our reach as instructors. The films we choose as pedagogical tools in the language classroom can provide a base for building empathy and as a result, community.

Note

1. All translations are the chapter authors' own unless otherwise stated.

References

Bissiere, Michele. *Séquences*. Cengage Learning, 2008.

Blickenstaff, Jacob. "I'll Bring the Popcorn! Using Popular Movies in Science Class." *The Science Teacher*, vol. 78, no. 6, 2011, pp. 42–46.

Buchanan, Lisa Brown. "Fostering Historical Thinking Toward Civil Rights Movement Counter-Narratives: Documentary Film in Elementary Social Studies." *The Social Studies*, vol. 106, no. 2, 2015, pp. 47–56.

Byram, Michael. *Teaching and Assessing Intercultural Communicative Competence*. Multilingual Matters, 1997.

Campos, David. "Understanding Transgender Students. Helping Transgender Students Feel Accepted Starts With Understanding." *American School Board Journal*, vol. 3, no. 205, 2018.

———, and Ericka Knudson. "Using Films to Expand Horizons." *Educational Leadership*, vol. 77, no. 1, in press.

Dodman, Benjamin. "French LGBT Groups Denounce 'Culture of Hate' After Spate of Attacks." *France 24*, 2018. www.france24.com/en/20181022-france-lgbt-homophobia-attacks-gay-marriage-lesbian-procreation. Accessed October 28 2018.

Dubreil, Sébastien. "Rebels With a Cause: (Re)Defining Identities and Culture in Contemporary French Cinema," *L2 Journal*, vol. 3, no. 2, 2011, pp. 176–200.

Kaiser, Mark. "New Approaches to Exploiting Film in the Foreign Language Classroom." *L2 Journal*, vol. 3, no. 2, 2011, pp. 232–249.

"Laurence Anyways the Movie." *Laurence Anyways*, 2019. laurenceanyways themovie.com/home/. Accessed 29 March 2019.

Marcus, Alan S. "'It Is as It Was': Feature Film in the History Classroom." *The Social Studies*, vol. 96, no. 2, 2005, pp. 61–67.

———, and Jeremy Stoddard. "Tinsel Town as Teacher: Hollywood Film in the High School Classroom." *The History Teacher*, vol. 40, no. 3, 2007, pp. 303–330.

Marques, Sandrine. "Xavier Dolan 'Dégoûté' par les Prix Récompensant les Films Gays." *Le Monde*, 2014. www.lemonde.fr/culture/article/2014/09/20/xavier-dolan-degoute-par-les-prix-recompensant-les-films-gays_4490979_3246.html. Accessed 29 March 2019.

MLA Report. *Foreign Languages and Higher Education: New Structures for a Changed World*, 2007. www.mla.org/flreport. Accessed 28 October 2018.

Nielsen, Greg. "Media Literacy in the Social Studies Classroom." *Education Digest*, vol. 76, no. 7, 2011, pp. 43–45.

Rice, Anne-Christine. *Cinema for French Conversation*. Focus, 1999.

———. *La France Contemporaine à Travers ses Films*. Focus, 2011.

Russell, William B. "The Art of Teaching Social Studies With Film." *The Clearing House*, vol. 85, no. 4, 2012, pp. 157–164.

Saltau, Margaret. "Not Just Another Teen Movie: Juno – A Study Guide." *Screen Education*, vol. 52, 2008, pp. 110–116.

Schwarz, Gretchen. "Expanding Literacies Through Graphic Novels." *English Journal*, vol. 95, no. 6, 2006, pp. 58–64.

Sommer, Paul. "Using Film in the English Classroom: Why and How." *Journal of Adolescent & Adult Literacy*, vol. 44, no. 5, 2001, pp. 485–487.

"Terminology." *Harvard College Office of BGLTQ Student Life*, The President and Fellows of Harvard College, 2019. bgltq.fas.harvard.edu/terminology. Accessed 29 March 2019.

Timsit, Annabelle. "The Push to Make French Gender-Neutral." *The Atlantic*, 2017. www.theatlantic.com/international/archive/2017/11/inclusive-writing-france-feminism/545048/. Accessed 14 October 2018.

Williams, Neil. "The Comic Book as Course Book: Why and How." *Paper presented at the 29th Annual Meeting of TESOL*, 1995.

Index

Printed in Great Britain
by Amazon

45642679R00159